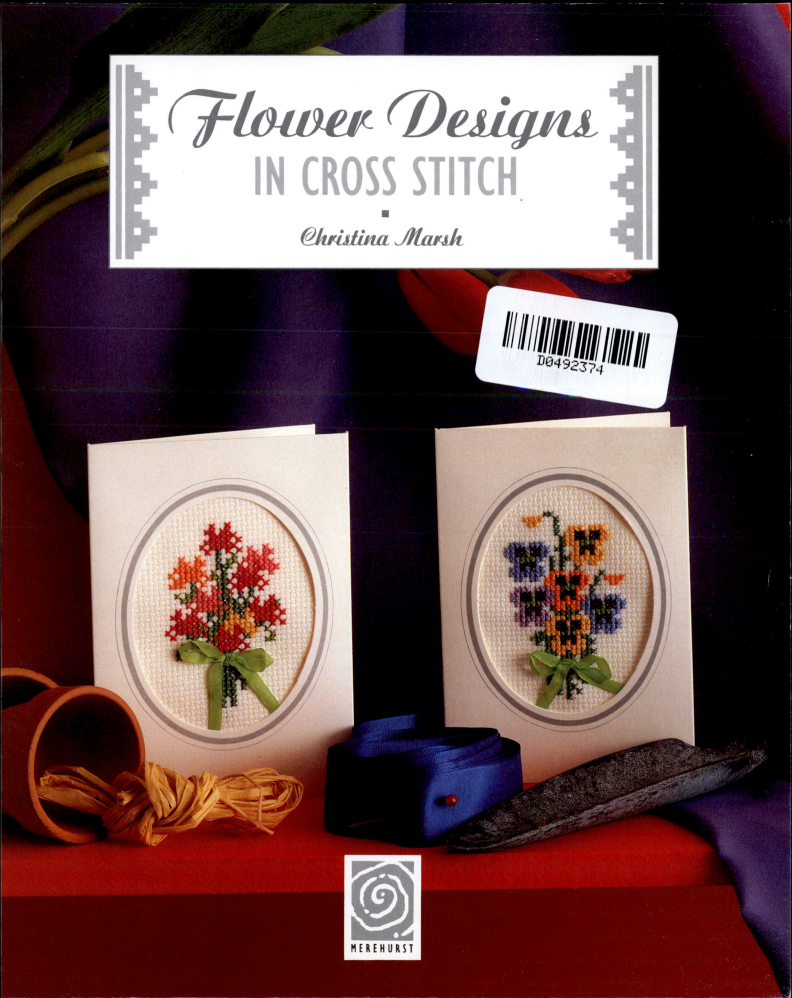

Flower Designs
IN CROSS STITCH

Christina Marsh

MEREHURST

THE CHARTS

Some of the designs in this book are very detailed and due to inevitable space limitations, the charts may be shown on a comparatively small scale; in such cases, readers may find it helpful to have the particular chart with which they are currently working enlarged.

THREADS

The projects in this book were all stitched with Anchor stranded cotton embroidery threads. The keys given with each chart also list thread combinations for those who wish to use DMC or Madeira threads. It should be pointed out that the shades produced by different companies vary slightly, and it is not always possible to find identical colours in a different range.

Published in 1997 by Merehurst Limited
Ferry House, 51-57 Lacy Road, Putney, London SW15 1PR
Copyright © 1997 Merehurst Limited
ISBN 1 85391 645 5

A catalogue record for this book is available from the British Library.

Edited by Diana Lodge
Designed by Maggie Aldred
Photography by Juliet Piddington
Illustrations by John Hutchinson (pp.5-7 and 34) and King & King (p.38)
Typesetting by Dacorum Type & Print, Hemel Hempstead
Colour separation by Fotographics Limited, UK – Hong Kong
Printed in Hong Kong by Wing King Tong

Merehurst is the leading publisher of craft books and has an excellent range of titles to suit all levels. Please send to the address above for our free catalogue, stating the title of this book.

CONTENTS

INTRODUCTION

As a keen gardener I am delighted to have had the opportunity to design and stitch for this book. I have tried to include as many of my favourite flowers as possible and I hope some of these are your favourites too.

If you are new to cross stitch or have a limited amount of time for stitching, then the Floral Bouquet cards are designed just for you. These quick and easy-to-sew card designs are ideal for the beginner and are suitable for a wide range of occasions. The desktop projects are also designed with the beginner in mind and make beautiful gifts.

On a slightly more ambitious level, why not brighten up your home with the sunflower cushion and your table with linen decorated with cottage garden flowers? The bathroom is not forgotten – stitch ever-popular daisies on towels and create eye-catching matching accessories. There are also pictures for the wall, a beautiful jewellery box and much more.

The projects have been chosen to cover a wide range of abilities, from the beginner to the more proficient stitcher. Many of the designs are stitched on easy-to-sew Aida fabric, which is ideal for the beginner, but if you prefer to work on linen you can substitute the 14-count Aida with a 28-count evenweave, taking each stitch over two fabric threads.

Finally, whether you are a newcomer to cross stitch or a skilled embroiderer, I am sure you will enjoy stitching these projects, not only for yourself but for those dear to you.

BASIC SKILLS

BEFORE YOU BEGIN

PREPARING THE FABRIC
Even with an average amount of handling, many evenweave fabrics tend to fray at the edges, so it is a good idea to overcast the raw edges, using ordinary sewing thread, before you begin.

FABRIC
The projects in this book use Aida fabric, which is ideal both for beginners and more advanced stitchers as it has a surface of clearly designated squares. All Aida fabric has a count, which refers to the number of squares (each stitch covers one square) to one inch (2.5cm); the higher the count, the smaller the finished stitching. Projects in this book use 11-, 14- and 18- count Aida, popular and readily available sizes, in a wide variety of colours.

THE INSTRUCTIONS
Each project begins with a full list of the materials that you will require. The measurements given for the embroidery fabric include a minimum of 5cm (2in) all around to allow for stretching it in a frame and preparing the edges to prevent them from fraying.

Colour keys for stranded embroidery cottons – Anchor, DMC, or Madeira – are given with each chart. It is assumed that you will need to buy one skein of each colour mentioned in a particular key, even though you may use less, but where two or more skeins are needed, this information is included in the main list of requirements.

Before you begin to embroider, always mark the centre of the design with two lines of basting stitches, one vertical and one horizontal, running from edge to edge of the fabric, as indicated by the arrows on the charts.

As you stitch, use the centre lines given on the chart and the basting threads on your fabric as reference points for counting the squares and threads to position your design accurately.

WORKING IN A HOOP

A hoop is the most popular frame for use with small areas of embroidery. It consists of two rings, one fitted inside the other; the outer ring usually has an adjustable screw attachment so that it can be tightened to hold the stretched fabric in place. Hoops are available in several sizes, ranging from 10cm (4in) in diameter to quilting hoops with a diameter of 38cm (15in). Hoops with table stands or floor stands attached are also available.

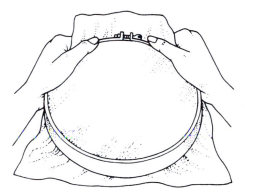

1 To stretch your fabric in a hoop, place the area to be embroidered over the inner ring and press the outer ring over it, with the tension screw released. Tissue paper can be placed between the outer ring and the embroidery, so that the hoop does not mark the fabric. Lay the tissue paper over the fabric when you set it in the hoop, then tear away the central embroidery area.

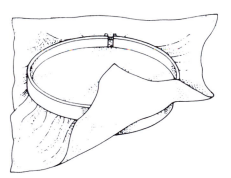

2 Smooth the fabric and, if necessary, straighten the grain before tightening the screw. The fabric should be evenly stretched.

WORKING IN A RECTANGULAR FRAME

Rectangular frames are more suitable for larger pieces of embroidery. They consist of two rollers, with tapes attached, and two flat side pieces, which slot into the rollers and are held in place by pegs or screw attachments. Available in different sizes, either alone or with adjustable table or floor stands, frames are measured by the length of the roller tape, and range in size from 30cm (12in) to 68cm (27in).

As alternatives to a slate frame, canvas stretchers and the backs of old picture frames can be used. Provided there is sufficient extra fabric around the finished size of the embroidery, the edges can be turned under and simply attached with drawing pins (thumb tacks) or staples.

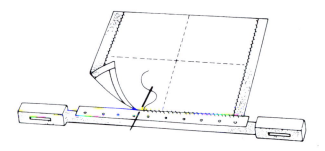

1 To stretch your fabric in a rectangular frame, cut out the fabric, allowing at least an extra 5cm (2in) all around the finished size of the embroidery. Baste a single 12mm ($\frac{1}{2}$in) turning on the top and bottom edges and oversew strong tape, 2.5cm (1in) wide, to the other two sides. Mark the centre line both ways with basting stitches. Working from the centre outward and using strong thread, oversew the top and bottom edges to the roller tapes. Fit the side pieces into the slots, and roll any extra fabric on one roller until the fabric is taut.

2 Insert the pegs or adjust the screw attachments to secure the frame. Thread a large-eyed needle (chenille needle) with strong thread or fine string and lace both edges, securing the ends around the intersections of the frame. Lace the webbing at 2.5cm (1in) intervals, stretching the fabric evenly.

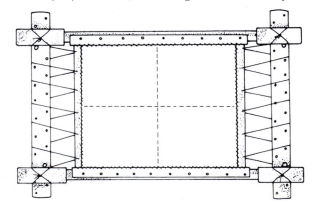

EXTENDING EMBROIDERY FABRIC

It is easy to extend a piece of embroidery fabric, such as a bookmark, to stretch it in a hoop.

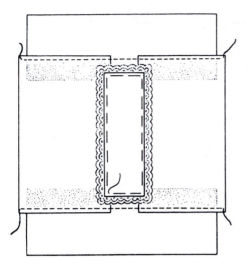

● Fabric oddments of a similar weight can be used. Simply cut four pieces to size (in other words, to the measurement that will fit both the embroidery fabric and your hoop) and baste them to each side of the embroidery fabric before stretching it in the hoop in the usual way.

THE STITCHES

CROSS STITCH

For all cross stitch embroidery, the following two methods of working are used. In each case, neat rows of vertical stitches are produced on the back of the fabric.

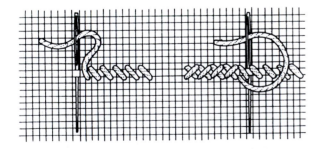

● When stitching large areas, work in horizontal rows. Working from right to left, complete the first row of evenly spaced diagonal stitches over the number of threads specified in the project instructions. Then, working from left to right, repeat the process. Continue in this way, making sure each stitch crosses in the same direction.

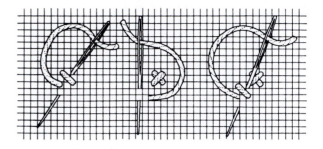

● When stitching diagonal lines, work downwards, completing each stitch before moving to the next. When starting a project always begin to embroider at the centre of the design and work outwards to ensure that the design will be placed centrally on the fabric.

BACKSTITCH

Backstitch is used in the projects to give emphasis to a particular foldline, an outline or a shadow. The stitches are worked over the same number of threads as the cross stitch, forming continuous straight or diagonal lines.

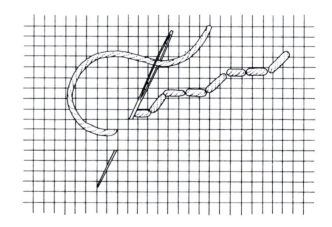

● Make the first stitch from left to right; pass the needle behind the fabric and bring it out one stitch length ahead to the left. Repeat and continue in this way along the line.

THREE-QUARTER CROSS STITCHES

Some fractional stitches are used on certain projects in this book; although they strike fear into the hearts of less experienced stitchers they are not difficult to master, and give a more natural line in certain instances. Should you find it difficult to pierce the centre of the Aida block, simply use a sharp needle to make a small hole in the centre before making a stitch.

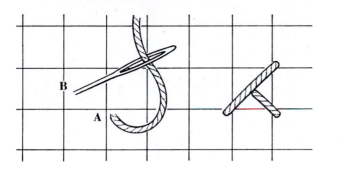

To work a three-quarter cross, bring the needle up at point A and down through the centre of the square at B. Later, the diagonal back stitch finishes the stitch. A chart square with two different symbols separated by a diagonal line requires two 'three-quarter' stitches. Backstitch will later finish the square.

FRENCH KNOTS

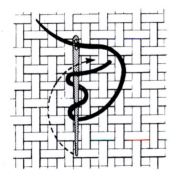

To work a french knot, bring your needle and cotton out slightly to the right of where you want your knot to be. Wind the thread once or twice around the needle, depending on how big you want your knot to be, and insert the needle to the left of the point where you brought it out.

Be careful not to pull too hard or the knot will disappear through the fabric. The instructions state the number of strands of cotton to be used for the french knots.

FINISHING

MOUNTING EMBROIDERY
The cardboard should be cut to the size of the finished embroidery, with an extra amount added all round to allow for the recess in the frame.

LIGHTWEIGHT FABRICS

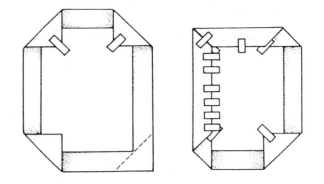

1 Place embroidery face down, with the cardboard centred on top, and basting and pencil lines matching. Begin by folding over the fabric at each corner and securing it with masking tape.

2 Working first on one side and then the other, fold over the fabric on all sides and secure it firmly with pieces of masking tape, placed about 2.5cm (1in) apart. Also neaten the mitred corners with masking tape, pulling the fabric tightly to give a firm, smooth finish.

HEAVIER FABRICS

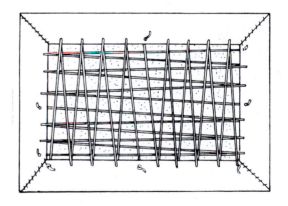

● Lay the embroidery face down, with the cardboard centred on top; fold over the edges of the fabric on opposite sides, making mitred folds at the corners, and lace across, using strong thread. Repeat on the other two sides. Finally, pull up the fabric firmly over the cardboard. Overstitch the mitred corners.

A Woodland Garden

Capture the delicate magic of a
woodland garden in springtime.
The bright colours of the tulip beds,
mixed with the fresh greens of
spring foliage, make this a delightful
picture both to embroider
and to own.

A WOODLAND GARDEN

YOU WILL NEED

For the picture, set in a frame with an internal measurement of 22.5cm × 17.5cm (9in × 7in):

30cm × 25cm (12in × 10in) of white, 14-count Aida fabric
Stranded embroidery cotton in the colours listed
No26 tapestry needle
Frame of your choice, with measurements as specified above
Firm card to fit the frame (for the embroidery to be laced over)
Card mount to fit the frame, with an oval aperture measuring 17.5cm × 12.5cm (7in × 5in)

•

THE EMBROIDERY

Prepare the fabric as described on page 4; find the centre either by folding the fabric in half and then in half again, and lightly pressing the folded corner, or by marking the horizontal and vertical centre lines with basting stitches in a light-coloured thread. Mount the fabric in a frame (see page 5) and count out from the centre to start the design at an appropriate point.

Following the chart, complete all the cross stitching first, using two strands of thread in the needle. Where two colours are given for a symbol, use one strand of each colour in the needle.

MOUNTING AND FRAMING

Remove the finished embroidery from the frame, leaving the basting stitches (if any) in place. Wash if necessary, then press lightly on the wrong side, using a steam iron. Lace the embroidery over the firm card (see page 7), using the basted centre lines to check that the embroidery is centred over the card.

Remove the basting stitches; place the oval mount and the mounted embroidery in the frame and assemble it according to the manufacturer's instructions.

COMPLETE THREAD LIST			
	ANCHOR	DMC	MADEIRA
White	2	White	White
Yellow	292	3078	0102
Orange	302	743	0114
Pale green	259	772	1604
Light green	241	703	1401
Medium green	243	701	1402
Green	245	986	1404
Dark green	879	890	1705
Pink	50	605	0613
Red	19	821	0212
Blue	131	798	0911
Medium blue	133	796	0913
Purple	101	550	0713

A WOODLAND GARDEN ▶	ANCHOR	DMC	MADEIRA
· White	2	White	White
∷ Yellow mix	302/292	743/3078	0114/0102
V Orange	302	743	0114
O Orange mix	302/19	743/821	0114/0212
● Red	19	821	0212
U Pink mix	302/50	743/605	0114/0613
∕ Pale green	259	772	1604
▬ Light green	241	703	1401
⊞ Medium green	243	701	1402
☐ Green	245	986	1404
■ Dark green	879	890	1705
Y Green mix	879/241	890/703	1705/1401
◇ Light blue mix	131/133	798/796	0911/0913
◆ Dark blue mix	133/101	796/550	0913/0713

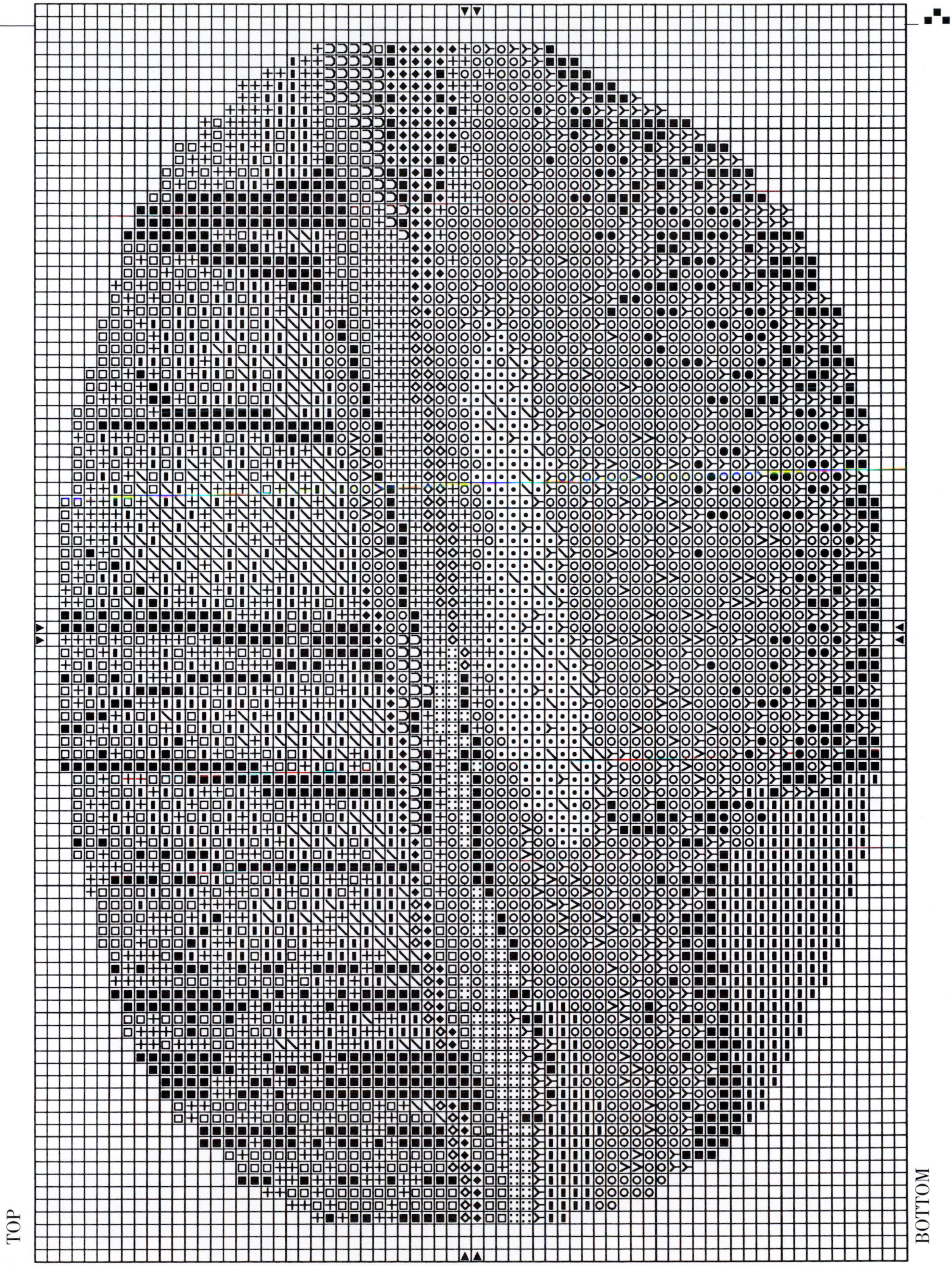
TOP
BOTTOM

Floral Bouquet Cards

Equally suitable for a birthday, to
wish a friend the best of luck, or
to offer congratulations or thanks,
these pretty cards are quick
and easy to stitch.

FLORAL BOUQUET CARDS

YOU WILL NEED

For each card, with an oval aperture measuring
8.5cm × 6cm (3½in × 2½in):

15cm (6in) square of white, 14-count Aida fabric
Stranded embroidery cotton in the colours given in
the appropriate panel
No26 tapestry needle
15cm (6in) of ribbon, 4mm wide
Card as specified above (for suppliers, see page 40)

NOTE: one skein of each colour on the combined list is
sufficient for all four designs

•

THE EMBROIDERY

Prepare the fabric as described on page 4; find the
centre either by folding the fabric in half and then in
half again, and lightly pressing the folded corner, or
by marking the horizontal and vertical centre lines
with basting stitches in a light-coloured thread.
Mount the fabric in a small hoop.

Following the chart, complete all the cross stitching first, using two strands of thread in the needle.
Be careful not to take dark threads across the back
of the work in such a way that they show through on
the right side.

FINISHING

Remove the basting stitches (if any) and lightly
press. Tie the ribbon in a small bow and secure it to
the embroidery with a couple of neat stitches.

Trim the embroidery to measure 12mm (½in)
larger all around than the size of the card window.
Position the embroidery behind the window; open
out the self-adhesive mount; fold the card, and press
firmly to secure it. Some cards require a dab of glue
to ensure a secure and neat finish.

PANSIES ▼		ANCHOR	DMC	MADEIRA
⠿	Gold	306	725	0114
□	Orange	324	721	0309
○	Light green	239	702	1306
●	Medium green	210	561	1312
X	Blue	145	799	0910
+	Lilac	109	209	0803
■	Purple	102	550	0714

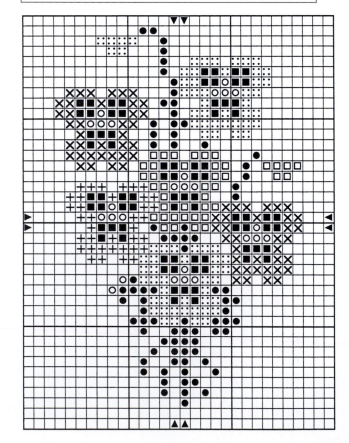

COMPLETE THREAD LIST				
		ANCHOR	DMC	MADEIRA
⠿	Gold	306	725	0114
□	Orange	324	721	0309
·	Pink	38	335	0610
▬	Red	59	600	0704
○	Light green	239	702	1306
●	Medium green	210	561	1312
X	Blue	145	799	0910
+	Lilac	109	209	0803
■	Purple	102	550	0714

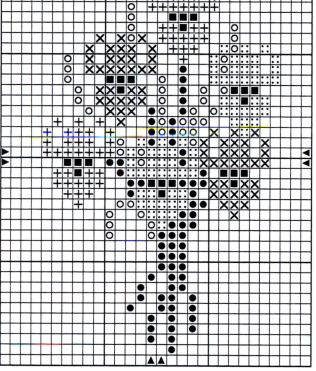

DAHLIAS ◀		ANCHOR	DMC	MADEIRA
⣿	Gold	306	725	0114
☐	Orange	324	721	0309
·	Pink	38	335	0610
▬	Red	59	600	0704
○	Light green	239	702	1306
●	Medium green	210	561	1312

IRISES ▲		ANCHOR	DMC	MADEIRA
⣿	Gold	306	725	0114
○	Light green	239	702	1306
●	Medium green	210	561	1312
X	Blue	145	799	0910
+	Lilac	109	209	0803
■	Purple	102	550	0714

TULIPS ◀		ANCHOR	DMC	MADEIRA
⣿	Gold	306	725	0114
·	Pink	38	335	0610
▬	Red	59	600	0704
○	Light green	239	702	1306
●	Medium green	210	561	1312

Rose Jewellery Box

Embroider this beautiful cluster of
old roses and set them in an
unusual jewellery box.
Alternatively, you could embroider
the design as a picture.

ROSE JEWELLERY BOX

YOU WILL NEED

For the jewellery box, measuring approximately 19cm (7½in) square and 8cm (3¼in) high:

25cm (10in) square of white, 14-count Aida fabric
Stranded embroidery cotton in the colours listed in the panel
No26 tapestry needle
50cm (18in) of cotton fabric for the box cover, cut as follows: four 21.5cm (8½in) squares and four pieces 21.5cm × 17.5cm (8½in × 7in)
Lightweight wadding (batting): one piece 19cm (7½in) square and four pieces 19cm × 7.5cm (7½in × 3in)
Medium-weight card: three 19cm (7½in) squares, one of them with a 15cm (6in) circular aperture, one 18cm (7in) square, and four pieces 19cm × 7.5cm (7½in × 3in)
Lightweight card: one 16cm (6½in) square
38cm (15in) of medium-weight piping cord
Matching sewing cotton
5cm (2in) of ribbon, 12mm (½in) wide
Glue stick and masking tape

•

THE EMBROIDERY

Prepare the fabric as described on page 4; find the centre either by folding the fabric in half and then in half again, and lightly pressing the folded corner, or by marking the horizontal and vertical centre lines with basting stitches in a light-coloured thread. Mount the fabric in a frame (see page 5) and start the design from the centre.

Following the chart, complete all the cross stitching first, using two strands of thread in the needle. Finish with the backstitching, using one strand of thread in the needle. Be careful not to take dark threads across the back of the work in such a way that they show through on the right side. Remove the finished embroidery from the hoop or frame and wash if necessary, then press lightly on the wrong side, using a steam iron.

THE BOX

To prepare the side sections, first glue a piece of wadding to one side of each of the four 19cm × 7.5cm

(7½in × 3in) pieces of card. For each side, take a piece of cotton fabric 21.5cm × 17.5cm (8½in × 7in) and lay a card, padded side down, on the wrong side of the fabric, with an allowance of 12mm (½in) of fabric showing at each side and the bottom edge. Fold the sides and tape them; bring the upper section of fabric over the card and turn the raw edge under stitch along the lower edge, so that the stitching line is just slightly to the back of the card (not along the bottom). Oversewing the edges with neat stitches, join the four sides of the box together to make a square, with the padded sides facing out and the stitched lower edges facing inward.

Take two of the square cards (for the base) and cover one side of each with a piece of fabric; fold in the sides, mitring the corners, and secure with tape (see page 7). Push one piece, fabric side down, into the base of the box, and neatly oversew the base to the bottom edges. Turn the box over and neatly stitch the cord along the top edge of one side (now the back edge), allowing the ends to run down the inside corners and on to the base. Push the second base piece, fabric side up, into the box, covering the cord ends and the back of the first base section.

Cover the 18cm (7½in) card (inside lid), using the same method as for the base card. Glue the remaining piece of wadding to the card with the aperture and cut around the edge of the circle to remove the wadding from the centre. Do this carefully, because this piece of wadding is then glued to the centre of the lightweight card.

Place the card with the aperture on the final piece of fabric and fold in the sides; mitre the corners, and secure with glue. When the glue has dried, cut out the centre, leaving an allowance of approximately 12mm (½in) of fabric for the turning. Snip into the fabric allowance at intervals of 12mm

ROSE JEWELLERY BOX ▶	ANCHOR	DMC	MADEIRA
⋅ White	1	White	White
⦿ Yellow	305	726	0112
● Deep yellow	306	725	0113
⠿ Pale pink	73	3689	0607
X Light plum	76	3731	0610
☐ Medium plum	65	816	0704
■ Dark plum	45	814	0513
⊟ Pale green	254	472	1409
V Light green	256	906	1411
◇ Medium green	258	904	1413
◆ Dark green	246	319	1406

Note: outline the leaves and stems in dark green and the flowers in dark plum, using one strand of thread in the needle.

(½in); turn the fabric back over the card, and secure at the back with masking tape. Next, place the embroidery so that the design is positioned exactly over the circular piece of wadding that you have already glued to the lightweight card. Lace the embroidery over the back of the card (see page 7).

To assemble the lid, centre the mount over the embroidery, then place the inside lid at the back, forming a sandwich with the embroidery in the middle. The mount should overlap the inside lid by a margin of about 6mm (¼in). Insert the ribbon, folded in half, between the inside lid and the mount to make the front opening tag. Neatly stitch the inside lid to the mounted embroidery. Finally, oversew the back of the lid to the cord at the back edge of the box.

A Summer Table

Add a touch of magic to your table with these beautiful cottage garden floral designs. We show a cake band, napkin and matching napkin ring, but the designs could also be used for a border or corner motifs around a tablecloth.

SUMMER TABLE

YOU WILL NEED

For the cake band:

*1m (1yd) of 14-count Aida cake band,
5cm (2in) wide
Stranded embroidery cotton in the colours given
in the panel
No26 tapestry needle*

For the napkin:

*Stranded embroidery cotton in the colours given
in the panel
Sharp needle
10cm (4in) square of waste canvas
Napkin of your choice*

For the napkin ring:

*10cm (4in) square of yellow, 14-count Aida fabric
10cm (4in) square of iron-on interfacing
Stranded embroidery cotton in the colours given
in the panel
No26 tapestry needle
Napkin ring (for suppliers, see page 40)*

*NOTE: one skein of each colour listed will be
sufficient for the cake band and a set of four napkins
and napkin rings*

•

THE CAKE BAND

This project is unsuitable for stitching in a frame and the band should be held in the hand. Find the centre by counting the number of squares between the top and bottom of the cake band, and run a horizontal line of basting stitches in a light-coloured sewing cotton along the full length of the band.

Start the embroidery at the left-hand edge of the band, taking care that the design is centred. The design is repeated every 5.5cm (2¼in), and it is suggested that you have a number of photocopies of the chart so that you can mark off the patterns as you stitch. Following the chart, complete the cross stitching, using two strands of thread in the needle. On completion, wash if necessary and press lightly on the wrong side, using a steam iron.

THE NAPKIN

Place the waste canvas in one corner of the napkin, aligning the edges, and pin to hold. Start the embroidery in the corner, 12mm (½in) in from the edge at each side, treating each pair of canvas threads as one. Following the chart, cross stitch in the usual manner, using three strands of thread in a sharp-pointed needle. Take care to stitch through the holes and not the canvas, as the latter would make it difficult to withdraw the threads.

When you have finished the embroidery, remove the pins and cut away surplus canvas around the design. Dampen the right side with slightly warm water and leave it for a few minutes until the sizing in the canvas softens. Gently remove the canvas threads one at a time, using tweezers. The threads should come out easily, but the operation requires patience; if you try to remove several threads at once this could spoil your embroidery.

THE NAPKIN RING

Prepare the fabric as described on page 4, and find the centre either by folding the fabric in half and then in half again, and lightly pressing the folded corner, or by marking the horizontal and vertical centre lines with basting stitches in a light-coloured thread. You will not require a frame as this small project can be worked in the hand. Following the chart, complete all the cross stitching, using two strands of thread in the needle. On completion, remove the basting stitches; wash if necessary, and lightly press on the wrong side. Finally, place the iron-on interfacing, glue side down, on the back of the work and lightly press with a steam iron. Trim the fabric to the required size, and assemble the napkin ring according to the manufacturer's instructions.

SUMMER TABLE ▶		ANCHOR	DMC	MADEIRA
⊡	Yellow	295	726	0109
⠿	Gold	306	725	0113
⊞	Pink	57	956	0611
○	Medium plum	59	600	0704
●	Dark plum	44	814	0514
☐	Light green	225	703	1307
■	Medium green	227	701	1305
◇	Pale blue	140	809	0910
◆	Medium blue	142	799	0911
⊟	Dark blue	143	797	0912

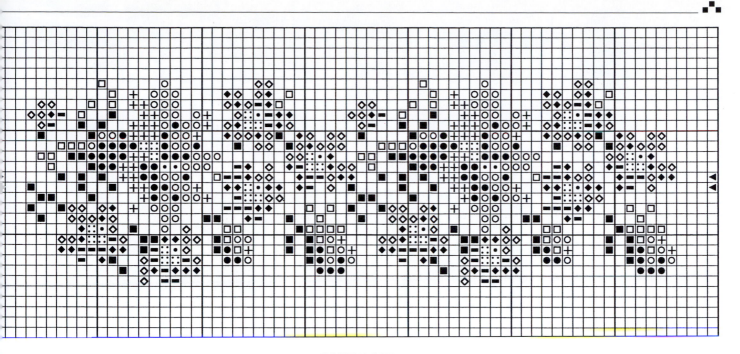

CAKE BAND

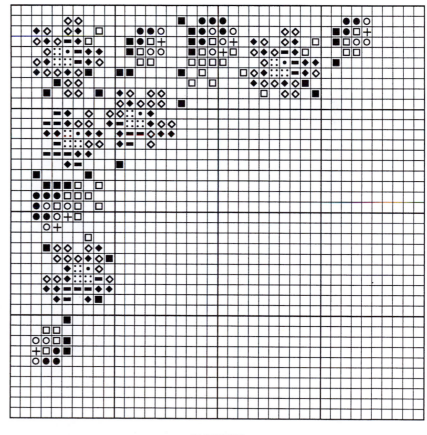

NAPKIN

NAPKIN RING

Summer Spice

The rich colours of the flowers in
this garden are truly hot and spicy,
like a sizzling summer's day.
Stitch this beautiful scene in a
mixture of shimmering rayons
and soft cottons to capture the warm
glow of summer.

SUMMER SPICE

YOU WILL NEED

For the picture, set in a frame with an internal measurement of 35cm × 30cm (14in × 12in):

45.5cm × 40.5cm (18in × 16in) of emerald green, 14-count Aida fabric
Stranded embroidery rayon and cotton in the colours listed
No26 tapestry needle
Frame, as specified above
Firm card (for the embroidery to be laced over) to fit the frame
Wadding (batting) to fit the frame
Two cardboard mounts to fit the frame, one with a 22.5cm × 17.5cm (9in × 7in) aperture, and one with a 23cm × 18cm (9¼in × 7¼in) aperture
Glue stick

•

THE EMBROIDERY

Prepare the fabric as described on page 4; find the centre by folding the fabric in half and then in half again, and lightly pressing the corner, or by marking the horizontal and vertical centre lines with basting stitches in a light-coloured thread. Mount the fabric in a frame (see page 5) and start the design from the centre.

Following the chart, complete all the cross stitching first, using three strands of thread in the needle. Where two colours are given for a symbol be careful to check that you are using the correct colours and thread types. Finally, long stitch stems, using two strands of light green in the needle.

FINISHING

Remove the embroidery from the frame and wash if necessary, then press lightly on the wrong side, using a steam iron. Spread glue evenly on one side of the mounting card, and lightly press the wadding (batting) to the surface. Lace the embroidery over the padded surface (see page 7), using the basting stitches (if any) to check that the embroidery is centred over the card.

Remove basting stitches; place the cardboard mounts and the embroidery in the frame, and assemble according to the manufacturer's instructions.

COMPLETE THREAD LIST
STRANDED EMBROIDERY COTTON

	ANCHOR	DMC	MADEIRA
Silver green	875	966	1702
Light green	255	907	1410
Medium green	257	905	1411
Yellow	298	972	0107
Mustard	306	783	0114
Orange red	332	608	0206
Medium red	19	347	0211
Deep red	20	498	0513
Violet	101	552	0713
Brown	381	938	2005

STRANDED RAYON THREAD

	MARLITT
Gold	821
Orange	850
Red	843
Pink	813
Lilac	858
Purple	859

SUMMER SPICE ▶	ANCHOR	DMC	MADEIRA
▬ Silver green	875	966	1702
❙ Light green	255	907	1410
❙❙❙ Medium green	257	905	1411
↓ Mustard	306	783	0114
✕ Dark red	20	498	0513
● Brown	381	938	2005

Note: for the above symbols, use three strands of cotton in the needle. Straight stitch stems using two strands of light green.

	MARLITT
◩ Pink	813

Note: for the above symbol use three strands of rayon in the needle.

	MAR/ANC	MAR/DMC	MAR/MAD
⊞ Gold/yellow	821/298	821/972	821/0107
◯ Orange/orange red	850/332	850/608	850/0206
⊻ Red/medium red	843/19	843/347	843/0211
☐ Lilac/violet	858/101	858/552	858/0713
■ Purple/violet	859/101	859/552	859/0713

Note: for the above symbols, use two strands of rayon with one strand of cotton.

	MAR/ANC	MAR/DMC	MAR/MAD
⸬ Red/orange red	843/332	843/608	843/0206

Note: for the above symbol. use one strand of rayon with two strands of cotton.

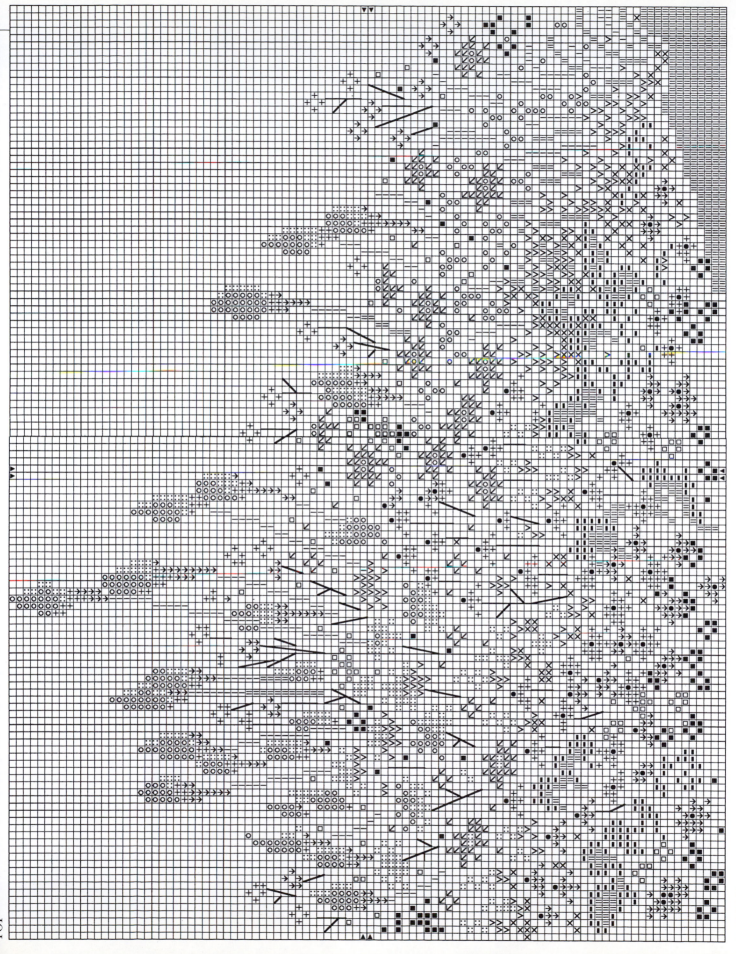

TOP

BOTTOM

Desktop Flowers

Either individually or as a set, these embroideries make ideal gifts. The versatile designs can be used in many ways – the oval and circular shapes are ideal for cards or miniatures, while the bookmark could be adapted for a cake band.

DESKTOP FLOWERS

YOU WILL NEED

For the bookmark, measuring 21cm × 5cm (8½in × 2in):

33cm x 20cm (13in x 8in) of antique white, 14-count Aida fabric
Stranded cotton in the colours given in the panel
No26 tapestry needle

For the address book, with an aperture measuring, 13.5cm × 10cm (5½in × 4in):

25cm × 20cm (10in × 8in) of antique white, 14-count Aida fabric
Stranded cotton in the colours given in the panel
No26 tapestry needle
16.5cm × 12.5cm (6½in × 5in) of lightweight card
Address book (for suppliers, see page 40)

For the paperweight, with a diameter of 7.5cm (3in)

17.5cm (7in) square of antique white, 14-count Aida fabric
Stranded cotton in the colours given in the panel
No26 tapestry needle
10cm (4in) square of iron-on interfacing
7.5cm (3in) paperweight (for suppliers, see page 40)

NOTE: one skein of each of the colours listed will be sufficient for all designs

•

THE EMBROIDERY

Follow the same instructions for each of the designs shown. Prepare the fabric as described on page 4; find the centre either by folding the fabric in half and then in half again, and lightly pressing the folded corner, or by marking the horizontal and vertical centre lines with basting stitches in a light-coloured thread. If you are stitching all three designs on one piece of fabric, find the centre of each embroidery area. Mount the fabric in a small hoop (see page 5).

Following the chart, complete all the cross stitching, using two strands of thread in the needle. Outline in backstitch, using one strand of dark pink in the needle. Remove the embroidery from the hoop and wash if necessary, then press lightly on the wrong side, using a steam iron.

THE BOOKMARK

Trim the fabric to measure 21cm × 12.5cm (8½in × 5in). Fray the top and bottom of the fabric by removing horizontal threads, leaving about 2cm (¾in) of vertical threads showing. Oversew the fabric at the base of the frayed edges with matching sewing cotton to prevent further fraying. Fold under the fabric on each side of the work, leaving about 3mm (⅛in) clearance at each side of the embroidery, and press the folds lightly with a steam iron. At the back of the work, place one flap over the other; turn under a narrow allowance along the overlapping edge, and finish by hemming the length of the bookmark.

THE ADDRESS BOOK

Lace the embroidery over the card (see page 7), using the basting stitches (if any) to check that the design is centred over the card. Finally, slip the design into the address book, taking care that the design is centred in the oval aperture.

THE PAPERWEIGHT

Turn the embroidery face down and place the interfacing, glue side down, over the back of it; press lightly with a steam iron. The interfacing will help to prevent fraying when the circle is cut. Assemble the paperweight, following the manufacturer's instructions.

DESKTOP FLOWERS ▶		ANCHOR	DMC	MADEIRA
⊡	Pale yellow	300	745	0111
⊡	Pale pink	893	224	0814
◯	Light pink	894	223	0813
●	Medium pink	895	3722	0812
⊟	Dark pink	896	3721	0810
☐	Light green	266	3347	1402
☐	Medium green	267	3346	1403
■	Dark green	268	3345	1404

Note: for the Backstitch outline, use one strand of dark pink.

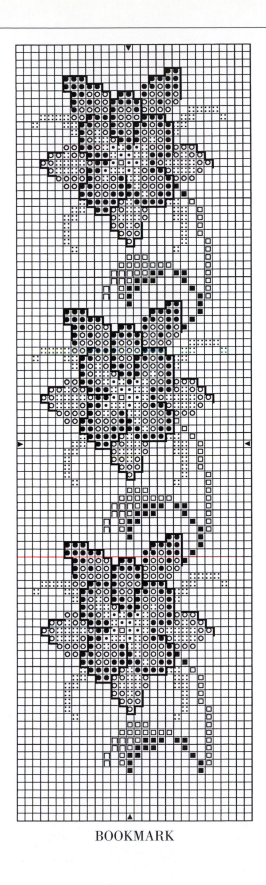

BOOKMARK

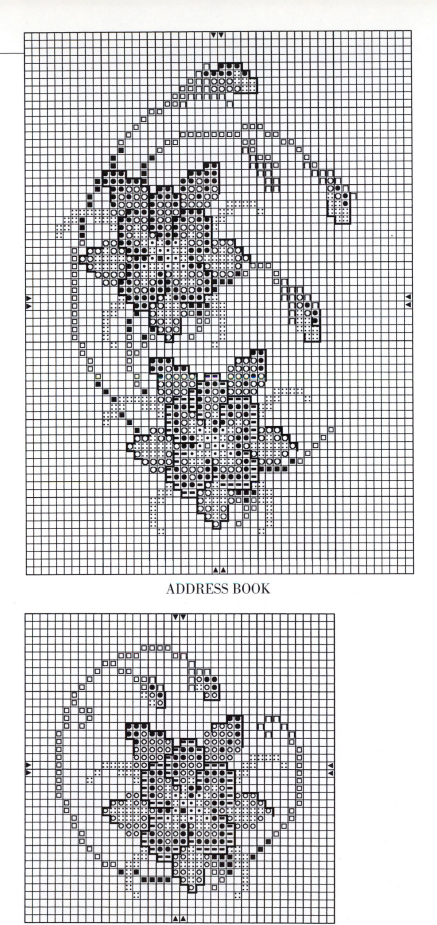

ADDRESS BOOK

PAPERWEIGHT

Sunflower Cushion

Stitch this colourful cushion and capture the warmth of long summer days. This project would be guaranteed to brighten any corner of your home, but it would also make a practical and very unusual golden wedding present.

SUNFLOWER CUSHION

●

THE EMBROIDERY

Run a basting line (using ordinary sewing cotton) from the top to the bottom of the Aida fabric, 16cm (6½in) in from the left-hand side. Mount the fabric in a frame as shown on page 5.

Start the embroidery 4cm (1½in) below the top raw edge of the fabric and one square to the right of the basting line. The design is repeated every 11cm (4½in) and it is suggested that you have a number of photocopies of the chart so that you can mark off the pattern as you stitch. Finish 4cm (1½in) above the bottom raw edge.

Following the chart, complete all the cross stitching, using two strands of thread in the needle. Be careful not to take dark threads across the back of the work in such a way that they show through on the right side.

MAKING THE COVER

Take the finished embroidery from the frame and remove the basting line. Wash the fabric if necessary and press the work lightly on the wrong side, using a steam iron. Trim the fabric to measure 45.5cm (18in) square, making sure that the embroidery is no closer than 11cm (4½in) to the left-hand edge. Place the embroidery and backing fabric with right sides together and machine stitch round the edges, taking a 12mm (½in) seam allowance and leaving an opening of 38cm (15in) at the bottom of the cushion. Trim across the seam allowance at the corners,

to remove excess fabric, and turn the cover right side out. Insert the cushion pad into the cover; fold in the remaining seam allowances, and slipstitch the opening, leaving a small gap at one end for the cord ends. Pin the cord trim around the edge of the cushion cover, tucking one end into the opening. Neatly slipstitch the cord in place, tucking the remaining end into the opening when you reach the starting point again, and stitching across the opening to seal it.

COVERED PIPING

You may, if you prefer, cover the piping with either bias-cut fabric of your choice or a bias binding; alternatively, ready-covered piping cord is available in several widths and many colours.

1 To apply piping, pin and baste it to the right side of the fabric, with seam lines matching. Clip into the seam allowance where necessary.

2 With right sides together, place the second piece of fabric on top, enclosing the piping. Baste and then either hand stitch in place or machine stitch, using a zipper foot. Stitch as close to the piping as possible, covering the first line of stitching.

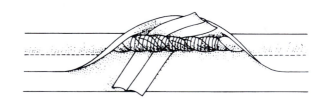

3 To join ends of piping cord together, first overlap the two ends by about 2.5cm (1in). Unpick the two cut ends of bias to reveal the cord. Join the bias strip as shown. Trim and press the seam open. Unravel and splice the two ends of the cord. Fold the bias strip over it, and finish basting around the edge.

SUNFLOWER CUSHION ▶		ANCHOR	DMC	MADEIRA
·	Light gold	306	725	0113
❙❙	Medium gold	307	783	0114
⊞	Dark gold	308	782	2212
V	Light green	256	906	1411
☐	Medium green	258	904	1412
■	Dark green	246	986	1404
X	Brown	310	780	2303

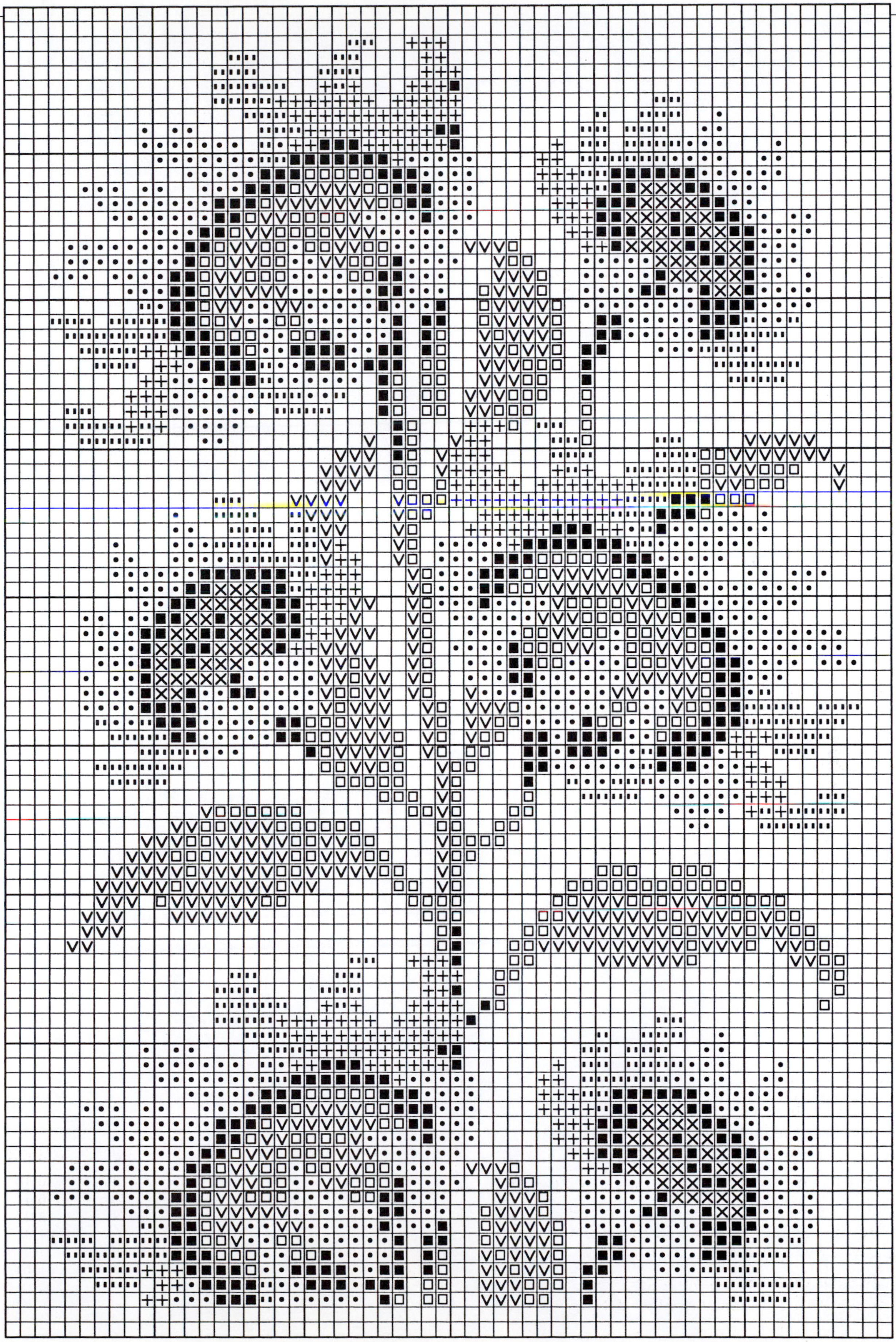

Lazy Daisy Bathroom Set

Brighten up your bathroom with ever-popular daisies. These quick, versatile designs would look equally good as a colourful trim for bed linen and curtains.

LAZY DAISY BATHROOM SET

YOU WILL NEED

*14-count waste canvas (for suppliers, see page 40) –
the canvas should always be at least 2.5cm (1in)
larger each way than the finished motif(s)
Stranded embroidery cotton in the colours given in
the panel
Sharp needle
Items of your choice*

*NOTE: for best results, use items made from non-
stretch fabrics; you can, if preferred, decorate the
towels with strips of Aida band, embroidered with the
repeat motifs, instead of using the waste canvas
technique to embroider directly on the towels.*

●

WASH BAG AND SLIPPERS

For the wash bag, cut a 10cm (4in) square of waste
canvas. Centre the canvas over the area where the
motif is to be stitched and pin it in position; use the
blue threads in the canvas to ensure that the finished
embroidery lies straight on the bag, aligning it either
with the weave of the fabric or with the pattern (if
any). Start the design from the centre, treating each
pair of canvas threads as one. The pins may be
removed after a few stitches have secured the canvas
to the bag.

Following the chart, cross stitch in the usual
manner, using three strands of thread in a sharp-
pointed needle. Take care to stitch through the holes
and not the canvas, as the latter would make it difficult to withdraw the threads. Finally, stitch the
petals of the daisies, using six strands of thread.
These are indicated on the chart by a straight line
and are made by a single chain stitch. This stitch is
called lazy daisy stitch and it can be found in the
general instructions. If you find this stitch is difficult
to work on the canvas it can be stitched after
the waste canvas has been removed. Although it is
easier to stitch afterwards, you will need to estimate
the length of the stitches.

Exactly the same method is used to stitch the
slippers. For these you will need two pieces of
canvas, each 5cm (2in) square (one piece for each
slipper). Please note that there are two separate

designs, one for the left and the other for the right
slipper. After pinning the waste canvas in position,
follow the above instructions.

For the bath towels, you will need 3.5cm × 5cm
(1½in × 2in) and for the hand towels, a 3cm (1¼in)
square of waste canvas for each motif. The design is
repeated every 2.5cm (1in) on the hand towels and
worked in groups of three (one set of three at each
end and one in the centre) on the bath towel.

FINISHING

When you have finished the embroidery, cut away
surplus canvas around the design. Dampen the right
side with slightly warm water and leave it for a few
minutes until the sizing in the canvas softens. Gently
remove the canvas threads, one at a time, with
tweezers. The threads should come out easily, but
the operation requires patience; if you try to remove
several threads at once, this could spoil your
embroidery.

LAZY DAISY

Bring your needle out at the base of the petal shape;
hold the thread down with your thumb as you re-
insert the needle slightly to the right of the starting
point. Bring the point of the needle out, inside the
loop, at the required length of the stitch (petal); pull
the thread through, and make a small stitch over the
end of the loop, to hold it. Bring the needle out again
at the base of the next stitch (petal).

LAZY DAISIES ▶	ANCHOR	DMC	MADEIRA
White	1	White	White
☐ Yellow	298	972	0107
☒ Red	46	666	0210
■ Green	238	703	1307

*Note: use all six strands of white thread for lazy daisy stitches; back-
stitch stem outlines using three strands of green thread.*

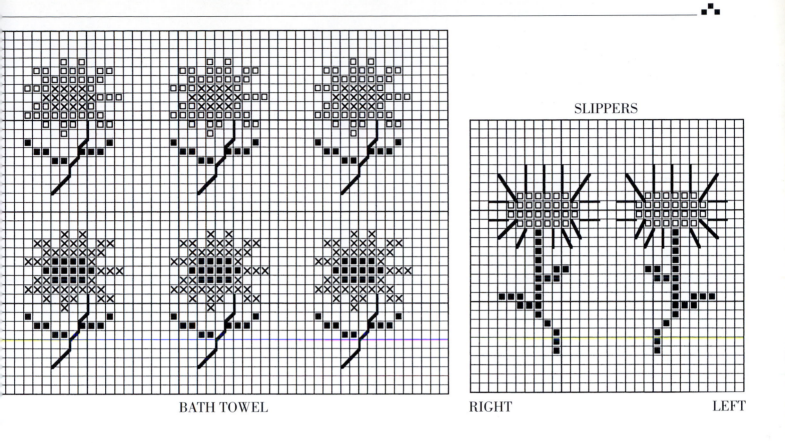

BATH TOWEL

SLIPPERS

RIGHT   **LEFT**

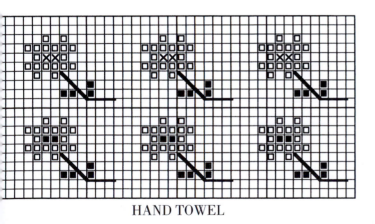

HAND TOWEL

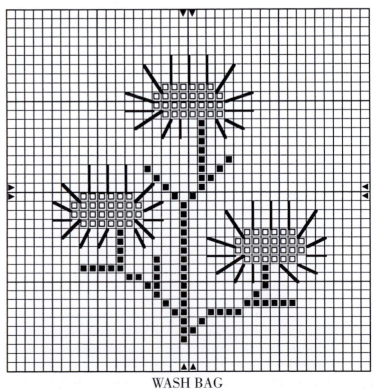

WASH BAG

ACKNOWLEDGEMENTS

My grateful thanks go to my family for their invaluable help, with special thanks to my daughter Elizabeth for her beautiful stitching.

I also wish to thank Coats Paton Crafts and Framecraft Miniatures Ltd for supplying the materials for this book.

SUPPLIERS

All fabrics and threads were supplied by Coats Paton Crafts, and the cards (page 12), napkin rings (page 20), address book and paperweight (page 28) were supplied by Framecraft Miniatures Limited, a mail order company that is also a useful source of supply for other cross stitch items, including blank embroidery cards, picture frames and linens:

Framecraft Miniatures Limited
372/376 Summer Lane
Hockley
Birmingham, B19 3QA
England
Telephone: 0121 212 4442

Addresses for Framecraft stockists worldwide
Ireland Needlecraft Pty Ltd
2-4 Keppel Drive
Hallam, Victoria 3803
Australia

Danish Art Needlework
PO Box 442, Lethbridge
Alberta T1J 3Z1
Canada

Sanyei Imports
PO Box 5, Hashima Shi
Gifu 501-62
Japan

The Embroidery Shop
286 Queen Street
Masterton
New Zealand

Anne Brinkley Designs Inc.
246 Walnut Street
Newton
Mass. 02160
USA

S A Threads and Cottons Ltd.
43 Somerset Road
Cape Town
South Africa

For information on your nearest stockist of embroidery cotton, contact the following:

DMC
(also distributors of Zweigart fabrics)

UK
DMC Creative World Limited
62 Pullman Road, Wigston
Leicester, LE8 2DY
Telephone: 0116 2811040

USA
The DMC Corporation
Port Kearney Bld.
10 South Kearney
N.J. 07032-0650
Telephone: 201 589 0606

AUSTRALIA
DMC Needlecraft Pty
P.O. Box 317
Earlswood 2206
NSW 2204
Telephone: 02599 3088

COATS AND ANCHOR
Coats Paton Crafts
McMullen Road
Darlington
Co. Durham DL1 1YQ
Telephone: 01325 381010

USA
Coats & Clark
P.O. Box 27067
Dept CO1
Greenville SC 29616
Telephone: 803 234 0103

AUSTRALIA
Coats Patons Crafts
Thistle Street
Launceston
Tasmania 7250
Telephone: 00344 4222

MADEIRA

UK
Madeira Threads (UK) Limited
Thirsk Industrial Park
York Road, Thirsk
N. Yorkshire, YO7 3BX
Telephone: 01845 524880

USA
Madeira Marketing Limited
600 East 9th Street
Michigan City
IN 46360
Telephone: 219 873 1000

AUSTRALIA
Penguin Threads Pty Limited
25-27 Izett Street
Prahran
Victoria 3181
Telephone: 03529 4400

Dominique Morin

How to Understand God

SCM PRESS LTD

Translated by John Bowden from the French
Pour dire Dieu
published 1989 by Les Editions du Cerf,
29 bd Latour-Maubourg, Paris

British Library Cataloguing in Publication Data

Morin, Dominique
How to understand God.
1. God
I. Title II. Pour dire Dieu. *English*
211

ISBN 0–334–02451–X

211

20024 594x

First published in English 1990
by SCM Press Ltd, 26–30 Tottenham Road, London N1 4BZ

Typeset at The Spartan Press Ltd, Lymington, Hants
and printed in Great Britain by Clays Ltd, St Ives plc

Contents

Preface

In this book we are going to risk talking about God. We shall be doing so from a 'philosophical' perspective. That is, we shall begin more from our human questioning and experience, by investigating the great thinkers, both believers and atheists, who have considered this problem.

It is clear that it will not be possible to provide 'the' solution to this question. After we have thought about it, it is for each reader to decide for himself or herself, personally and freely. What I want to do is just to provide, in as simple and approachable a way as possible, further elements for reflection to those who are interested, no matter what their relationship to God may be: whether they believe in God, reject God or cannot make up their minds either way.

When people talk about God, they often do so in a very imprecise way. Whether affirming or denying God, they sometimes use arguments which are scarcely notable for their clarity or their coherence, and which often end up by posing the problem very badly, as a result of insufficient information. So they end up by being extremely discouraging. Consequently, instead of embarking on a quest, those who listen to these arguments remain confused and simply go by their impressions, whether positive or negative, without being able to justify them or make them more profound. Here I want simply to provide some basic elements for consideration by those who want to go a step further.

Of course I am writing from a particular standpoint. It cannot be otherwise, since on being confronted with such a problem one cannot remain neutral – even if the choice is always difficult for everyone, and will always remain so. But my perspective is a clear one: while recognizing the logic and consistency of those who deny God – and we shall see why – I affirm his existence, and it will become clear that this affirmation of God is as logical and consistent as the denial of God. But we shall also see that it is not a matter of affirming the existence of just any God on any conditions, and perhaps that is the essential thing in this debate.

In other words, I shall try to present the problem with the utmost clarity and rigour, setting out the arguments on both sides carefully, in order to allow readers to make their choice in full knowledge, in possession of what they need to know.

I shall be referring to a number of books about the question in the text. Bibliographical details about all of them will be found in the section 'For Further Reading' at the end of this book.

PART ONE

The Question of God Today

'Do modern men and women still ask questions about God?'

Heinz Zahrnt, *What Kind of God?*, p.69

'Whether a decision today is made for or against God, it must be made realistically, not in the light of a Greek or mediaeval but of a modern understanding of God.'

Hans Küng, *Does God Exist?*, p.127

'Do modern men and women still ask questions about God?' The answer to this is clearly 'Yes!' Certainly, at least in our Western civilizations, a great many people very rarely ask questions, if at all. (Things are different in other civilizations, for example the Islamic world, India and Latin America, where religion is almost omnipresent.) But the question of God still means something to a great many others – perhaps more than one might think – even if the replies given to it are very different.

In saying this I am not just reassuring believers, but acknowledging the facts. The phenomenon is easy enough to see, even if it is difficult to interpret. There is evidence of it in the numerous books which have been published recently on the problem of God; in the vitality of believers who reflect on the problem individually or in groups; and in the thought and writing of all those who, whether unbelievers or 'semi-believers', keep asking the question. There is also evidence of it in the massive and often ambiguous phenomenon of the 'return of the religious' (sects, spiritualism, magic, astrology) and even in the cinema!

Why do people keep asking this question about God? That is hard to say, because motives are very different. But one might suppose that here, in many forms, in the end we find the problem of the meaning of life. Without doubt, when many people ask about the meaning of their existence, they find it difficult to avoid raising the question of God – though (and we shall return to this point later) it is also possible to refuse outright to raise this question of God or to be utterly indifferent to it.

While the problem is at the heart of the preoccupations of believers, it can also preoccupy unbelievers, and it is from the unbeliever's perspective that we shall begin this book. Why and how can we raise the question of God today?

As I have said, our reflection will be more of a 'philosophical' type. It will begin from our questions and the image of God that we have when we say 'God', in other words when we try to say who God is on the basis of our experience (Chapter 1). Our conception of God, whether or not we are believers, is necessarily more or less dependent on our culture. For us this culture is rooted simultaneously in the tradition of Greek

1

philosophy and the tradition of Judaism and Christianity, and this two-fold origin colours our idea of God, whether we are aware of it or not (Chapter 2). But this is a culture which is strongly marked by what one might call 'modernity', by the fantastic social and cultural evolution which has been human experience for around two centuries, with repercussions which are of prime importance for the way in which we raise the question of God today (Chapter 3).

1

The Philosophical Approach

God, a question arising out of our concrete experience

We shall not be approaching the question of God from the Bible and Christian revelation, as Christians have often done, but from the human realities that we experience and see today: we shall be approaching the problem of God by way of philosophy.

Why a 'philosophical approach'?

Don't be afraid of the word 'philosophy'! The reality denoted by the word is in fact quite simple. We all do philosophy. We do philosophy when we begin to reflect on and ask questions about the meaning of our existence and the specific everyday experience we have of ourselves, of others, and of the universe around us and in which we live. In this way we put ourselves in an 'existential' perspective, and these questions may (or may not) raise the question of God.

So if we give priority to this orientation, instead of supposing that the question is settled by immediately affirming belief in God with a reference to his revelation, we shall begin by reflecting on the reality around us. We shall ask about the meaning of our life and the significance of the universe by looking at various solutions put forward today, by both atheism and a theism inspired by Judaism and Christianity, asking whether God might not ultimately provide the answer to the questions we ask ourselves.

In adopting this approach I am in no way minimizing the importance of revelation and the act of faith, but only stressing that for the believer, this philosophical approach is quite inseparable from the other more familiar approach which consists in moving from God to human beings by receiving the word of God and his revelation in faith.

Speaking of God today, and speaking of God in a philosophical perspective, is not a secondary task for the believer. It is a task which is both urgent and topical for at least two important reasons. First, because as human beings, starting from our experience, we cannot avoid reflecting on the meaning of our lives and the value of the response which our faith in God prompts. Secondly, because this is a task which often corresponds to a very lively expectation, since despite the religious indifference and atheism around us, many of our contemporaries also raise these questions, and expect believers to help them to provide some answers. Here Christians have something to say.

4

The Christian and the Philosophical Problem of God

In faith, believers encounter a living God . . .

Believers can never forget that in faith they encounter a living God and never a simple idea or a simple concept. Important though it may be, the philosophical approach is not enough for the believer. The God arrived at in this way is strictly rational, a very different idea from the living God of religious faith. God is not an idea that we can arrive at after a good rational argument. The God whom the Christian arrives at in his or her faith is a living reality, a personal God who has revealed himself to men and women, in particular through Jesus Christ. This God is a God whom believers can address and with whom they can enter into dialogue.

To this extent, faith does not mean that people have to be intellectuals, since one can be an authentic believer without ever having studied philosophy or religious science. Ignorance in this area does not prevent anyone from reflecting on his or her religious convictions. Sometimes such people can do so more deeply than certain 'intellectuals'.

. . . but this must never lead to fideism

The real danger here for the believer is in not having a religious culture equivalent to his or her secular culture. Where that happens believers in fact risk succumbing to fideism, a concern simply to justify their own faith, without reflecting more widely. In the long run that could even lead to atheism, once the usefulness of a faith in God totally disconnected with real and concrete everyday life came to be doubted.

That is why the Catholic Church has always condemned fideism, which it sees as being an extremely dangerous attitude, since it most often ends up in subjectivism, sentimentalism, fanaticism, superstition and obscurantism, since the believer tends to see a mystery where in fact there is only ignorance! Fideism is blind submission to the deity in an inhuman and irrational approach, utter childishness.

So believers can no longer agree with the nineteenth-century Danish philosopher Søren Kierkegaard that they must close their mouths to reason. They must be able to justify their faith simultaneously in the eyes of others and in their own eyes. And the need to do that is all the greater, since they are constantly confronted with atheism and religious indifference, so that they cannot avoid giving increasingly clear reasons for their belief in God. Faith cannot simply make affirmations; in the famous words of St Anselm, it 'seeks understanding'.

A necessary effort at reflection and rationality

If reason is not everything when we touch on the problem of God, since (as we have just recalled and as we shall again have occasion to note in due course), the will is a necessary part of affirming or denying God, it is out of the question to neglect reason or even to relativize it. If we do so, we risk leaving aside an essential human dimension, our intelligence.

This is our present perspective, in continuity with the vast majority of theistic philosophers and theologians. While recognizing that there is always something in this sphere which is beyond us, these thinkers have constantly tried to bring out the *rationality* of faith by making this faith deeper and giving it rational justification by presenting reasons for believing in God.

Can we speak of God?

This is obviously the first question that we are led to ask when we touch on this problem of God.

There are very different views on the matter. First of all, even some believers think that all we can say of God is that God exists. They believe that it is impossible to go further than this, since God infinitely surpasses us; and since God is radically different from us by virtue of his very perfection, we cannot say more.

Others, like the philosophers Immanuel Kant and Ludwig Wittgenstein, also think that we cannot say anything about God because God is outside the world of our existence. For that reason we cannot apprehend God correctly; moreover, our language is quite inadequate for speaking correctly of God, since it can relate only to what we know within our own horizons.

Finally, others think that we cannot say anything about God – because God does not exist! This is the atheistic position.

I personally think, following numerous philosophers and theologians, that we *can* speak of God, even if what we say is always insufficient and partly inadequate because in fact God is fundamentally different from us. Here we have the problem of 'naming' God.

The importance and the difficulty of 'names' for God

Einstein, we are told, replied to a journalist who asked him whether he believed in God: 'First tell me what you mean by this word "God" and then I will tell you whether I believe in him.' That was a good answer, because when we talk of God, the crucial question is indeed what we mean by 'God'.

Why is it so important to know whether we can thus seek to say who God is without being content to affirm that God exists, and before even affirming or denying God's existence? Because before we know whether or not God exists, we have to agree on the meaning of this word 'God'.

It is often because people do not take enough time to answer this first question that discussion of God becomes a discussion between deaf people: the word is used in such different ways. Thus we shall see in due course that when the French philosopher Jean-Paul Sartre says that he does not believe in God, paradoxically the believer can agree with him, because the God in whom Sartre does not believe does not have much to do with the God of the Christian revelation. Similarly, when two people argue that God exists, they can in fact have very different conceptions of God and in the end be unable to agree, though they cannot always see why.

Nicolas Malebranche, a Christian philosopher living at the end of the seventeenth century, noted in his *Treatise on Morality*: 'This word "God" is equivocal, and infinitely more so than one believes.' He then went on to add: 'And so people think that they are loving God when in fact they are only loving a huge phantom which they have created for themselves.' The word 'god' has in fact been used to denote natural phenomena, like Neptune the sea-god or Pluto the god of the underworld in Roman times, as well as the God of Christian revelation or the many gods of the many religions through time and space. Nor should we forget the 'God of the philosophers', who also takes many forms, with which theistic, deistic or atheistic philosophers are confronted.

So we should be very attentive to what people say when they are talking about God, and should constantly purify our ideas of God, since despite the very real risks of confusion which arise from

Emmanuel Kant.
'It is not possible to speak of
God, because he is outside the
world of our experience.'

Søren Kierkegaard.
'God can only be approached
through faith.'

such different, not to say contradictory conceptions, we cannot abandon the term 'God' when
we want to talk of God.

The theologian Henri de Lubac has suggested
that we might compare someone trying to
'understand' God to a swimmer who, in order to
keep above the waves, swims out into the ocean,
at each stroke confronted with a new wave. He
constantly pushes back the new pictures which
keep forming, well aware that they are holding
him up but that to stop at them would be to
perish. Any image is in fact dangerous, because
it necessarily distorts God like the distorting
mirrors in travelling fairs. And yet we have to
use these images and to 'name' God if we want to
talk of God; otherwise we must remain silent and
risk falling into indifference or atheism. So these
images allow us to talk of God, and quite often
reveal something of the truth; but the important
thing is constantly to criticize them and take
them up in order to refine them and keep making
them more precise.

How do we speak of God?
Using analogies

So knowing God is neither easy nor obvious. All
the great theologians and philosophers who
have believed in God have been the first to stress
this point: we do not know much about God, and
when it comes to talk of God we can do little
more than stammer.

Why? Because God is absolute perfection and
in essentials that perfection escapes us. All that
we can do is to try to be more specific about this
perfection by taking to an absolute degree all the
relative perfections which are in us and which
we know in our world. For example, when we
say that God is love, we are inevitably referring
to our own capacity to love in order to try to
imagine this love in all its fullness and all its
perfection in God.

We call this the 'method of analogy'. It allows
us to establish a certain resemblance, a certain
'analogy', between God and us. This method is

7

The word 'God' is the most loaded of all human words

God . . . is the most heavy-laden of all human words. None has become so soiled, so mutilated. Just for this reason I may not abandon it. Generations of men have laid the burden of their anxious lives upon this word and weighed it to the ground; it lies in the dust and bears their whole burden. The races of men with their religious factions have torn the word to pieces; they have killed for it and died for it, and it bears their finger-marks and their blood. Whence might I find a word like it to describe the highest? . . . We must esteem those who interdict it because they rebel against the injustice and wrong which are so readily referred to 'God' for authorization. But we may not give it up . . .

Martin Buber, *The Eclipse of God*, pp.17f.

extremely valuable, even indispensable, if we are to try to come a little closer to the mystery of God. However, it is far from being completely satisfactory, because this resemblance is always very imperfect and therefore always misleading.

All that we can say of God by using the 'method of analogy' therefore remains vague, inadequate, imperfect and finally full of danger, since for the reasons that I have just stressed, what we can say of God is always unsatisfactory and runs the risk of leading to serious errors, which can become formidable obstacles to any knowledge that we can have of God.

For all these reasons, when we use this method of analogy, it is worth paying great attention to what we are saying, without hesitating constantly to keep questioning our 'knowledge'. We need to be particularly mistrustful when we 'understand' God too easily, since, as St Augustine was fond of saying, 'if you understand, it is not God'.

That having been said, once we begin to talk of God we cannot do without the appeal to analogy, which adds much greater penetration to our thought.

Names for God today

So it is indispensable for us to try to give to God the best names we can, and to do so without being vague, since far from taking away the true God, rigour and clarity can only help us to get close to God, and to do so while taking account of our contemporary cultural universe.

The way in which we give names to God can never in fact be independent of our culture and the way in which it came into being. So first we must go backwards to see the origin of the conception of God which we have today.

2

The History of God

Nowadays, the most common image of God in our civilization with its Judaeo-Christian tradition is that of a perfect and omnipotent being, creator of the world. This image is the result of a long development which has deep roots in human history, apparently from the time when human beings first led a conscious existence.

The origin of the idea of God

For a long time, it was thought that there was a progression in the development of this notion of God through the ages, beginning from a very vague notion of the divine and ending with the idea of God that we have nowadays in our Western societies. The idea of God would thus have undergone a kind of progress, a development from 'inferior' to 'superior' beliefs, in three major stages: first of all a very vague idea of God, or rather of the divine, through magical, animal or fetishist cults; then the transition to polytheism (belief in the simultaneous existence of several gods); and finally the transition to monotheism (belief in the existence of a single God). In this perspective one could claim that the idea of God as transcendent and personal was finally a distillation of former religious experiences and thus was acquired at a late stage by humanity.

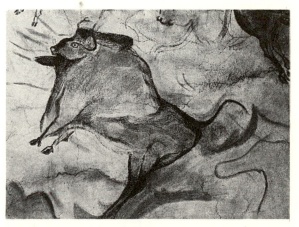

Cave painting from Altamira.
The idea of the divine seems to have developed with the emergence of the human consciousness.

However, these so-called 'evolutionary theories' have been questioned since the beginning of the twentieth century by specialists who, after long research, have concluded that so-called 'inferior' religions would have derived from a primitive monotheism. That is above all the view of Mircea Eliade, a great expert in the history of religions. He rejects any evolutionist theory and thinks that he can attest from the beginning belief in a supreme Being who has the attributes of the creator God. And it seems that in

The God of Non-Christian Religions

The conception of God in Judaism and Christianity is only one among numerous others . . . which are not necessarily absurd or uninteresting!

Is it permissible for us Westerners and Christians still to talk about God as if our understanding of him is the only one possible? From the standpoint of the comparative study of religions . . . Christianity is one religion among others. Is it not a sign of provincialism if we raise universal claims from a very particular viewpoint? Might it not be evidence of a higher universalism if we remained continually aware of our own sociocultural limitations and restrictions even in the field of religion?

The religious experiences, forms, structures and ideas of humanity are infinitely rich; the problems they raise are infinitely complex . . . The images of God are diverse: their divergences and convergences, distinctions and blendings are incalculable . . .

We want to recognize, respect and appreciate the truth of other conceptions of God, but without relativizing the Christian faith in the true God or reducing it to general truths. In this way mutual contempt might give way to mutual appreciation, disregard to understanding, attempts at conversion to study and dialogue.

Hans Küng, *Does God Exist?*, p.587

---

fact experience of the divine has taken many forms without it being possible to discover in any detail the stages of the stumbling quest for God.

What we can, though, be certain of, is that the idea of a divine reality has always been a human preoccupation, regardless of how this reality is perceived and thought of. In it lie the roots of the philosophical research and religious reflection in Judaism and Christianity, which we shall now go on to consider.

The God of modern theism in the tradition of Greek philosophy and Judaism/Christianity

Throughout the history of Western thought, philosophers and theologians have offered us many images of God, converging and diverging, sometimes even diametrically opposed. So there are immediately both similarities and marked differences – sometimes real oppositions – between the god or gods of the first Greek thinkers, the creator God of mediaeval philosophy, the God of Kant who guarantees the moral law, the oppressor God denounced by atheistic modern philosophers and the image of God in contemporary Christian theology.

And yet all those who have come across these views, no matter what their personal convictions, have contributed to a constantly better perception of the idea of God, by their research, their reflections, their affirmations, their rejections and their hesitations.

From the first century this reflection has been found at the confluence of two traditions, the tradition of Greek philosophy and the tradition of Judaism/Christianity.

Plato and Aristotle. Rome, the Vatican.
Our conception of God is partly rooted in the Greek philosophical tradition.

The God of the Greek philosophers

Although we often find among the philosophers of ancient Greece a remarkable mixture of popular polytheistic belief and the affirmation of the divine, or a God of a monotheistic kind, it should be noted that there are great differences between them over their conceptions of God. However, the details of these differences are unimportant here; all we need note are three main characteristics.

The first is that God is conceived as an impersonal principle with no interest in the world. God is not perceived as a person.

The second is that the Greek philosophers had no idea of creation. For them the world exists from all eternity. God is only the principle of order. He organizes the world. Some, notably Aristotle, even thought that God has nothing to do with the world and plays no part in it. That was to pose certain problems to philosophers and Christian theologians, serious problems which we shall be discussing in more detail in due course.

The third important characteristic is that God is not conceived of as infinite, since for these philosophers infinity is synonymous with imperfection. It is whatever is unfinished, unaccomplished, incomplete. In a word, it is that which is imperfect.

The God of Judaism and Christianity

However, the current image of God today in the Western world is equally dependent on Jewish-Christian tradition. In fact the first Christians very rapidly sought to fuse the philosophical conceptions of the Greeks with those of growing Christianity. They sought to endow God with attributes arising from the teaching of the Bible of which the ancient philosophers had made no mention.

By contrast to the philosophers, the Christians affirmed in particular that God is a person, that he is creator, that he is omnipotent and infinite, and that he is the perfect Being, infinitely good, the source of all existence and all value. Finally, on top of all that, Christian doctrine added that 'God is love'.

The essential affirmation here, the one which finally takes in all the others and which introduces a completely new dimension in comparison with Greek philosophy, is that God is a person. How are we to understand that?

11

Theism and Deism

These two terms are not synonyms

The term 'theism' comes from the Greek *theos*, God

This conception of God is very familiar to us. It is quite simply the one people usually have when they talk about God. It arose out of the encounter between Greek philosophy and the great monotheistic religions (Judaism, Christianity and Islam).

So the term 'theism' is a general description of all the doctrines, even purely philosophical ones, which affirm the existence of a personal God who transcends the world (that is, who is external to it and superior to it), a world which is the result of his creative action.

This conception of God is that of Christianity. So it is that which is generally accepted by Christian philosophers. And it is still the conception to which atheistic philosophers generally refer in order to reject it.

The term 'deism' comes from the Latin *deus*, God

Deism originated in the nineteenth century, under the influence of violently anti-Christian philosophers like Voltaire.

This term denotes the doctrine of those who, while rejecting the God of Christian revelation, nevertheless accept the existence of a supreme Being whose nature remains somewhat indeterminate. This God does not have anything in particular to do with God conceived of as a person as one finds him in theism, as described above. In a variety of forms this deism invaded Western Europe, leading to indifference and atheism, and winning over many people who had previously been Christians.

The great contribution of Judaism and Christianity: God is a person

For believers, and for philosophers who relate to the conception of God which has arisen from Jewish-Christian revelation, God is not a simple principle. God is a person. God is really a person, because one cannot imagine God without reason, without intelligence, without freedom, without love, without will, without feelings. God is one whom men and women can address in full confidence. That is particularly important for believers, since if they believe in God, they can believe only in a personal God and can express their belief only in personal categories.

However, this is one of the main difficulties for belief today, because there is still too often a tendency to imagine God as a person more or less in our image, as a majestic old man in a white beard living in heaven with his court of angels and saints. The source of catastrophic ambiguities, this dreadful picture has prompted many extremely dangerous and damaging errors of interpretation – so much so that certain journalists asked Yuri Gagarin, the first cosmonaut to travel in space, whether he had met God on his journey.

God is certainly not a person as human beings are persons, even with all human perfections and more. God is not just a superman; God is even more than that. However, this 'more' can be expressed only in an extremely imprecise and confusing way. Even if we use all the possibilities of the 'method of analogy', we can scarcely say more than that God is beyond all representations.

So that, overall, is the image of God which we have inherited from our cultural tradition. But this image of God has equally been very much influenced over the past two centuries by the new picture that we have progressively made of our universe, by the fantastic explosion of our knowledge in all spheres . . . and by two particularly important phenomena relating to this problem of God. First there is the problem of secularization, which, as we shall see, far from necessarily leading to atheism, can be the occasion for a better approach to God. Then there is the massive phenomenon of modern atheism, to which we shall be returning later.

It is clear that nowadays – without abandoning the numerous findings of our predecessors, which remain vital on a great many points – we can only envisage the problem of God against this background of modernity.

The mystery of God

If an ordinary human being – your fiancé, your wife, your child – is already an ocean of mystery, why should not God be the mystery of mysteries? We must respect God by not claiming to understand him as though he were the page of a newspaper. If we claim to understand him perfectly, we reduce him to our own little level, and God is no longer the personal God, the God who is as mysterious as any person, the God who is more mysterious than any person. He becomes a false God of our making.

T. Rey-Mermet

3

The Influence of the Modern World on Images of God Today

Human beings in control of the world: the phenomenon of secularization

The use of the term 'secularization' in philosophy and theology is fairly recent. It used to belong in the legal sphere and denoted a move from religious to lay life or the transfer of church property to the state. Nowadays it denotes the way in which the realities of the world and human life tend to establish an increasing autonomy, removing themselves from any sacral, religious or church order.

This development in our civilizations corresponds to the emergence of the modern world. In fact one can say that until the beginning of the eighteenth century people in the West lived in a very religious world. The world, the church and God formed as it were three concentric circles which almost coincided and which fitted together very well. Subsequently, however, these three circles very rapidly became detached, as human beings became aware that they could take over the world completely and ignore the two other circles. They discovered that science no longer needs God as a hypothesis, that politics no longer has anything to do with the

church, and that morality is no longer under religious control.

Paul Hazard began his famous book, *The Crisis of the European Conscience*, like this: 'What people of the seventeenth century loved was hierarchy, discipline, order provided by the authorities, dogmas which offered a firm rule for life. But constraint, authority and dogmas were what the people of the eighteenth century, their immediate successors, detested. The former were Christians and the latter anti-Christians . . . The majority of· French people used to think like Bossuet; suddenly they all thought like Voltaire. That was a revolution.'

So people progressively left the tutelage of the church and God and found in themselves the resources and the main lines of their individual and collective development. From then on they refused to count on an omnipotent God who was more or less a magician. Freed from the tutelage of the church and religion, they were no longer willing to be guided by them. They took the risk of thinking and acting by themselves and took

The world from above and the world from below

The 'divinized world' has become the 'hominized world'. The world of God has become the world of man . . . And when he looks about him, man no longer sees the 'footprints of God' everywhere, but only the 'footprints of man', the consequences of his own transforming action upon the world.

A new vision of the world derived from the syntheses of Hellenism and Christianity which had endured throughout the middle ages into modern times. According to this dualism, there stand opposed to each other two different worlds, thought of as each possessing substantial existence: the higher and the lower, the supernatural and the natural, the spiritual and the physical, the heavenly divine world and the earthly human world . . . Of these, the higher, supernatural, spiritual divine world was regarded as the only real and true one. It defined the horizon of the lower, natural and physical world, and was set above all earthly and human life like the light of the sun above the earth, lighting it from above and making it what it is. But as the process of the enlightenment, that activity on the part of man which illuminated and changed the world, came to its conclusion, the ends of the world as it were grew together over our head . . . and became our new heaven.

This happened in the process of secularization which has just been described, by which the world became worldly. Through this process the world beyond, the supernatural divine world, which hitherto had been regarded as the only real and effective world, has become unreal and ineffective. It has lost its power and no longer gives life.

There are more and more people who no longer believe in heaven, hell and eternal life, and yet live and act responsibly here in time. The background to their attitude is a shift of consciousness from the world beyond to this world. The orientation of life has swung through exactly 180°. New priorities have been substituted for old, and a real 'revaluation of all values' has taken place. It seems as though what the young Hegel said is now being fulfilled:

'Apart from some earlier attempts, it has been reserved in the main for our own epoch to vindicate at least in theory the human ownership of the treasures formerly squandered in heaven.'

In this age man has begun to build himself a house in a world which has ceased to be divine, to make himself 'at home' on earth.

Heinz Zahrnt, *What Kind of God?*, pp.22f.

---

full advantage of their freedom by giving themselves their own laws and their own values. They took complete charge of the world in which they lived. The fantastic progress of science and technology gave them increasingly effective and practical means of dominating the world. They became masters of their universe.

In fact, if on the one hand Copernicus and Galileo made people aware that their earth was no longer the centre of the world, on the other the first great scientific and technological discoveries made them aware that the planet earth was their sphere and not primarily that of God.

Then, little by little, this emancipation extended from the sphere of the sciences and technology to all the other spheres of human life: politics, economics, the law, the state, culture, education, medicine, welfare, etc.

It is worth remembering the speed with which new ideas came into circulation and discoveries multiplied: the telegraph was invented in 1684, the weaving machine in 1735, the steam engine in 1764, gas lighting in 1786, the year of the first ascent by balloon. The thirty-five volumes of *The Encyclopaedia* which appeared between 1751 and 1772 rightly aimed at taking stock of human

The Encyclopaedia. New ideas came into circulation and discoveries multiplied.

knowledge: scientific progress, the mechanical arts, the marvellous machines which were invented. It also brought together in a common enterprise all those who in the name of reason were engaged in shaking off the yoke of prejudice and authority.

Intoxicated by their scientific and technological triumphs, people ended up by rejecting God: God was dead! From now on human beings felt perfectly capable of taking charge of their world. Also, in a gigantic movement, they progressively went on to eliminate God and to take his place. They became, as Descartes put it, 'masters and owners of nature', and suddenly God in practice ceased to be part of their habitual preoccupations, even if sometimes they would refer to him in moments of crisis. In all essentials God was well and truly dead. From now on human beings were making their own history.

The challenge to God

Nowadays we conceive of the world as a history, that is, as something in the making, as the unbounded scene of the action of human transformation, and we conceive of human beings as having creative freedom to transform themselves and the world. Human beings, and no longer God, produce this history and are responsible for it. By acquiring their autonomy, in both thought and action, human beings are delivered at a stroke from an omnipotent God whose servants and slaves they were, and a God who would make good the defects of their existence – the one who provided consolation for the human condition, for suffering and for death – as being gaps in human knowledge.

So men and women today have come to understand that if there is a God, he cannot be the one who denies their freedom, nor a God who is at the disposal of human beings and can be adapted to their needs, nor a God who can be used to supply our deficiencies and to justify our actions and our enterprises. God cannot be other than a free God, a God who respects the freedom and the growth of human beings and the world, a God who is not useful, but gratuitous.

This first observation is reinforced by the insight that this omnipotent God had been bound up with a certain stage of the world and society. There was a realization of the function which this God had exercised as the guardian of an established order, a powerful conserver, in the world as much as in the church.

There are plenty of examples of the role played by this image of God in the conservation of the order of things in which pride of place is given to the notions of order and hierarchy, while at the same time social disparities are largely hidden or justified.

This challenge to the social function exercised by this image of God ends up by making such a God unbelievable. If there is a God, if God is God, he cannot but be otherwise – a God who is useless and gratuitous, as we saw above. It has to be added that God must be a God who cannot be grasped by thought, a God who cannot be manipulated by human beings; a God who is not the one who endorses the domination and oppression of one human being by another. God must be a free God for free men and women who are making their own history.

These are some of the requirements for the naming of a God in our culture. We cannot distort them; they are the obligatory starting point for the question of God today.

Modern atheism rooted in a desire for independence

This human desire for liberation is matched by the main claims of modern atheism. In essentials, they revolve around three poles which we shall take up again later:

1. Claims in the name of science: science can explain everything and God is a hypothesis which is both useless and an encumbrance.

2. Claims in the name of human beings and their freedom: if God exists, he knows everything, has foreseen everything and human beings are finally just puppets in his hands.

3. Claims in the face of the scandal of evil and suffering: if God exists, why is there evil and suffering, when God cannot but be perfectly good?

The purifying role of atheism

Properly understood, even the modern atheism which originates in the enlightenment has had a purifying and refining effect on theology. Think of the things we took for God! Think of the things we claimed to be the work of God! Think of the things that we have said and done in the name of God! How often have we made God in our own image! From now on this kind of idolatry is impossible. The positive achievement of atheism is the vigorous purification which Christianity, together with its theology, has undergone, bringing the rejection of every kind of idolatry. The French Christian Jean Lacroix once expressed this in the words: 'I am grateful to my atheist friends, for they have taught me not to cheat.'

Heinz Zahrnt, *What Kind of God?*, p.45

A new more satisfying concept of God

But if this powerful movement of secularization has indubitably favoured the development of modern atheism, it has equally had the great merit of leading Christian philosophers and theologians to revise their talk of God in the modern world. In this sense, far from leading to atheism, secularization has played an essential role of purification for the believer today.

It has allowed believers to become aware that the God of Christian revelation has nothing to do with the all too common conception of a sovereign absolute God who is the omnipotent master of a world totally subject to him in which human beings have no margin of freedom.

This erroneous image of God has been rightly criticized by modern Christian thinkers who have stressed the essential importance of human freedom, responsibility and autonomy, an importance which has also been strongly emphasized by the Second Vatican Council: 'The people of our time prize freedom very highly and strive eagerly for it. In this they are right . . . Man's dignity requires him to act out of conscious and free choice' (*Gaudium et Spes* 17). In fact, far from being the gravedigger of human freedom, God is its foundation and guarantor.

This phenomenon of secularization is thus very complex: it proves to be simultaneously the source of atheism and the source of reflection which may help believers to deepen their thought. Seen closely, it is never a simple phenomenon, but has two aspects, one negative and one positive. The negative aspect is its rejection of the religious enterprise; the positive aspect is the access of human beings to their autonomy. Because religion is rejected, the modern world is structured on values which are no longer specifically Christian, even if they have derived from the Christian world. But positively, this means that men and women come of age are responsible for their world. Christians do not have any

An astronaut. Scientific and technical discoveries do not necessarily lead to atheism.

special knowledge from God which is not given to others. They too must take responsibility in full freedom, along with the risks inherent in any choice. Initially sensitive to the threat of secularization, which they identified with de-Christianization, Christians have ended up recognizing a legitimate tendency in it.

That is why we have to distinguish carefully between two attitudes when it comes to secularization: secularism and secularity.

Secularism denotes the movement of human autonomy directed against God and thus leading to atheism.

By contrast, for the believer, secularity denotes the conviction of being able to live a human life in full freedom while affirming the existence of God and his presence in the world, a presence which while real is very discreet and infinitely respectful of human freedom.

These are the main ideas which will form the basis of our reflection and which we shall now go on to consider. This approach will at the same time allow us to examine responses to the objections of atheistic philosophers and to think about God in our present setting, that of the modern world.

PART TWO

Is Science a Way to God?

'From now on it is science, often more than philosophy and perhaps even than religion, which has the privilege of compelling all of humanity to consider collectively the question of its being and its destiny.'

J. Lacroix

'The naive positivistic claim of the nineteenth century has been abandoned for ever . . . The human spirit is now assured of only one certainty, that of its uncertainty.'

Jean Milet

A serious conflict contributed decisively to the advent of modern atheism and to a most important (and most beneficial) revision of the conception of God among believing philosophers and theologians: the conflict between theology and the natural sciences.

Because the church had for too long had a negative and sterile attitude to scientific discoveries, a catastrophic break developed between it and the modern world. So great was this break that, in the 'struggle' between science and religion, at one point it seemed as though the former would definitively obliterate the latter and totally eliminate God from our contemporary culture (Chapter 1). That did not turn out to be the case in the end because the two sides ultimately became aware, particularly after the sorry affair of Galileo and the problem of evolu-

tion, that things were far more complex than had been believed at the moment when a triumphant positivism attacked a church stuck in its conservatism and its mistrust. It steadily emerged that not only did science not contradict the affirmation of God and Christian revelation but sometimes it could even contribute to it.

Finally, cannot the prodigious discoveries of modern science, by making us discover more and more of the unimaginable complexity of our universe, lead us to pose the problem of the creation of the world once again? Is our universe sufficient in itself, or is it the result of a creative act of God? In this way science leads us once again to raise the question of meaning, to ask why this universe exists and why we exist, and hence to restate the problem of God in a definitive way (Chapter 3).

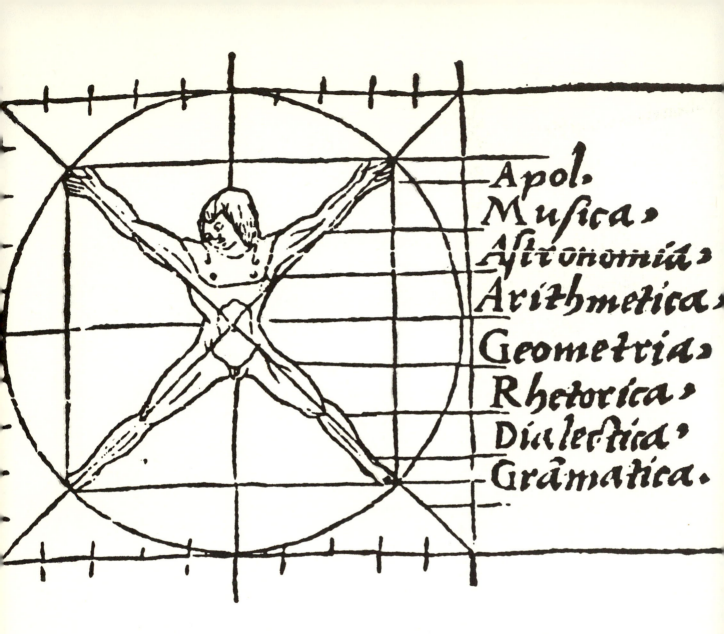

Apol.
Musica.
Astronomia.
Arithmetica.
Geometria.
Rhetorica.
Dialectica.
Gramatica.

'Man is the measure of all things' (Pythagoras).

1

God and Science

For almost two millennia, Christians in the Western world believed, on the basis of statements in the Bible, that the universe had been created in seven days and that this creation dated from about four thousand years before Christ.

The traditional chronology, in particular of the creation and flood, was disseminated throughout the English-speaking world from the seventeenth-century Archbishop Ussher's book *Annales Veteris et Novi Testamenti* (*Annals of the Old and New Testament*), the dates from which were printed in the margins of many Bibles. This chronology continued to be taught in many places right down to the nineteenth century, and in some cases such teaching even lasted into the twentieth century.

Nowadays, however, astrophysicists estimate that our universe is around fifteen thousand million years old, and they are virtually able to reconstruct the main stages of this history from the initial 'big bang' which is supposed to be the 'beginning' of the world. We have moved from a fixed world to a world which is in process of transformation, from a closed and stable world to a universe in expansion and in constant evolution. (Those interested in looking at mod-

ern views of the universe should consult *How to Read the World: Creation in Evolution*, by Christian Montenat, Luc Plateaux and Pascal Roux, also in this series.)

So these amazing discoveries are apparently a long way from the two biblical accounts of the creation of the world which show us, for example, God fashioning earth as the potter fashions clay or operating on Adam by removing a rib in order to be able to form Eve.

Unfortunately, for a long time, the concern was to take these images as scientific truths – which they are not, though they are rich in meaning on another level. This encouraged many non-believers – and some believers ill at ease in their faith – to think that one could not accept both what science affirmed and what the Bible said. So one could not believe both in science and in God.

Here lie the roots of the violent controversies on the relationship between science and faith, and of many people's atheism. The debate is not a new one, but it is always topical. Perhaps it is even more so today, since we live in a world in which science and technology are taking an increasingly important place.

A universe in constant evolution

The 'big bang' is the name given to the explosion (which is thought to have taken place about a thousand million years ago) of the first nucleus of matter, so unimaginably dense that it produced the whole universe, which since then has been in a state of constant expansion.

The galaxies which form it – around 500 million, each containing around a 100 million stars – are moving apart at colossal speeds. Most thinkers, regardless of their philosophical or theological opinions, are now in virtual agreement that this theory is now the most probable one, but note the need of other discoveries to confirm it – or disprove it!

Our earth contains many elements without which we cannot conceive life, and which are indeed vital for the maintenance of life on earth. In particular carbon is a crucial ingredient of all living systems. Where did these elements come from? Only hydrogen and helium formed in the first moments of the universe after the big bang, before the density decreased so as to prevent further fusion of protons and neutrons. However, when stars formed, nuclear reactions began to take place, and the heavier elements were synthesized inside stars by nuclear process. When a heavy star exhausts its supplies of nuclear fuel, the core may implode rapidly and shrink to nuclear densities. This releases huge gravitational energy as a result of which the surface area of the star explodes. The explosion of a supernova, creating enormous luminosity, may be observed from earth by telescope. The force of the explosion disperses the heavier elements into the area around the galaxy, and later when stars and planets form, they incorporate these debris into themselves. Life as we know it could only occur because of the death of an earlier generation of stars. The process leading to this explosion is dependent on the strength of the 'weak interaction'. *It seems remarkable that the possibility of a planet where life as we know it could evolve should depend upon the precise value of this particular constant.*

The most recent theories concerning the origin of the cosmos can take us one step forward: they can explain how it was *possible* for some of these 'coincidences' to occur. What they cannot do is to explain their actual occurrence. In the same way, the latest attempts at Grand Unified Theory (the object of which is to relate together the fundamental forces of the cosmos) may be able to show how 'constants' came into being, but what they cannot do is to explain the actual 'constants' themselves which have made possible the emergence of life on this planet.

Hugh Montefiore, *The Probability of God*, pp.29, 30

A relatively recent conflict

Contrary to what is often believed, the church has not always been systematically opposed to scientific progress. For a long time it at least allowed scientific progress and the development of technology along with the elimination of deities which were thought to rule the universe, even if it did not encourage this progress. It did so in continuity with the Bible which had 'desacralized' the universe.

In Genesis the stars and animals are no longer worshipped. Stripped of their divinity they can become the objects of study. Moreover, Genesis assigns to human beings as their primordial role the exploitation of the whole earth. So it is possible to see the first biblical accounts as encouragement towards a rational exploitation of the universe.

Taken overall, at least a fairly positive attitude of the church in this sphere allowed scholars to develop progressively a fairly rigorous knowledge of reality. We should remember that this had also been done among the host of Greek philosophers like Aristotle, who sought to understand the universe in a rational way.

From this point of view it can be said that despite some barriers which were more cultural than strictly religious, the church helped the sciences to develop as such and to regain their independence, at least up to the modern era. Then, however, there developed those violent conflicts between the church and scientists to which I have just referred, because the scientists' discoveries seemed to eliminate God.

As Bishop Walter Kasper has put it: 'Initially there was a widespread conviction that faith and knowledge were reconcilable. The work of G. W. Leibniz (1646–1716), one of the last universal scholars, was representative of the attempt to find a new synthesis of faith and knowledge. But the more the scientists discovered the regularities of nature, the more they were forced to eliminate God from the world. They needed him now only on the periphery and to fill up lacunae in human knowledge' (*The God of Jesus Christ*, p.22).

Science seemed increasingly able to explain everything in a precise and rigorous manner which satisfied reason, while the Bible seemed to be no more than a naive collection of archaic legends, particularly when it came to problems about the universe and its origins. Hence it appeared that one could not both accept scientific discoveries and believe in God. The opposition became absolute, and so obvious did it seem that the scientific mentality was incompatible with the religious mentality of the believer that the situation of God seemed to be particularly compromised.

Positivism

Scientism, or positivism, was the most elaborate form of this scientific atheism. Auguste Comte, who largely contributed to the development of this positivist movement in the nineteenth century, and Jacques Monod, who has recently illustrated it, are probably its best-known and most typical representatives.

Auguste Comte

Faced with the fantastic progress of the sciences, Comte came to think that they should be enough to explain everything, so that it was useless to appeal to God or to supernatural forces to understand the world around us and to understand ourselves.

In his view it was also necessary firmly to renounce any religious or metaphysical explanation, i.e. any explanation going beyond the framework of specific sense-experience. Such explanations were sheer imagination and totally devoid of interest because they appealed to factors which could not be verified scientifically. It was necessary to keep exclusively to facts known by observation and concrete experience, in other words, to what was known by science. From this perspective God and religion become useless and even harmful, to the degree that they fettered scientific progress and put a brake on human flourishing.

That is the foundation of 'positive' philosophy. According to Auguste Comte, the term

Auguste Comte. Science ought to explain everything.

What is positivism?

A philosophical position belonging to the empirical tradition, according to which man can have no knowledge of anything but phenomena, that is, of what is directly apprehended by the senses, or one of them. 'Positive' knowledge is here associated with the various fields of science; there must be no question of going beyond the limits of what is given in observation: inevitably, both theology and metaphysics are regarded as speculation.

John Kent, in *A New Dictionary of Christian Theology*

'positive' (evident, sure, attested, certain, concrete) indicates that in the modern period philosophy can be interested only in reality as it is open to scientific examination. Whatever the truth may be, it can come *only* and exclusively from science.

Jacques Monod

Comte affirmed that in the nineteenth century. In the twentieth century his position was taken up again by a brilliant French biochemist and Nobel prize winner, Jacques Monod, who died in 1976.

From the same perspective as Comte, Monod utterly rejected any idea of God. In his view the Christian religion, like all religions, can only lead people into error. These archaic attempts at explanation are simply dangerous illusions, monstrous lies, which happily have been gradually demolished by modern science. Modern science must do all that it can to remove 'the repugnant mess of Jewish-Christian religion' which still underlies our modern civilization.

In his view, this supposed truth is simply the product of the delirious imagination of people seeking desperately to allay their anxieties and fears in the face of death by appealing to a supernatural power: God. In fact that is pure fantasy. God does not exist and human beings are simply the product of matter and change (cf. further, p. 42 below). Like Comte, Monod thus categorically rejects any religious or metaphysical perspective and condemns out of hand any attempt to find any sort of truth outside a rigorously materialist and positivist framework.

Scientific objectivity and the problem of God

From a strictly scientific point of view, Comte and Monod are quite right to demand total objectivity and to reject any dependence on metaphysical and/or religious questions in the scientific sphere. They are equally right to refuse to see God as the possible stop-gap for our ignorance. We cannot but agree with them completely on this point. Here is an absolute necessity. Experts must *never* allow their philosophical views to intrude into their specifically scientific work, no matter what these may be. They must not be believers or atheists, but exclusively scientists (see below, p. 37).

But contrary to certain contemporary positivists like François Jacob or Claude Lévi-Strauss, who in fact refuse to associate scientific problems with metaphysical problems, Comte and Monod can be accused of not having totally respected this principle themselves, and of having presented affirmations of a metaphysical kind as scientific truths.

When on the basis of their scientific work they affirm that the hypothesis of God must be rejected, or when Monod argues that the world is solely the result of chance, they are giving a *metaphysical* interpretation of the results of their scientific work and thus adopting a philosophical standpoint. They certainly have the right to do this, but only on condition that they recognize that they are making affirmations of a philosophical kind, indeed specifically metaphysical affirmations, and are not stating scientific truths.

This distinction between facts established scientifically and the philosophical conclusions that can be drawn from them is quite vital here. For reasons that we shall go into in detail in the next chapter, it would seem that while science provides essential elements to reflect on, it is neutral over the problem of God: it cannot prove either that God exists or that God does not exist.

However, in my view this neutrality does not signify that the option for God or the rejection of God are no more than a matter of taste, as Jacob affirms or Lévi-Strauss suggests. On the contrary, for reasons which I have already stressed (see above, pp. 4–6), it seems to me that believers or theistic philosophers cannot dispense with rigorous reflection, here on the basis of the results of scientific discoveries, if they really want to arrive at a standpoint which is neither subjective nor fragile, but based on reason, and which is solid because it rests on as precise and objective a knowledge of reality as possible. This demand for rationality seems to me to be essential, and will be the subject of the following chapters.

François Jacob: God is a matter of taste

Winner of the Nobel Prize for biochemistry in 1965 with Jacques Monod and Lwoff, François Jacob has no interest whatsoever in metaphysics. He is concerned only with scientific research. In his view, the option for God or the rejection of God are exclusively matters of subjective and emotional assessments.

For the scientist engaged in science the question of the existence of God does not arise. His reasoning and his hand are never guided by the search for a proof of the existence or non-existence of God. I believe that this problem is completely irrelevant to the practice of science. Since it is no longer a matter for science, as far as I am concerned it becomes purely a question of taste. That is why some scientists are believers and some are not. Some love, some do not; some need it to live, others do not.

There are perfectly respectable scientists, excellent scientists, who believe in the existence of God. But once again, that has nothing to do with science; it is another matter. →

Claude Lévi-Strauss: scientific research is all that matters

An anthropologist who is also a structuralist (see p.61 below), Claude Lévi-Strauss, while accepting that the science cannot prove that God exists, asserts that this problem does not concern him. All that matters to him is scientific research.

The question of God is a question which I do not ask, and have never asked as long as I remember. I have never had any problems here. In discussing with believers I have always felt that the basic difference between them and me is that they raise problems that I do not. I refuse to put forward philosophical claims and meta-scientific claims. On the contrary, scientific claims seem to me to have priority, and metaphysics, which we can completely do without, must be confined to the more modest role of intimate dreams. If you ask me the meaning of existence, my answer is that existence has no meaning.

2

Science and God: New Perspectives

It is worth while our reminding ourselves briefly of two major conflicts between science and faith. The first broke out in the sixteenth century, when Galileo asserted that the earth was not at the centre of the universe but revolved around the sun, and the second in the nineteenth century, when Darwin stressed in turn that all the living species in the universe, human beings included, were the result of natural evolution.

The Galileo affair

In 1543 a Polish astronomer, Copernicus, published a book entitled *The Revolution of the Celestial Orbits*, in which he demonstrated the two-fold movement of the planets on themselves and around the sun. In his view the earth was not at the centre of the universe, as had hitherto been believed (a theory called geocentric), but the sun (the new theory is called heliocentric). This heliocentric theory, later established on an even more precise scientific basis by another astronomer, a German called Kepler, provoked little reaction at the time.

By contrast, in 1600 an Italian religious, Giordano Bruno, was condemned and publicly burned as a heretic for having put forward the same arguments and having drawn philosophical and theological conclusions from them which were judged erroneous by the church. In particular he argued that the universe was infinite. (He also affirmed that this infinite universe coincided with God. Pantheistic statements of this kind certainly weighed very heavily at his trial.)

Why was Copernicus not condemned?

Doubtless because at that time there was less interest in the sciences than there was three-quarters of a century later, and above all, it seems, because the Roman Catholic Church was not yet very preoccupied with the growth of Protestantism nor obsessed by attacks on doctrine and deviations from it, as it was to be in the time of Giordano Bruno and Galileo.

Finally, the best-known figure in this context, Galileo Galilei, another Italian and an astronomer, after a first warning in 1616 was condemned by the church on 22 June 1633. He was declared to be 'suspect of heresy as having believed and put forward a false doctrine, contrary to Holy Scripture'. His theory was that the earth was not the centre of the world but, like all the other planets, revolved on itself and round the sun. Following his condemnation, at least officially Galileo abjured his errors and devoted himself to other scientific work, carefully leaving on one side his research into the structure of the solar system.

This judgment would have had limited consequences had the church quickly recognized its mistake. Unfortunately, the mistake became a catastrophe because it was not recognized in time and became a symbol of the church's opposition to science. Traumatized by the fear of anything new, Rome persisted obstinately in a fierce and disastrous conservatism. And this mistrust of science, above all science which dared to investigate the traditional image of the world, gave the impression that the church thought nothing of scientists and their work and that from a religious point of view their research was devoid of all value.

Here we already have all the elements which crop up again later with the problem of evolution in creation. Why were Giordano Bruno and Galileo condemned? Because they put forward a theory which seemed in flagrant contradiction to the biblical statement that the earth is the centre of the world, and because their proposals also seemed to deny reality, since the sun really did seem to go round the earth. For this reason the church continued to keep to the theory of Ptolemy, a famous astrologer of the second century AD, which was strictly geocentric.

So theologians, seeing heliocentric theory as a very grave threat to the faith, rejected the scientific discoveries of Copernicus and Galileo. But they deceived themselves in supposing that these discoveries were contrary to the faith, since they were not so at all. As we shall see again

Giordano Bruno. Condemned and burnt as a heretic.

The Copernican
System.
The earth is no longer
the centre of the uni-
verse. (*Bodleian Library,
Oxford*)

32

shortly, the message of the Bible is not scientific at all. The church later recognized that the heliocentric theories were correct, but unfortunately did so too late; moreover, these theories were themselves superseded when it was discovered that the sun is only a very small star within a gigantic galaxy composed of millions of stars, often far bigger than the sun. And our galaxy is certainly not at the centre of the 500 million (at least) galaxies scattered through space.

The controversy over evolution

The same mistake arose in connection with the theory of evolution in creation, which is now well established. Fortunately it was rectified more rapidly.

The first transformist hypotheses saw the light at the end of the eighteenth century. Throughout the nineteenth century these hypotheses were developed in detail and were brilliantly confirmed, above all by Charles Darwin. However, on 30 June 1909 the Roman Catholic Church officially affirmed that the literal meaning of the first three chapters of the biblical book of Genesis – which contain the creation stories – could not be doubted. By a decree of the Biblical Commission it therefore condemned transformism and maintained the more rigorous fixism.

The Roman Catholic Church condemned the theory of evolution because once again it seemed to contradict the teaching of the Bible, which affirmed that the world had been created in seven days and that God had specially created the first man, Adam, of whom all other men and women were the descendants. Following this condemnation, for some time believing scholars

Galileo tragically and unjustly condemned

The measures which were taken at the time by the Roman authorities in connection with the theory of the movement of the earth and more particularly against its main advocate, Galileo, are indefensible. That can be affirmed in the light of the subsequent more correct insights of the Church in the respective spheres of science and faith. These measures did a great wrong to the Church.

François Russo

Later, 'under constraint and forcibly', the Church ended up recognizing its mistake, but even so it was not until 1757 that the works of Copernicus were withdrawn from the Index and authorized for publication and reading. And it was only in 1822 that the Church finally recognized that this doctrine was not *contrary to the teaching of the Bible, since that teaching was not scientific in nature. In 1979 John-Paul II, on the occasion of the centenary of the birth of Einstein, became the spokesman of the Roman Catholic Church, publicly regretting this unfortunate condemnation of Galileo, and in particular stating:*

The greatness of Galileo is known to all, as is that of Einstein, but the difference between Galileo and the man whom we are honouring today is that he had to suffer a great deal, and we must not conceal the fact that this was at the hands of individuals and institutions in the Church.

And John-Paul did not hesitate to take up the famous remark of Galileo himself: 'The Bible teaches us how to go to heaven, and not how the heavens move.'

and theologians tried to reconcile the Bible with scientific discoveries, attempting, for example, to make the different geological eras correspond to the seven days of creation in the Bible. They attempted to create a doctrine of concordism, a desperate and naive attempt which was doomed to failure.

Then finally, still 'forced and under constraint', in 1943, with Pius XII's encyclical *Divino afflante Spiritu*, the church indirectly recognized the validity of scientific discoveries relating to evolution by accepting the existence, in the Bible, of different literary genres expressing truths in languages other than our own. Similarly, it recognized that the narratives of Genesis were not explanations of a scientific kind.

Creationism and transformism

After the Galileo affair a second shock was caused with the appearance of evolutionary theories. Up to that point, creationist doctrines reigned in peace. According to these, the animal species had emerged as they were from the hands of the creator. For example Linnaeus (1707–1778) wrote: 'There are as many species as the divine Being created originally.'

The undisputed founder of transformist doctrines was Lamarck (1809). His theories were taken up by Darwin (1859) on new foundations. In 1900 De Vries gave them a solid basis with the theory of mutations. They explain how genetic variations are possible and can be transmitted, and thus can account for the relationship between species, whether animal or vegetable. The progress of genetics has confirmed these views: molecular biology, a recent branch of biochemistry, has demonstrated the mechanisms involved. Although at present our knowledge of them is not complete, evolution is not just a hypothesis but a fact. The rarity of well-preserved fossils prevents us from drawing the genealogical tree of the human race with the precision we would like, but it is certain that the human branch separated from the animal trunk millions of years ago; it has evolved progressively and doubtless will continue to do so.

J. F. Catalan and J. M. Moretti, *La foi devant le science*

For more details see Christian Montenat, Luc Plateaux and Pascal Roux, *How to Read the World: Creation in Evolution*, also published in this series.

The literary genres in the Bible

In everyday life we distinguish quite clearly between 'literary genres'. We do not confuse a detective story with a collection of poems or a scientific work with a comic strip: they are different literary genres. Now the Bible is a collection of seventy-three books which belong to very different literary genres. In this collection the book of Genesis, which contains the creation stories, is certainly not of a 'scientific' genre in terms of our own day.

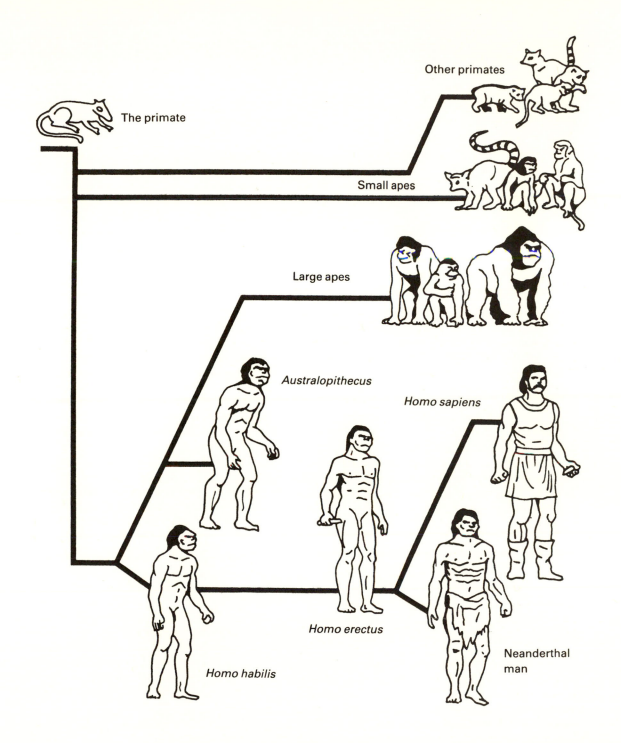

The primate

Other primates

Small apes

Large apes

Australopithecus

Homo sapiens

Homo erectus

Neanderthal man

Homo habilis

The Bible is not a scientific work

So the aim of the Bible is not to deliver a scientific message but a spiritual message. As Wilfred Harrington has put it, 'The religious writers are certainly religious thinkers. They are also very often poets, but they never claim to be scholars. If we look for scientific truth in the Bible, we shall not find it, simply because it is not there. That is why, for example, the creation of the universe is described in a way which matches views of the time in which the narratives were written, a way which has no scientific value.'

The best indication of this is that there are two *contradictory accounts* of creation in the Bible. In the first (Genesis 1), everything comes from the water: originally there was nothing but an enormous mass of water, and after God had separated the waters of the firmament and the waters of the earth, he further separated the latter to make dry land appear. By contrast, in the other account (Genesis 2), everything came from the land. Originally there was only dry and barren land, and God made water spring from it later. Clearly the author who put these two texts into the same account was not fooled by their contradictions. The reason why he put them side by side was that as far as he was concerned, the 'scientific' aspect of the texts was a secondary matter.

The Bible does not seek to explain how the universe works – that is the specific role of scientific research – but to answer questions like: Why does the universe exist at all? Why this development? Why human beings? The biblical narratives do not set out to give us scientific theory to satisfy our curiosity. They seek to make us reflect on essentials: our human condition, our situation before God, our tragic divisions, the way we are faced with a hostile nature and finally the sense of a history in which we are both spectators and actors.

From this philosophical and religious perspective, these biblical accounts of creation affirm at least three very important things:

1. The world is the object of a creative act of God: it is not sufficient in itself.

2. The universe is not eternal: it had a beginning.

3. God created a world and beings different from him and – in particular where conscious beings, men and women, are concerned – free and autonomous beings.

We shall not dwell on the second point here, because it is not essential to our study. St Thomas Aquinas recognized that the world could well be created and yet eternal. However, we shall return to the first and third points, since they are essential to our approach to the problem of God.

The need to respect different approaches

Like the French naturalist Laplace, who when Napoleon asked him what place he reserved for God in his 'system of nature', replied, 'Sire, I have no need of that hypothesis', researchers adopt a 'methodological' atheism. They set God aside in their scientific work, rightly refusing to mix up strictly scientific problems with philosophical or religious ones.

Scientists as such seek constantly to know more of reality as it appears to them, independently of the significance it can take. They study 'how' things happened, how they are produced. But it is not directly their task, as scientists, to ask 'why' reality is, why creation, why evolution, why the universe exists, whether it was created by God, and if not, where it comes from. These questions are essentially philosophical and/or religious ones.

The dialogue needed between science and faith

Science is confronted with a number of major questions in which the distinction between what is strictly science and what goes beyond science is difficult, if not impossible, to make. The questions relate to the beginning of the universe, the formation and the development first of matter and then of life, from the first cell to humankind, to the generation of the human being. We cannot treat these processes purely in terms of positivist materialism, since we 'feel' that what we call, for better or for worse, spirit, purpose and (with human beings) freedom are involved in them. All these are aspects of 'things' which, despite the claims of a certain number of theologians and indeed scientists, cannot really be kept apart.

That is why science and faith must continue to engage in dialogue. It is to be hoped that this dialogue will be marked by the serenity and understanding which were so sadly lacking in the Galileo affair.

François Russo

Certainly, for the believer these three approaches – scientific, philosophical and religious – are intimately connected, but we must be always very careful to dissociate them, since it would be catastrophic all round – for the objectivity and value of scientific research on the one hand and for the credibility of philosophy and/or the believer on the other – to mix them up. It is essential for this indispensable dialogue of science, philosophy and faith to rest on a clear foundation and on mutual respect for the scientific approach to reality.

The scientific approach to reality and the question of God

Science is neither 'for' nor 'against' God . . .

Since it is content to study 'how' phenomena take place and cannot as such go beyond that, science is not in fact either 'for' or 'against' God. As we have already seen in connection with positivism, it is perfectly neutral in this respect. It cannot prove either God's existence or God's non-existence. As Claude Lévi-Strauss, an atheistic scientist, said of atheism: 'An atheism which justifies itself on a scientific basis cannot be defended because it would imply that science is capable of answering all questions. Clearly it is not, and never will be.'

Science is neither for nor against God

If, from the indubitable fact that the world exists, someone wants to infer a cause of this existence, his inference does not contradict our scientific knowledge at any point. No scientist has at his disposal even a single argument or any kind of fact with which he could oppose such an assumption.

Hoimar von Diffurth, contemporary scientist

Galileo.
'The measures which were taken against Galileo are indefensible' (François Russo).

. . . but the scientific approach to reality can lead to raising the question of God

Science certainly raises formidable questions which can lead to philosophical and religious questioning. On the one hand it poses extremely delicate and complex ethical problems, like those raised by the use of atomic energy (both military and civil) or by discoveries in genetics and bioethics. On the other hand, by bringing us a fantastic amount of information and knowledge, and showing us at the same time the prodigious wonders of nature – and its defects – science invites us at least to reflect. What is the origin of this prodigious richness of life which sometimes seems to be as much the result of purposeful thought as of blind fumbling? Where can this headlong scientific and technological progress lead? Is it the source of happiness or unhappiness for humanity?

Whether we like it or not, these questions arise inescapably, and they can lead some people to consider (or reconsider) the hypothesis of God. Putting ourselves in this latter perspective, starting from the reality of the universe in which we find ourselves, we shall ask about its existence and its appearance. Are the universe and human beings sufficient in themselves or are they the result of the creative act of God?

New openness

We should not believe too quickly that from now on relations between science and religion will improve. The personal positions of scientists vary widely, ranging from the most categorical atheism to the most authentic and unambiguous affirmation of Christian belief, through the great majority of scientists who seem finally to have opted for a prudent scepticism. These personal differences are related to particular scientific disciplines, the human sciences generally being more 'suspicious' than the natural scientists. However, generally speaking, following the example of Lévi-Strauss, a great many scientists now acknowledge that they do not have answers to all questions. Hans Küng sees a new and promising opening in this situation.

→

Can the fact be overlooked that, despite continuing mutual mistrust, the relationship between religion and science has slowly improved toward a new openness?

The trend is most striking with physicists. Many today see the inadequacy of the materialistic-positivistic world view and understanding of reality and also the relativity of their own methods. Particularly among the physicists, we now find very few militant atheists, even though there are still many agnostics. The invention of the atom bomb in the first place, but increasingly also the negative consequences of scientific and technical progress as a whole, have raised at the present time, especially among atomic physicists, the question of responsibility in scientific and technical activity and consequently the question of ethics. But ethics implies the question of discovering meaning, of a scale of values, of models and – for their justification – of religion.

Hans Küng, *Does God Exist?*, p.553

3

The Origin of the Universe and the Creation of the World

The idea of creation was unknown to the Greek philosophers, who thought that the universe existed from all eternity. This idea was introduced into philosophical and theological reflection by the Jewish-Christian revelation. For example II Maccabees 7.28 affirms, 'Look at the heaven and the earth and see everything that is in them, and recognize that God did not make them out of things that existed', taking up an idea already expressed in the book of Genesis and in several other places in the Bible. What is it?

It is impossible to prove whether or not the world has been created

The first thing that needs to be understood here – and it is extremely important – is that the problem of creation is not primarily a scientific problem, as is often believed. It is above all a philosophical and/or religious problem. In fact science cannot prove whether the world was created or not, any more than it can prove the existence or non-existence of God. Science provides numerous elements which are indispensable for dealing with this problem, but it cannot solve it as such.

Nothing can give a definitive and evident answer to the apparently simple question 'Is or is not the universe the object of divine creation?', since no proof can be advanced either way.

Why? Because, as we have just seen, while scientists may be able to explain 'how' the universe is – and their information is clearly very important in this respect – they cannot *qua* scientists answer the question why the universe is and why it has evolved. Here we are in the sphere of philosophical and – for the believer – religious positions. Science as such is neutral.

This explains the diversity of views in this connection both among philosophers and among scientists themselves, who are far from being in accord. Some reject the creation of the world for excellent reasons and others accept it for reasons which are no less good. Some remain sceptical and are not sure which way to lean.

The rejection of the idea of creation

A certain number of scientists and scholars therefore think that it is useless to appeal to any kind of God or to a hypothetical spiritual power to explain the appearance of the universe and its development; in their view matter contains within itself the principles of its existence and its development.

From a philosophical point of view all these thinkers are materialists. For them there is only one reality, matter. This matter exists of necessity. It is uncreated, eternal and infinite in space and time. Moreover it is in constant evolution, an evolution in the course of which we see the progressive appearance of life, first in vegetable form, then in animal form and finally, with human beings, who have thought and conscience.

To explain this evolutionary process such philosophers generally appeal first either to a principle of evolution inherent in matter (Marxism) or to pure chance (Monod).

Marxism

Marx and his faithful friend and disciple Engels thought that matter formed itself, and Marx, to explain its origin, spoke of 'spontaneous generation'. 'A rude shock has been given to creation by science, which has represented the formation of the earth, its coming to be, as a phenomenon of spontaneous generation. Spontaneous generation is the only practical refutation of the theory of creation' (Karl Marx, *Political Economics and Philosophy*).

This matter bears within itself the principle of its evolution. Matter makes itself, and by virtue of its own resources becomes living matter, then thinking matter. It is self-creative. The world, nature and human beings are self-sufficient. They do not owe their existence to anyone else: they are the fruit of the dialectical evolution of matter. Matter is naturally movement, and this movement which, as Engels said in *Anti-Dühring*, 'is as impossible to create as it is to destroy', explains its evolution.

So the positions of Marx and Engels are clear: neither matter nor movement are created. They exist by themselves and for all eternity.

In fact this theory does not seem very convincing because one has some difficulty in imagining this mysterious internal force which would explain its evolution . . . These difficulties are shared today by numerous scientists, not necessarily only believers, who find this explanation quite unsatisfactory.

Materialism – a brief history

Materialism is far from being a discovery by Marx. As early as the fifth and fourth centuries BC, the Greek philosophers Democritus and Epicurus (Marx did his doctorate in philosophy on them!) had developed materialist theories, and these were taken up in the first century AD by the Latin philosopher and poet Lucretius.

After Lucretius and up to the seventeenth century there were virtually no materialist philosophers in the Christian West.

Materialism began to reappear in England in the seventeenth century, and then in France with the whole current of the *Encyclopaedia*, focused on Diderot, for whom material became a weapon to use against God, religion and the established order.

This current came to full flood with Feuerbach, whose vigorous arguments in favour of materialism were to influence Marx and Engels, who praised him for having 'restored materialism to its throne'.

Monod

For Jacques Monod, on the other hand, if matter is the only reality, its evolution can be explained purely by chance. 'Pure chance, absolutely free but blind, is at the very root of the stupendous edifice of evolution' (*Chance and Necessity*, p.110). It is as a result of successive mutations due to chance that the changes develop which constitute evolution and allow life to appear. (Chance has full play at this stage, but the situation is different in the selection of mutations. There necessity appears since, by a process of rigorous selection, living beings integrate or reject these mutations and, if they retain them, they transmit them genetically.) So there is no pre-established plan in nature. All evolution is simply the result of sheer chance. That is why Monod, who clearly rejected any idea of God and divine creation (see above, p. 27) was also violently opposed to the dialectical materialism of Marx and Engels.

In effect he charges them with affirming that matter has its own inherent principle of evolution, which would suggest that this evolution of a 'dialectical' kind was in some way 'programmed' in advance. In Monod's view this 'principle of evolution', this kind of mysterious force inherent in matter, cannot but strangely recall the fallacious idea of a divine power governing the world which – again according to Monod – would all in all be a way of surreptitiously reintroducing the divine into matter. This is an 'animist projection . . . an interpretation not only foreign to science but incompatible with it' (*Chance and Necessity*, p.46). In fact, he argues, only chance can explain everything.

Monod finally accuses all these 'old philosophies' – in which he includes not only the religions but Marxism – of wanting to soothe men and women in the face of their anxieties and their deaths. Even if it is very hard to be lucid and realistic on this point, since it is extremely agonizing, he argues that man should know 'that he is alone in the unfeeling immensity of the universe out of which he emerged only by chance' (p.167).

This theory of Monod's does not seem to be much more satisfactory than that of Marx and Engels. While the vast majority of scientists and philosophers of all convictions are indeed agreed in recognizing that chance plays a by no means negligible role in the process of evolution, it would seem difficult for many of them to accept that *everything* which exists in the universe is solely the result of this chance! Though agnostic and leaning more towards atheism, the biologist Jean Rostand commented: 'Something else has to be found.'

Jacques Monod.
'Pure chance is at the very root of evolution.'

The God of Christian revelation as creator of the world

Faced with this inadequacy, other scholars do not hesitate explicitly to affirm the existence of a superior creative intelligence. In their eyes, this alone could explain the appearance and development of the universe.

That is, for example, the testimony of the naturalist Pierre-Paul Grasse who also not only affirms, like some of the members of 'Princeton Gnosis', the existence of 'a powerful and superior reason' (Einstein), but the God of Christian revelation: 'If I have returned to faith, it is through science, through a scientific approach . . . If the universe is comprehensible, it is because the universe is ordered. Chaos is incomprehensible. But where does this order in the universe come from? We live in an ordered world. "Ordered" entails an ordering intelligence. This intelligence can only be that of God.'

We find this perspective again among a certain number of other scientists, for example Pierre Teilhard de Chardin or the historian and sociologist Jean Delumeau, whose book *Ce que je crois* is worth quoting at some length because he explains it very well.

After stresssing that science must never cease to go forward boldly, knowing that it will never reach the horizon, the limits of which extend further, the further we progress, and that 'we shall never exhaust the immensity of space nor the complexity of living structures', he adds:

'The question then arises. Is not God in the depths of this night? Who can be certain that he is not there? What proof do we have that the immensity has no sense? And that "evolution does not have a plan"? Science does not seem to me to lead to the denial of God, but rather to invite human beings both to keep in their place and to ask themselves about that which is greater than they.

So I would gladly take up a thought of Jean Hamburger's: "In addition to being the sumptuous adventure that it can be for the human spirit, science could indirectly be the source of meditations capable of freeing us from the feeling of absurdity. But scientific knowledge remains quite inadequate to our profound need for transcendence."

At other times theologians have talked too much, declaring themselves to be competent on everything. Does not the reversal of the situation lead certain scientists in our day to commit the same type of error and to claim authority in areas which escape science and will always escape it? Science explains one stage in the way. But it cannot explain where this way leads. It is not for science to affirm that it leads nowhere. On the other hand, the scientific community now seems agreed in thinking that the way had a beginning and that we can already say something about this beginning. It is true that the biologist sees programmes being realized under his microscope without ever meeting the programmer. But does that mean that the programmer does not exist? No scientific knowledge will ever be complete or definitive. Science does not have the last word.

Science must go as far as it can. Its results, read from a Christian perspective, can only shed a little more light on the infinite riches of creation. As far as I am concerned, science is an invitation to turn towards the message of religion and seek an explanation of the way in which it illuminates mechanisms. The hundred thousand million stars in our galaxies, the thousands of millions of galaxies known in the universe, the complexity of the human brain with its hundred thousand million neurones . . . Do not these amazing realities provoke the wonderment of the observer?

Then why not draw the logical conclusions from these marvels, which is to call on religion to complement our information? So science and religion would seem to me to stand side by side and to lean towards one another.'

So the scientific knowledge of the universe can

lead us to affirm the existence of a creator God. And even if this idea of the creation of the world is not totally satisfactory, to the degree that it would be difficult to understand how God could have brought matter out of nothing, and how God could have created a universe in which evil, suffering and death reign, we must note here that at any rate such an explanation seems more satisfactory than explanations of a materialistic kind.

The world cannot be understood without a creative principle: Princeton Gnosis

After often having rejected the idea of creation throughout the nineteenth century and at the beginning of the twentieth, a number of scientists have now become more cautious. Though some still categorically reject any idea of creation and others maintain a prudent scepticism, more than might be supposed are considering it again: they do not think that it is necessarily stupid or anti-scientific.

That is the case with thousands of scholars, including a certain number of Nobel prize winners, who belong to a vast international movement known as 'Princeton Gnosis', from the name of the American university where the movement began. The existence of God seems to them more than probable to the degree that they feel that we have to conclude the existence of an intelligence which encompasses and animates the universe.

Certainly this 'God' is not unambiguous, since the idea they have of God is often very vague. Thus Einstein remarked: 'My religion consists in a humble admiration of the superior being, without limits, who reveals himself in the smallest details that we can see with our weak and feeble spirits. This profound conviction of the presence of a powerful and superior reason which reveals itself in the incomprehensible universe is my idea of God.'

Despite this, one can only stress how interesting this quest is, for while the religious approach of Princeton Gnosis may seem inadequate to believers, and above all to Christians, it is nevertheless remarkable that at a time during which the death of God has been proclaimed, when so many people, including Christians, feel that faith will not hold when confronted by science, highly distinguished scientists conclude that not only does science not reject God, but feels constrained to affirm his existence.

Teilhard de Chardin

One man played a very prominent role here in encouraging this rapprochement between science and faith: Pierre Teilhard de Chardin (1881–1955). A profound believer, this Jesuit was also a brilliant scientist who specialized in palaeontology (a science dependent on geology which is particularly concerned with the study of fossils, and thus with the scientific reality of evolution). In a vast synthesis he sought to show that the Christian religion was quite compatible with modern science.

His standpoints are sometimes doubtful from both a scientific and a philosophical or theological perspective, but he nevertheless remains a powerful thinker from whom one can always learn something. His best-known book is *The Phenomenon of Man* (see the section For Further Reading).

For more about Teilhard de Chardin see also *How to Understand the World: Creation in Evolution*, also published in this series.

The idea of creation in the Jewish-Christian perspective

So Christianity affirms that God created the world. But precisely what do we mean by that? What does this idea of creation entail?

In fact the affirmation of creation involves three complementary things:

1. God creates a world different and distinct from himself.
2. God creates free beings.
3. Creation cannot be reduced to the problem of the beginning of the universe.

God creates a world different and distinct from himself

This distinction between the creator and his creation is of prime importance. It would be a serious mistake to suppose, like the pantheistic thinkers, that God and the world more or less coincide, since if there were no differentiation between God and the world we would be mixed up with God and consequently we would not be autonomous, free or responsible.

In his creative act God produces something which is different from him, distinct from him. Particularly where men and women are concerned, God has created beings who are free and autonomous in relation to him.

God creates free beings

Creation is not just a simple matter of making. Because of the biblical images, which are inadequate here, God is sometimes imagined as making us as a craftsman makes an object. Here perhaps more than elsewhere, there is a need to avoid all temptations to anthropomorphism, for if we were only products of the divine worship we would indeed be no more than objects! But we are conscious, free, autonomous and responsible beings. As we shall see in due course, that is extremely important: in creating us, God created free beings which in their turn will be creative.

Creation cannot be reduced to the problem of the beginning of the universe

Certainly the beginning of the universe is also a problem. But it is far from being the only problem. The creative act of God carries on through time. And that is essential. One can say with St Thomas Aquinas that God continues at each moment to create the world to the degree that he keeps it ceaselessly in existence. That is why some theologians talk of 'continuous creation'. This action is as necessary on the part of God as the action by which he initially produced the universe, since the world has no more intrinsic reason to continue to exist than it does to appear in the first place.

Jean Delameau.
'Science is an invitation to turn to God.'

An essential affirmation

This kind of metaphysical and religious affirmation does not satisfy our curiosity . . .

So, for the believer, to affirm that the universe is created is finally to affirm that it depends on God in its existence, and that this dependence continues through time. But it is also to affirm that creation is the action through which God gives life by creating a universe distinct from himself, and above all by creating autonomous freedoms in this universe.

These affirmations doubtless do not really satisfy our curiosity, and this conclusion could therefore seem disappointing, since we would very much like to know the specific details of how God could have created the universe. However, legitimate though it may be, this curiosity can never be satisfied. Even if it could partly be satisfied by all that scholars teach us about the universe, its life and its evolution, the fact remains that when we come to the origin of this universe, no one knows more than what I have just said . . . and in the end that is not very much. It explains why there are several theories which explain this 'origin' of the universe!

. . . but it is nevertheless essential for believers today

Present-day believers can express this conviction that the world was created by God without feeling in the least opposed to the most recent scientific facts.

As far as they are concerned, the conviction allows them to give a valid response to the question why the universe of which they are a part exists and to give it an ultimate meaning. 'Believing in the Creator of the world means affirming in enlightened trust that the world and man are not pointlessly hurled from nothing into nothing, but that in their totality they are meaningful and valuable' (Hans Küng, *Does God Exist?*, p.641).

Well understood and correctly interpreted, it also allows believers to affirm, contrary to the statements of modern atheistic humanism, that far from being opposed to or in competition with human freedom, the creative freedom of God is its foundation. God created men and women free, autonomous and fully responsible for their own existence. He created human beings to be really and authentically creative.

Creation is taking place today

Creation covers the totality of time: past, present and future. Creation is taking place today. It is not yet finished. Humankind is a permanent process of growth. Today is the day of creation, and time is bringing forth something new. Furthermore, if we want to envisage creation as a finished reality, it is to the future that we shall have to turn, for our history, the history of humankind, is like the showing of a film. We do not understand it by dwelling on a single frame, but by knowing the whole screenplay. Today we are not yet created; humankind has not yet appeared in its fullness.

P. Gane, *La création*

The end of the world?

There is neither an unambiguous scientific extrapolation nor an exact prophetic prognosis of the definitive future of humanity and the cosmos.

Neither the first things nor the last things, neither primordial time nor the end time, are accessible to any direct experience. There are no human witnesses. Poetic images and narrative represent what is unsearchable by pure reason, what is hoped for and feared.

The biblical statements about the end of the world have authority not as scientific statements about the end of the universe but as faith's testimony to the way the universe is going, which natural science can neither confirm nor refute. We can therefore give up any attempt to harmonize the biblical statements with the various scientific theories of the end.

The biblical testimony of faith sees the end essentially as the completion of God's work on his creation. Both at the beginning of the world and at its end, there is not nothing, but God.

Hans Küng, *Does God Exist?*, p.656

PART THREE

God and Human Freedom

'Man will ever rise higher and higher from that point outward when he no longer flows out into a God.'

Nietzsche, *The Gay Knowledge* (also known as *The Joyful Wisdom*), no.285

'It is as liberator that God is Creator of the world and of history. Moreover, God is at this point infinitely free, and that alone allows God to make possible, support and achieve human freedom.'

Alexandre Ganoczy

'Contemporary atheism has an accent of its own which is immediately recognizable, regardless of the differences of content in doctrines and of style in attitudes. Whether boastful or desperate, contemporary atheism seeks to affirm humanity totally by denying God; it defines itself as a humanism, and bears witness that it has itself taken human beings to the limits of their possibilities. Hence the presupposition that belief in God is, conversely, a kind of dehumanization of men and women. Here we come up against what is common to contemporary atheists in all senses of the word.'

This comment by the Christian philosopher Etienne Borne describes a perspective already present in the scientific humanism which we have just considered and which is characterized by the total rejection of God in the name of human beings. This God is conceived of as one who denies human freedom.

The ultimate problem here is the notion of divine creation. This idea of creation is not at all well understood by those atheistic philosophers who, following Sartre, think that if God created the world, he could only have created beings totally dependent on him, devoid of all freedom. If that were true, human beings would be totally manipulated by God, who would have foreseen everything in advance (Chapter 1).

Now we have just seen that when we talk of divine creation from the Christian perspective we are talking of something very different. Far from being a manipulator, the tyrant that he has so often been thought to be, God created human beings not only totally free and responsible, but as creators themselves (Chapter 2).

49

The rejection of creation for the sake of human freedom

Basically, what atheists deny is not so much transcendence as such, but a creator God. If God created us, they say, it is impossible for us to be truly free men and women. In some sense we would be objects in the hands of the creator, 'puppets in the hands of the gods', as one of Plato's characters says. Now that is obviously contrary to human dignity. Here we have a subject of basic importance.

François Varillon

1

The Challenge of Contemporary Atheism: Atheistic Humanism

This opposition to a tyrannical and oppressive God which has appeared progressively in popular consciousness has been thought out, systematized and argued by atheistic philosophers who have violently rejected it in the name of human beings and their freedom.

The beginnings: Descartes and Kant

However, if we are to understand the significance of these atheistic philosophers for reflection on God today, it is important to go back in time, to see how this two-fold movement of secularization and rejection of God in contemporary atheism was paradoxically encouraged by theistic philosophers, notably Descartes and Kant, who overturned the classical perspectives of philosophy and hence indirectly of theology, by first putting stress on human beings themselves and no longer on nature and its creator, God.

Generally speaking, up to Descartes philosophers and theologians were primarily interested in God and nature, the work of divine creation into which human beings, who came

later, were integrated.

In asserting that human beings must rely solely on the power of reason to know the truth (except for truths of faith taught by the church), Descartes brought about a kind of Copernican revolution. In fact he reversed the traditional perspective of his time which tended more to be content with repeating the 'truths' handed down by tradition. Descartes tried systematically to eliminate prejudices, arguments from authority and unproven truths, and invited man to use his reason and his own power of knowledge.

Leaving aside all other approaches than his own human reason, Descartes thus sought a first 'indubitable truth' on which to base his thought. For that he put everything in doubt – the famous methodical doubt – in order to find a first truth which, because it resisted this doubt, seemed to him to be absolutely certain. He noted one can apparently doubt everything: not only the existence of God, since one cannot verify whether or not God exists, but reality itself, since it could be part of a dream. Only one thing resists this doubt, and that is the fact that if I think, I must necessarily exist. 'I think, therefore I am' was to be the starting point of his philosophy, and it was only at a second stage that he touched on the problems of God and the universe.

What is freedom?

Like the word 'God' (cf. above, pp. 6ff.), the word 'freedom' is extremely ambiguous. It can take on very different, sometimes contradictory meanings. As such, Paul Valery has called it a 'detestable' word. But it is also an indispensable word, since it denotes an essential value, even though we recognize that we have difficulty in defining this value correctly.

First of all one might think that freedom is simply the absence of all constraint, the possibility to do what one wants, when one wants, as one wants. Though that might seem obvious, as a definition it is really most unsatisfactory. On the one hand that is because we have many limitations. And on the other hand, it does not take sufficient account of the essential fact that we are beings with a conscience, beings who plan, beings endowed with the power of reflection and who are responsible for their actions.

From this point of view, for human beings, to be free cannot consist in being content to follow one's instincts, impulses or desires. To be really free is in fact to do what we judge to be the best. Now this 'best' will vary a great deal depending on the individual and the values to which he or she gives priority, but the important thing to note is that unless we behave in an inhuman, non-human way, when making choices, taking decisions, or performing actions, we have to appeal to our conscience, our reflection, our responsibility.

So freedom is not a synonym for capricious, unthinking, irresponsible behaviour. On the contrary, freedom is the way in which men and women act who are endowed with reason. It is the fact of making realistic, consistent and responsible choices in their particular circumstances, conditioned in many different ways by education, personal and collective history, character, professional and social position, and the concrete situations in which they find themselves.

The question raised in the following chapters is raised from this perspective: does God refuse to allow us to take responsibility in this way by more or less insidiously influencing our choices and foreseeing everything in advance, or on the contrary does he allow us to assume our responsibility completely by totally respecting our freedom?

So with Descartes man is brought to the fore; Kant merely accentuated this process by equally bringing out the importance of the thinking subject in knowledge and stressing the dignity of this subject and the importance of freedom for human beings, who alone are competent to organize the universe which is theirs.

By favouring reason and the subject in this way, Descartes and Kant facilitated the movement to secularization that I described earlier and thus had the merit of inviting believers to become open to modernity and, from there, to rethink the problem of God in a major way. However, unknown to them, unaware of the consequences, they also opened the way to the modern atheistic philosophers who were concerned to preserve human beings simply and purely by eliminating God.

We could make a diagram of this development towards atheism like this:

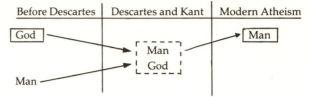

Of course this diagram does not suggest that all philosophers today are atheists – far from it. It simply stresses a development which led some of them to stress human beings to the detriment of God, by contrasting God the creator and human freedom. For other philosophers there is no contradiction in affirming the existence of God and human freedom simultaneously, and later we shall see why.

Human autonomy as the claim of modern atheism

Why this elimination of God? Because in the eyes of atheistic philosophers human beings can only be themselves if God does not exist. If God is the creator, human beings cannot be. Or, if they wish to be, they must eliminate God.

In this view belief in God corresponds in reality to an infantile age of humanity, and like the child who has to become independent of its parents really to enter into life, human beings must free themselves from the illusory protection of God if they are to become adult. Today, like all the religions which go with it, this belief in God must disappear for the exclusive benefit of human beings themselves. According to all these philosophers, the death of God is the absolute condition for the true life and real flourishing of human beings, for God can only be an insatiable

tyrant. As the anarchist Bakunin put it: 'God is, so man is a slave. Man is intelligent, just, free, so God does not exist. We defy anyone to get out of this circle, and now a choice has to be made.'

The choice for the atheistic philosophers is clear. They opt for human beings at the expense of God. In their eyes only this choice could save us. That is the reason why they claim the title humanists: they always put human beings first. But this is an atheistic humanism, which does not cease to state that God must die for human beings to live. For these philosophers whom we shall now consider, things are clear: contrary to what had been believed for too long, God did not create human beings, but human beings created God. God is a pure product of human desire and imagination.

Ludwig Feuerbach: God as the product of human imagination and desire

This idea is far from being new in philosophy. It could already be found in Xenophanes, a Greek philosopher from the sixth century BC. But the first profound analysis of this process which is said to have led human beings to 'create' God was put forward by Ludwig Feuerbach in a book which was a landmark in the history of philosophy, a real trigger in the war that some modern philosophers have declared on God. The book is called *The Essence of Christianity*.

Human beings, Feuerbach observes, are made to know, to love, to act, but in all these spheres, and even more generally in all that they do, they are aware that they are very limited, that they can always only know, love and act very imperfectly. They also note that they are subject to suffering, that they are confronted with evil, and finally that they are doomed to die.

Human beings project themselves on God . . .

Now human beings are convinced that they are incapable, of their own accord, of overcoming these limits. They also try to find a satisfactory way of fulfilling their needs and conquering their fears by inventing a perfect and omnipotent being who would have all these qualities and would never be subject to evil, suffering or death.

By projecting on to heaven this being whom they call God and who possesses all the perfections the lack of which they feel so cruelly, human beings simply escape into pure fantasy. God is nothing more than the product of their delirious imagination. He is only the gigantic, hypertrophied and idealized reflection of human beings themselves. In reality, the attributes that religion recognizes in the divine being – knowledge, love, wisdom and justice – are properties of the human species. In contemplating God

men and women are simply contemplating themselves.

This God has no reality. He is only the product of the desires for perfection entertained by human beings who in creating God are expressing their own aspirations. For Feuerbach human beings are merely realizing a chimaera, a dream: 'Religion is the dream of the human spirit.'

. . . and submit to the God they have created

Feuerbach continues his analysis by pointing out that human beings are not content to alienate themselves by thus projecting themselves on to God – a process by which they already strip themselves of what belongs to them for the benefit of this illusory God – but that they perhaps alienate themselves still more by submitting to this God through the religious principles which are equally the fruit of their imagination. So they alienate his freedom twice over for the benefit of an imaginary God whose slave they become.

This slavery cannot last for ever. Human beings must ultimately grow up and reject God. This is a matter of their survival, for 'the prime object of man is man'.

This point is of vital importance for Feuerbach and, following him, for all the philosophers with the same perspective. 'The supreme and first law must be the love of man for man, *homo homini Deus est* (man is God to man). That is the supreme practical principle; that is the turning point in world history'. In another book, *The Essence of Religion*, Feuerbach went on to explain: 'I deny God: for me that means that I deny the negation of man . . . The question of the existence or non-existence of God is for me simply the question of the existence or non-existence of man.'

Feuerbach's *Essence of Christianity*

Feuerbach wrote this book in 1841 and it was translated into English by George Eliot. It immediately proved a great success. In particular it was adopted with fervent enthusiasm by Marx and Engels, who were to be very much influenced by it. Some years later Engels noted: 'One has to have felt in person the liberating action of this book to have any idea of it. The enthusiasm was general.'

The importance of the book cannot be underestimated. Since then it has so nourished modern atheisms that one could legitimately call Feuerbach 'the father of modern atheism'.

Is God simply the product of human projection?

Feuerbach was quite right in saying that human beings necessarily project themselves on to God when they try to think of him, and that they inevitably tend to imagine him in an idealized human form.

But that does not mean that God is only that, only a simple projection of human desires and fantasies, and that God does not exist in himself. A simple example might help us to understand this better. In practice we almost always imagine that others are different from what they are because we have a tendency to 'project' on to them what we are, what we think, what we like or what we detest. We always see them more or less in our own image. But because we project ourselves on to them in this way, and necessarily do so, that does not mean that other people do not exist! Similarly, just because we project ourselves on to God, that does not mean that God does not exist.

Sartre: 'If God exists, human beings are nothing'

The French philosopher Jean-Paul Sartre did not spend long trying to 'prove' his atheism. He simply contented himself with denying God in the name of a certain vision of human beings – and that seemed enough to him.

If God existed, he could only be the one who rules the world from heaven, the one who has foreseen everything, who knows everything, who directs everything. So God would necessarily annihilate human freedom. For that reason men and women cannot but reject the very idea of the existence of this God who can only be the product of their delirious imagination. Those are the essential views of Sartre on this question.

If human beings are to live, God must die. 'If God exists,' asserts Goetz, one of Sartre's heroes,

Killing God to safeguard human beings

Marx and Engels

A being can only claim to be independent when he is his own master, and he is only his own master when he owes his existence to himself . . . Atheism is a denial of God, and by that denial of God atheism allows human beings to exist.

Karl Marx, *Political Economy and Philosophy*

All religion is only the fantastic reflection, in the brains of men, of external powers which dominate their everyday existence, a reflection in which earthly powers take the form of super-terrestrial powers.

F. Engels, *Anti-Dühring*

Nietzsche

In fact, we philosophers and 'free spirits' feel ourselves irradiated as by a new dawn by the report that 'the old God is dead'; our hearts overflow with gratitude, astonishment, presentiment and expectation. At last the horizon seems open once more, granting even that it is not bright; our ships can at last put to sea in every danger; every hazard is again permitted to the discerner; the sea, *our* sea, again lies open before us; perhaps never before did such an open sea exist.

The Gay Knowledge, no.343

God is dead! You higher men, this God was your greatest danger. Only since he lay in the grave have you risen again. Only now does the great noontide come, now does the higher man become master. Have you understood this word, my brothers? You are frightened: do your hearts turn giddy? Does the abyss yawn for you? Does the hell hound here yelp for you? Take heart, you higher men. Only now is the mountain of the human future in travail. God is dead: now we desire superman to live.

Thus Spake Zarathustra, Part IV, 68,2

Freud

I must contradict you when you say that men are completely unable to do without the consolation of the religious illusion, that without it they could not bear the troubles of life and the cruelties of reality . . . But surely infantilism is destined to be surmounted? . . . You are afraid, probably, that they will not stand up to the hard test? Well, let us hope they will. It is something, at any rate, to know that one is thrown on one's own resources. One then learns to make a proper use of them. And men are not entirely without assistance. Their scientific knowledge has taught them much since the days of the deluge and it will increase their powers further.

And as for the great necessities of fate against which their is no help, they will learn to endure them with resignation . . . By withdrawing their expectations from the other world and concentrating all their liberated energies into their life on earth they will probably succeed in achieving a state of things in which life will be tolerable for everyone and civilization no longer oppressive to anyone. Then, with one of our fellow unbelievers, they will be able to say without regret: 'We leave heaven to the angels and the sparrows' (a reference to the German poet Heine's *Deutschland*).

Sigmund Freud, *The Future of an Illusion*, p. 233

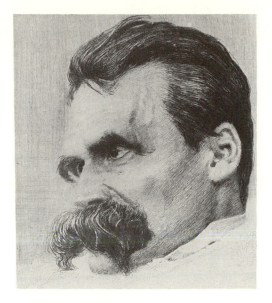

Friedrich Nietzsche.
'God is dead . . . we have killed him.'

Sigmund Freud with his daughter Matilda in London in 1938. 'Is not religion the result of an illusion which leads to infantilism?'

in *The Devil and the Good God*, 'man is nothing. If man exists . . . God does not.' For Sartre, things are thus very clear: creation and freedom are mutually exclusive. Why? Because Sartre imagines God creating human beings like a craftsman creating an object. In the all-powerful hands of God human beings could only be objects manipulable and manipulated at leisure. This God is unthinkable for Sartre. So he rejects him, because human beings must be the sole creators of their lives in the name of the freedom and the responsibility which are theirs, just as they must be the creators of the values by which they are going to direct their lives. As Goetz also says in the same play: 'I alone decided for evil; I invented good.'

In *The Flies*, Sartre imagines this dialogue between Zeus (God), who was imprudent enough to create a free man, and Orestes (the man), who uses this freedom to revolt against Zeus in the very name of his freedom:

'Zeus (to Orestes): Who, then made you?

Orestes: You. But you blundered; you should not have made me free.

Zeus: I gave you freedom so that you might serve me.

Orestes: Perhaps. But now it has turned against its giver. And neither you nor I can undo what has been done' (Act 3, scene 2).

This rejection of God is the absolute condition of all happiness. Parodying Pascal in his famous Memorial, Sartre makes his hero, Goetz, say: 'God does not exist. He does not exist. Joy, tears of joy. Alleluia! Mad! . . I will deliver you. No more heaven, no more hell, nothing but the earth' (*The Devil and the Good God*).

Thus it is faith in human beings which, in the wake of Feuerbach, leads all these philosophers to reject God. The pure and simple negation of God is then perceived as the postulate of freedom.

However, it should also be recognized that

Jean-Paul Sartre and Simone de Beauvoir in 1946. 'If God exists, human beings are not free.'

these philosophers are quite right to rebel against God or rather against the caricatures of God that they present to us, against these despotic, arbitrary, tyrannical, not to say cruel and perverse gods. And we must also recognize that Christianity has sometimes been the religion which has provided these unsatisfactory images of God and thus provoked the just criticism of atheistic philosophers!

Now we must go on to see whether, if one has a right idea of God, it is in fact necessary to 'kill God' in order to safeguard human freedom. And not only whether it is unnecessary to kill God, but in fact essential to affirm God's existence, to the degree that God is the only guarantor of human freedom and of human beings themselves.

I would be very happy for God not to exist . . .

One night I called on God, if he existed, to declare himself. He was coy and I never spoke to him again. Basically I was very happy for him not to exist. I would have detested it if the part that was being played out here below already had its dénouement in eternity.

Simone de Beauvoir

60

A false image of God

After watching a performance of Sartre's play The Flies, *Julien Green noted in his Journal on 20 January 1951:*

In it the author's atheism is given free reign, and I am sure that it will trouble many of the audience, but the God whom Sartre presents to us is so mediocre and so limited that we have no difficulty in understanding the author's atheism in relation to a God of this kind. If God were Sartre's God, I would be an atheist twenty times over, I would be a fanatical atheist as far as that God was concerned. But as it happens, he has the wrong person.

Structuralism and the disappearance of man

The movement which seeks to eliminate God also tends to suppress man. However, what it sought to do was the opposite. Feuerbach wanted to 'regain on earth the treasures which have been dispensed in heaven'. For Nietzsche, man come of age has to divest himself of the 'illusion of the final cause'. Sartre presented atheism as the only possible humanism. But Nietzsche and Sartre have been displaced by others more logical than they. 'We believe that the ultimate aim of the human sciences,' wrote Claude Lévi-Strauss, 'is not to constitute man but to dissolve him.' 'In our day,' Michel Foucault confirms, 'one can only think in the void of man who has disappeared. One can only utter a philosophical laugh at all those who still want man, his reign or his liberation, at all those who ask "What is man?"' These trenchant declarations are based on a coherent reasoning: if no creator God 'willed' man, man has no particular status, no proper vocation. Man is there by chance, provisionally, and will disappear. Man has no value in himself.

It is clear that God and man are bound together. If one kills the former, the latter is doomed to the same fate.

Jean Delumeau

2

God does not govern the world; God created creative men and women

Do the new directions given by Descartes and Kant to modern philosophy necessarily have to lead to atheism? Certainly not, provided that we understand properly what we are saying when we talk of God, of God's relations with the world and above all with men and women, for the formidable question posed by these changes in perspective is: what place does God give human beings in creation?

In other words, again following Descartes and Kant, and taking most careful account of the extraordinary contribution made by modernity, which we considered in Part One, can we not, despite Feuerbach and Sartre, imagine a relationship between God and human beings which is not a relationship of opposition and competition? Can we not imagine a relationship which takes into account both the existence of God and the existence of human beings with the utmost respect for the autonomy, the freedom and the responsibility proper to men and women?

Such a relationship might be depicted by the following diagram.

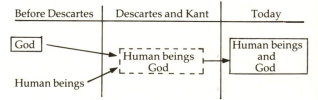

That is perfectly possible, but on condition that we take account of the development of thought and the contribution of the modern world to the image that we now have of God.

Human beings are totally responsible for their lives and their universe

In reality, God, the God of the Christian revelation of whom we are speaking here, is not at all as Sartre imagined him, a God who 'produced human beings precisely as the craftsman produces a paper-knife', a God who has foreseen everything in advance and who leaves human

62

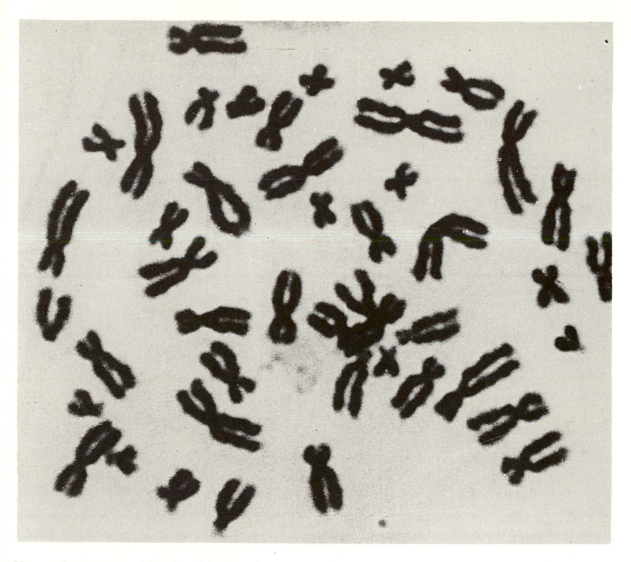

Human chromosomes. Man should become the 'master and possessor of the natural world' (Descartes).

beings no margin of freedom. If God created the world, he did not do so in the same way as a craftsman who produces material objects.

If one can make a comparison here, one could say that God created human beings rather like parents producing children: not to make them passive beings in their hands, but with a concern to make them free persons responsible for their own lives, beings capable of taking on their lives, beings which in turn may be creators. So we have to do away with the traditional image of a God with authoritarian omnipotence. Human beings have freely to find the way which leads to the best development of their creative faculties. It is clear that human beings are creative, and this characteristic has to be vigorously asserted.

That is also confirmed by the evidence of our secularized Western world: we live in a world which has discovered its true autonomy and proper responsibility. What above all concerns us here is that this affirmation is not in contradiction with the affirmation of God if we understand that God, far from seeming to act in competition with human beings, allows them to take on their own responsibilities.

And that is why, in agreement on this point with modern atheism, believers today can only affirm the autonomy of the world and of human beings, who alone are responsible for it. Men and women have become aware of their potential, of their effectiveness, of their genuinely creative power: the future of humankind is in our own hands. By becoming 'masters and owners of nature', as Descartes put it, human beings are finally realizing God's desire, which is to see them truly and freely taking their destiny in hand. It is for human beings, and human beings alone, to transform this world of ours in our own way. It is a world which is indeed 'secularized', a vast factory from which a 'new world' constantly emerges, that of human beings, the scene of their historical future which appears as the result of their creative action.

We in fact have a place in a history in which human beings and God are creators together. In this perspective there is room for God and room for human beings because their actions do not take place on the same level. The creator God is the one who makes things exist and sustains them in existence: God is the foundation on which everything rests. Human beings are in charge of modelling the reality given to them. Human beings and God are no longer in competition. In strictly human creation there is no place for a moment when God would intervene as an indispensable link without which human beings could do nothing. The creative act of God is of another order from the creative act of human beings. Although always present in his creation, God in no way threatens human freedom. He makes human beings exist. It is for human beings then to use their freedom as they will:

> # God takes human freedom very seriously
>
> There are those who see the deity as a blind destiny which weighs down on human beings and which they cannot escape. No matter what, they say, the chips are down. Some draw a good number, others a bad one. There's nothing you can do about it. It's fate.
>
> The Bible says precisely the opposite. Everyone is responsible for his or her own life. The creation is handed over to men and women to make it into a habitable world, a brotherly and sisterly world. People even have power to use their freedom badly.
>
> God is anything but paternalistic. God has confidence in his creatures. He is not an easy refuge which means that men and women need not assume their responsibilities. God takes human freedom seriously. He respects it. He seeks to be a discreet partner.
>
> Jacques Lacourt

men and women are totally and truly responsible for their action.

God gives men and women all the means of realizing themselves totally as human beings. While atheistic humanism is concerned to suppress God so that human beings can exist, we are now perhaps beginning to see the urgent need of a new humanism which discovers the ancient truth that God has to live for human beings to be.

However, the God in question here is not the God who emerged from the Greek philosophical tradition, namely a strictly immutable and transcendent God in the narrow sense of these terms, i.e. a God whose nature excludes any kind of change and who is superior and external to the world he has created.

A new image of God

As we have seen, the Greek philosophers did not have any idea of the creation of the world. For them the universe existed from all eternity and was conceived as a closed and very hierarchical entity in which everything, including human beings themselves, had a very precise place.

In this perspective, God was conceived of as not being at all concerned with the world. That is particularly clear in Aristotle, though he affirms that God draws the world to him. However, Aristotle immediately adds, if the world is attracted by God, it is only because God is perfect, and it is by reason of this very perfection which all beings ceaselessly seek that God attracts them. So to take up Aristotle's comparison, God attracts the world as the magnet attracts the iron. But that is all, since God is strictly indifferent to the world, which he completely ignores.

Of course Christian thinkers were to contradict Aristotle on this last point by affirming that God created the world and that there are reciprocal and very tight links between God and this world, and above all between God and human beings. But on the other hand, they retained the idea of the Greek philosophers about the order of the world. From his heaven on high, rigorously immutable and transcendent, God governs and directs all things. He has foreseen all things and willed the world to be as it is.

For a long time this scheme was accepted without too much difficulty, because the accent was not put so much on human beings themselves and the importance that has to be attached to their freedom. As we have seen, this development began in the modern era with the appearance of the phenomenon of secularization, the prodigious development of science and technology and, in philosophy, with the Cartesian revolution.

This over-rigid scheme – contrary to the Bible, which affirms precisely the opposite – was then put in question at the dawn of modern times. It is unthinkable today, even for believers, to accept that God has foreseen everything in advance and that he governs everything while remaining perfectly immutable and transcendent. Following modern philosophers and theologians, one can only affirm human autonomy. God is not the all-powerful demiurge who has forseen everything, but the one who loves men and women with an infinite love and, far from manipulating them, goes along with them in their history, totally respecting their freedom and their own responsibility.

But by very reason of this change of perspective, which is also a return to the biblical tradition, we can now no longer conceive God as a static being who would exclude from himself all true development and all true future. If God truly goes along with human beings, God can only do so in their becoming and in the process of their realization, so we are justified in going so far as to say that there is more newness in God than immutability defined once and for all. Eternally perfect, in this very perfection God has the freedom and the possibility to become historical, to go at our pace.

In other words, if God is indeed immutable in the sense that basically he always remains the same, God certainly is not immutable in the too narrow sense understood by classical Christian philosophy and theology, which at this point are too dependent on Greek philosophy, which imagined God as completely separate from the world. Similarly, if God is always transcendent in the sense that he infinitely surpasses the universe and humankind, the objects of his creation, he is not transcendent in the sense of being remote from the world and external to it.

Far from being an inadequacy in God, this divine will to be with human beings and to move to their rhythm is the consequence of this superabundance of being which is God's and from which there perpetually springs up a life which is both always the same and always new. As Hans Küng puts it, 'This is how the relationship between God and world, God and man, appears today. In the light of this historicity of God, the biblical message of a God who by no means persists unmoving and unchanging in an unhistorical or suprahistorical sphere, but is alive and active in history, can be understood better than in the light of classical Greek or mediaeval metaphysics' (*Does God Exist?*, p.188).

The progress of philosophical and theological reflection therefore leads us to imagine a different God. This change is important, because it provides new elements with which to give a different and doubtless better explanation of those difficult problems of the relationship between the creator God and free human beings on the one hand and evil on the other. We shall return to the problem of evil later on.

So this change is essential. To make the point once more, its main achievement lies in the fact that God is conceived simultaneously as the one who creates human beings and, while being extremely attentive to them, allows them to be totally free and fully responsible for their own lives. This leads to another question which is just as important for our reflection, that of divine providence.

Human freedom and divine providence

While deeply respecting human freedom, God is very attentive to men and women because he loves them deeply. That we call divine providence.

The notion of divine providence as it has been brought out in Christianity is based on this conviction that God is love, that God loves his creation and within it he particularly loves men and women.

However, this notion has been perverted by the ideas people had of this reality in antiquity when it appeared in an essentially superstitious

How are we to understand divine transcendence?

The word 'transcendence' is one of those words in religious vocabulary which contains a large number of ambiguities. For most people, to talk of transcendence means to lose oneself in unreality. In that case 'transcendent' means distant, external, and the expression denotes a solemn abstraction which paralyses us, a reality which we attain by deserting this world.

According to some people, the transcendence of God is affirmed the more that it is abstracted from human beings. In that case they create themselves in the image of an abstract and distant God. This divine despot who has no roots in human reality seems radically alien. Nothing that comes from God can penetrate a human life, human freedom.

In reality, the term 'transcendent' denotes a presence of such intensity that it surpasses all our limits of time and space, a universal power of loving without any egotism, total freedom. For human beings the fact of always being situated at a point of space and time limits their capacity to be present. If we follow our thought, our love, there are moments when we would like to be somewhere else, where we seek to surmount our limitations, to go beyond what we are. This experience, which is an essential fact of human life, can make us to some degree aware of the transcendence of God, who is always greater, always beyond the ideas and images that we can have of him.

Pierre Gane

form: it was a question above all of pleasing the gods and doing everything possible to disarm their hostility.

Too often, even today, even for many Christians, when one uses the words providence or providential, there is a tendency to mean something that arrives accidentally and by a 'happy chance'. So when they are applied to God we imagine that God intervenes to help us if the fancy takes him. From this perspective our ideas of God are very 'interventionist': God's action can not only be found in life and in history but also manifests itself in miraculous, fortuitous, marvellous events.

That would make God the author of the inexorable destiny of the world and of each individual. On this view God intervenes ceaselessly so that everything comes to pass as he had foreseen and according to his good pleasure or his whim. The role of human beings is then no more than to correspond, willingly or under compulsion, to this divine 'plan'.

That leads to two ideas which are as false as they are dangerous and which are more or less contradictory. On the one hand, it is in effect affirmed that God has rigorously and precisely foreseen everything in advance; everyone dies at his or her time: that is written in the great book of life and death. On the other hand, by contrast it is thought that God can intervene at will in creation, that he can overturn anything he wishes, and overwhelm us if we displease him or on the contrary keep us from misfortune, suffering and all that threatens our well being if we are 'very good'. (Of course this does not seem to work very well, for according to all the evidence, happiness and misfortune in this life are not distributed in accordance with the moral value of people's lives. This problem was already raised in the Bible, above all in the book of Job.)

Now, as we have just seen at some length, there is no divine 'plan' and God does not 'direct' the world in his own way, because he has too much respect for human freedom.

That is the Christian notion of divine providence. It is based on a two-fold conviction: on the one hand God loves his creation and, within it, human beings in particular; on the other hand he respects their freedom totally.

This is a great mystery, for how can God

Providence

Eusebius of Caesarea (c.265–339), who wrote the first great history of the church, to the time of Constantine, was in no doubt that God personally directed the fortunes of the church through his providence:

No one who reflects upon the matter can fail to be convinced that it was no mere human accident that the majority of the nations of the world never came under the unifying rule of Rome until the time of Jesus. For his wonderful visitation of humankind coincided with Rome's attainment of the acme of power . . . And no one can deny that it was not without God's help that this should have happened at the very same time that the teaching about our Saviour took its rise. Consider the difficulties involved in the disciples' journeying, had the nations been under separate governments and therefore not having any dealings with one another. But with those separate governments abolished, the disciples could accomplish their projects in safety. The supreme God had smoothed the way before them, controlling the animosities of those hostile to true religion through fear of a strong central government.

Eusebius, *Demonstration of the Gospel*, 3.7.30–3

And of his own time, he says:

Then the divine and heavenly grace showed how favourably and propitiously it watched over us, and even our rulers, the very people who had been waging war against us for so long, changed their attitude in the most remarkable way. They issued a recantation and, with merciful edicts and humane ordinances, they quenched the fire of persecution that had blazed so furiously against us. But this was not due to any human agency; it was not a result of anything that could be described as pity or humanity on the part of the rulers . . . It was divine providence itself, which became reconciled to the church and at the same time attacked the perpetrator of these evils . . . A divinely-sent punishment, I say, executed vengeance upon him beginning with his flesh and going on to the soul.

Eusebius, *Church History*, 8.16.1–4

---

simultaneously have a loving concern for men and women and yet leave them totally free to do or suffer evil? Does that not contradict his love?

It certainly seems to. And yet no matter what the cost, we must keep these two truths together: we are free, totally free, and yet God loves us so much that while completely respecting our freedom, he loves us with a deep love. That goes beyond us and is part of the mystery of God.

At this point we leave the sphere of philosophy and enter into that of theology. Here we must take account of the three following points:

1. The idea of divine providence is rooted in the idea of a covenant between God and human beings.

2. There is a mysterious action of God in the world.

3. But far from being alienating, this action is in fact the basis for our autonomy.

If God acts, he does not act outside the laws of the world and the consequences of our human actions. Moreover, his providence is the basis for our autonomy. He is present to us enough to allow us to be ourselves. And if that is true, God does not know in advance what we shall become.

It can be seen that the God who is infinitely concerned for human beings and at the same time has an infinite respect for their freedom is a long way from the God imagined by Sartre, a God who could only be a tyrant manipulating men and women. The God who created human beings is not their rival. He is the one who allows men and women to be fully themselves.

The Saint-Nazaire bridge. Men and women were created to be creative.

Does God know in advance what we are going to become?

Our freedom is not illusory, and because God has willed to safeguard it completely, some philosophers and theologians today do not hesitate to say that God does not know our future. The dice are not weighted.

God knows our time not only because he created it but because he bears it within himself as an indispensable characteristic of his love towards us. So there is no foresight in him, if we understand this word in its natural and spontaneous sense. If God really loves us, he cannot have this mythical superiority of the being who knows everything in advance. He cannot carry within himself this kind of knowledge of time which would alienate us and make our relationship with him a bait. We could go even further and say that God could not carry within himself foresight of our future, a full and anticipated vision of our future.

Henri Bourgeois

The power of God is a power of love

Can we Christians tranquilly assert that God is omnipotent, as if it were a matter of course, when on the contrary we feel ill at ease pronouncing these words? I think that many people do not find that difficult; in effect, if God is God, they do not see why he should not be omnipotent. For an increasing number of others, however, the affirmation of divine omnipotence is the most serious reason for not believing.

We should be careful not to take such people lightly: basically they think it more worthy of men and women, and therefore truer, to prefer a heaven void of the phantom of an emperor of the world, a potentate, a despot, a superb dramatist who manoeuvres the puppets of the human tragi-comedy, paralysing, petrifying and short-circuiting the freedoms which he is thought to have created. I think that the most numerous atheists are those who reject an omnipotence which would negate or destroy our freedom.

Far from being that, however, the divine omnipotence is the omnipotence of love. There is all the difference in the world, indeed an abyss, between omnipotence and an omnipotent love. Christians do not say that they believe that God is omnipotent; they say that they believe in God the omnipotent Father. For the Christian to say 'I believe in you' is to say, 'I know that your power is no danger to my freedom but that on the contrary it is in the service of my freedom.'

François Varillon

PART FOUR

Does God Exist?

'Man at last knows that he is alone in the unfeeling immensity of the universe, out of which he emerged only by chance.'

Jacques Monod, *Chance and Necessity*, p.167

'Is not perhaps God in the depths of this night? Who can be certain that God is not there? What proof do we have that the immensity has no meaning?'

Jean Delumeau

The Christian philosopher Etienne Borne has remarked that for the human spirit God is not self-evidently true but is a painful problem which needs patience and toil if it is to be resolved. It requires patience and toil because deciding about God is always an important and difficult decision to make.

The decision is important because it involves the whole person. It is no secondary matter. It is difficult and even painful to take because it is only by asking about the sense of our existence, an arduous question which is never definitively settled, that we can make the fundamental choice which orientates all our life (and sometimes make it again by modifying it): the recognition of God or the rejection of God.

It is equally possible to affirm or to deny God, and as we have already seen, there are weighty arguments on both sides. However – and this is the problem – none of these arguments is decisive, and there are no absolutely compelling reasons for deciding either for or against God.

But it does not follow from this equal possibility of affirming or denying God, or at least refusing to make this choice and remaining in scepticism or indifference, that the choice is neutral and must be left to chance or whim. All the more so since it is precisely on this choice that the meaning we attach to our lives will depend.

We have seen the main arguments put forward by atheists to justify their rejection of God, and I have also stressed that these arguments are far from being uninteresting. Believers for their part are no longer devoid of resources. Above all today, it can be shown perfectly well that this choice of God is reasonable and that it can be presented credibly to our contemporaries, since if we cannot 'prove' the existence of God, we can find the necessary arguments for justifying our belief in the existence of God. We have already been led inevitably to talk of this, but I shall now go on to take up the issue and explore it in more depth, by approaching it in a more systematic way.

When we talk of the existence of God, we might immediately think of the famous 'proofs' of God's existence which numerous philosophers and theologians have tried to develop down the centuries. So we too will begin by looking at these proofs. We shall see that if they are hardly decisive as proofs in the strict sense of the term, they are far from being devoid of interest, to the degree that they at least invite reflection by raising a certain number of essential questions about the meaning of our universe and our life (Chapter 1). It is from these questions that we shall again raise the question of the existence of God (Chapter 2).

1

Can we 'prove' the existence of God?

> 'We should expect more from the proofs of God's existence than a well-founded invitation to faith.'
>
> Walter Kasper, *The God of Jesus Christ*, p.100

The classical 'proofs' of the existence of God nowadays seem to have lost much of their power to convince. For atheists, they are reduced more or less to childish and sterile games. As for believers, often they do not find the proofs at all interesting. And neither side is prepared to accept them, seeing them as part of a bygone world.

However, we should not forget that the greatest thinkers of humanity have reflected on these proofs, so that they might be more interesting than is usually thought.

What are they, and what interest do they have for us today?

The main classical proofs of the existence of God

Three main sets of 'ways towards God', or to take up the traditional term, in full awareness that it must be used with great care, 'proofs' for the existence of God, are usually distinguished, depending on their starting points: from the reality of the world, from human beings, and from God himself.

'Proofs' from reality

These are also called 'cosmological' proofs because they are based on the fact of the existence of the material world and the universe (the cosmos).

These proofs are probably the oldest. We find them almost throughout the history of humankind in extremely different forms, from mythological expressions to rigorous formulations in philosophy. They respond to questions which are eternal and are still topical: Is our universe sufficient in itself or is it the result of divine creation? Why is there something rather than nothing? Why is the universe as it is and not otherwise? Why is it apparently organized (even if this organization leaves much to be desired – think of the problem of evil)?

Can one really talk of 'proofs' of the existence of God?

The term 'proof', used in connection with the problem of the existence of God, is very ambiguous and not in fact very adequate.

In fact when there is talk of 'proofs' of the existence of God there is often a tendency to imagine 'proofs' of a scientific kind, i.e. proofs which demonstrate in a certain and irrefutable way. One might also think, for example, of astronomers and astrophysicists who have demonstrated and proved that the earth is a minuscule grain of dust lost in a gigantic galaxy, itself lost in the midst of 500 million other galaxies all just as gigantic. They are absolutely certain of this, because they have been able to verify the fact both mathematically and experimentally, concretely, thanks to their powerful telescopes and radio-telescopes.

Now because we have no means of verifying experimentally what we are saying when we talk to God, we are far from arriving at the same certainty. Because God is not of the same nature as the reality which surrounds us and which we can know through the sciences, we cannot, as Kant has stressed, use the same means to discover God as we use to get to know our own universe. We cannot see God, speak to God or touch God. Contrary to the astrophysicist who can prove his or her theories, we cannot verify concretely and experimentally what we are saying when we affirm that God exists – or does not exist.

So when we talk of 'proofs' for the existence of God, we are talking more of indications of the direction we should take if we want to try to discover God and justify belief in God. That is why virtually all Christian philosophers and theologians are agreed in recognizing that the term 'proof' is not very satisfactory here, above all in our world which is increasingly characterized by scientific precision. They prefer to follow St Thomas Aquinas in talking of 'ways to God' or, to take up the illuminating phrase of Kasper which I put at the beginning of this chapter, 'a well-founded invitation to faith'.

In the light of revelation, the proofs were taken up by the first Christian theologians and philosophers, before being made precise and systematized by St Thomas Aquinas in the thirteenth century.

God the cause of the world

If we note first of all that everything that exists in the universe has a cause, it can be concluded that if the universe exists, it must necessarily have a cause. In the event, this cause can only be the all-powerful being God, for only he could create our prodigious universe.

We can also see that this universe is in constant evolution and that there is change and movement in it. Who can be the origin of this change and movement if not, as Aristotle said, the 'prime mover of the universe', God himself?

Noting, finally, that the universe is contingent, i.e. that it does not contain its own *raison d'être*, it can be asked whether God would not be the answer to this enigma. God would then be the necessary being in whom the world would find its justification and its *raison d'être*.

God the source of order in the world

This is the so-called teleological argument, the proof from purpose.

This argument begins from the real order which exists in the world (even if it is imperfect), from the amazement that one can feel when confronted with the spectacle of nature, from the observation that it becomes more complex through time, to produce life and finally human beings. Hence the question arises whether this

St Thomas Aquinas: The teleological proof

The fifth way is based on the guidedness of nature. An orderness of actions to an end is observed in all bodies obeying natural laws, even when they lack awareness. For their behaviour hardly ever varies, and will practically always turn out well; which shows that they truly tend to a goal, and do not merely hit it by accident. Nothing however that lacks awareness tends to a goal, except under the direction of someone with awareness and with understanding; the arrow, for example, requires an archer. Everything in nature, therefore, is directed to its goal by someone with understanding, and this we call 'God'.

Thomas Aquinas, *Summa Theologiae*, 1a q1, a3

---

world might not be the work of a sovereign intelligence.

The argument can be put in the form of a syllogism like this: purpose or order presupposes an intelligent cause. Now there is purpose and order in the world. So the world presupposes an intelligent cause. This cause can only be the omnipotent being God. So God exists.

In that way God would be the answer to a constant human questioning to which Voltaire gave famous expression: 'The universe embarrasses me, and I cannot think that this clock goes without a clockmaker.' The image was also used by the famous eighteenth-century clergyman William Paley in his *View of the Evidence of Christianity*, a book which contains many different forms of this argument.

This 'proof' is perhaps the most popular of all. Some Greek philosophers, like Plato and Aristotle, already put it forward in various forms. Through so much reality in the world, by asking themselves about its beauty, its order, its move-

ment, its defects (the problem of evil), they thought they could find in it the divine presence. This 'proof' has constantly been taken up ever since.

Although Kant himself did not find it at all convincing and criticized it severely, he nevertheless remarked: 'This proof always deserves to be mentioned with respect. It is the oldest, the clearest, and the most accordant with the common reason of mankind' (*Critique of Pure Reason*, p.520).

St Thomas Aquinas.
There are various possible 'ways to God'.

For a long time these 'proofs' seemed irrefutable, so much so that people had great difficulty in accepting any rejection of their apparent conclusiveness. That is the case in the Bible, in the book of Wisdom (13.1) and Paul's letter to the Romans (1.20); the idea was taken up again by Vatican I.

Nowadays, however, it is readily accepted that by themselves these proofs cannot lead us to accept the necessity of the existence of God. In the seventeenth century Pascal already stressed that it was naive and vain to tell those without faith that 'they only have to look at the smallest things which surround them, and they will see God openly' (*Pensées*, 242).

In fact, as is stressed by P. Roqueplo, a priest who is also a scientist, the universe is now less and less spontaneously a sign of the Creator to the modern mind. If it means anything to men and women today it is above all to convey the human power capable of deciphering its mysteries and the value of the science capable of expressing to us what the intelligence deciphers.

However – and we shall return to this – that does not mean that the questions which prompted these proofs have disappeared.

'Proofs' from the human side

These 'proofs' leave aside the external reality of the cosmos. They begin from the inner reality of the human spirit.

They stress first of all that human beings by nature have the idea of God within themselves and that they remain disquiet as long as they have not become aware of the effective presence of God within them. This perspective was very common among the church fathers, and there is a famous expression of it in St Augustine, who addresses God like this: 'You have made us for yourself, and our heart is restless until it finds rest in you' (*Confessions* 1.1).

Still in the same perspective, stress is then put on the profound dissatisfaction which seems to afflict men and women as long as they have not

found a solid foundation on which to base the values which give them life. Now as Bishop Walter Kasper puts it, 'the person cannot find full satisfaction in anything finite, in any finite values whether material or spiritual, nor even in finite persons. This accounts for the restless and unquiet constant movement and self-transcending of man. The human person can reach definitive fulfilment only if it encounters a person who is infinite not only in its intentional claims on reality but in its real being; that is, only if it encounters an absolute person' (*The God of Jesus Christ*, p.154).

In other words, it is vital for human beings that the important values which inspire and justify their actions, values which are commonly recognized as being essential from a human, moral and spiritual point of view, like justice, respect for others or the sense of duty, rest on some kind of solid basis. This 'some kind of' can only be absolute perfection, otherwise human beings would always feel unsatisfied. This absolute which they constantly seek more or less obscurely can only be God. So God exists.

Kant, who had severely criticized all the other proofs of the existence of God, retained this approach based on moral reflection, since in his view 'the only theology of reason that is possible is that which is based upon moral laws or seeks guidance from them' (*Critique of Pure Reason*, p.528). So he postulated the existence of God, supposing that only God could give meaning to our moral life and satisfy us fully from this perspective.

However, in his view this was a postulate, i.e. a reality which one has to accept as true without being able to prove its truth. So it is not a proof, since one cannot 'prove' God. One simply affirms his existence and believes in him because without that moral life would lose all justification.

These arguments do not seem to be any more compelling than the others.

In fact it is not because I have within myself the idea of God that God really exists, and besides, one could very well admit that there is nothing

Descartes: The ontological argument

Descartes thinks that if we try to conceive of God it is no more possible to conceive of God without the perfection which is existence than that the value of the three angles of a triangle are not equal to two right angles or to imagine a mountain without a valley.

Existence can be no more separated from the essence of God than the fact that the sum of its three angles is equal to two right-angles can be separated from the essence of a triangle or than the idea of a mountain can be separated from the idea of a valley; so that there is no less contradiction in conceiving a God, that is to say, a supremely perfect being, who lacks existence,

that is to say, who lacks some particular perfection, than in conceiving a mountain without a valley.

Meditations V, pp.144f.

Anselm's argument can be found put forward in his Proslogion, *chapters 2 and 3.*

Descartes also offers other 'proofs' of the existence of God 'by the idea of perfection' that we have within us. They can be found, along with the 'ontological proof' that I have just cited, in his Discourse on Method, *Part IV, and in a more difficult formulation in his* Meditations, *III and V.*

---

that corresponds to this need in human beings to transcend themselves and to justify the values which seem essential to them. The sole foundation for these values could be human beings themselves, in which case God, or the Absolute, would be nothing but a human projection, as Feuerbach thought, or the result of a desire of human beings for protection when in an infantile state, as Freud was to say.

'Proof' from God himself or the 'ontological argument'

This 'ontological argument' was first put forward by St Anselm in the eleventh century. It was taken up in various forms by certain modern philosophers, notably Descartes in the seventeenth century, Leibniz in the eighteenth and Hegel in the nineteenth.

It is based on one's idea of God. It can be put very simply: in speaking of God I have the idea of a perfect being. If this perfect being did not exist,

it would not be perfect because it would lack precisely the perfection of existence. So it exists.

This argument was strongly criticized by St Thomas before being criticized by Kant. Both stressed that one cannot move in this way from the realm of ideas (the ideas of perfection and the perfect being that I am thought to have) to that of the necessity of the existence of this perfect being.

This transition from the simple idea to the effective reality of this idea is very open to question. Kant stressed it by using the following comparison to show the weakness of the argument: it is not because I have the idea of a hundred thalers (German money at the time of Kant) that these hundred thalers really exist in my purse! 'The famous ontological argument of Descartes is therefore merely so much labour and effort lost', since one cannot prove God in this way any more than a merchant 'can better his position by adding a few noughts to his cash account' (*Critique of Pure Reason*, p.507).

The proofs: limitations and interest

The 'proofs' are far from being decisive . . .

These proofs certainly used to carry a good deal of weight, in a very religious world in which people naturally had a tendency to see God everywhere.

Nowadays they seem more fragile, even to the believer. Pascal already noted in the seventeenth century that 'The metaphysical proofs of God are so remote from the reasoning of men, and so complicated, that they make little impression; and if they should be of service to some, it would be only during the moment that they see such demonstration; but an hour afterwards they fear they have been mistaken' (*Pensées*, 542).

Cardinal Ratzinger has commented that no one is able to provide a mathematical proof of God, and he goes on to add that 'the believer is incapable of using it himself'.

There is nothing decisive about these 'proofs' as a demonstration. They do not prove anything in the strict sense of the term and, with relatively rare exceptions, in general they can only serve subsequently to strengthen the faith of those who already believe in God.

. . . but they do make us think!

Certainly these arguments are not enough to still human restlessness. However, they should not be thought negligible. Not only do they represent the rigorous thought of a number of thinkers, and this is no mean thing, but they correspond to an authentic and inevitable questioning by human beings. So they should not be rejected too quickly.

First of all, because even if they do not prove God, they are, as Bishop Kasper put it, 'argued invitations to faith'. They are ways to God, and as such they can lead some people to God.

Moreover, they can allow believers to express the feelings and the conviction that they have about the existence of God and give them means for justifying their faith rationally.

Finally, and perhaps above all, the arguments at least prompt reflection by raising questions which are not secondary, because they bear on the meaning we give to our lives and our universe, strictly existential questions which cannot leave anyone indifferent who takes

---

'Why is God not obvious?'

'Why is God not obvious?' one might ask. I shall content myself here with asking back, 'What would become of our freedom to know and love God if his existence imposed itself on us beyond any discussion?' However, we must not conclude from the non-evident nature of God that faith is only a matter of sentiment or mere chance. Intelligence has its full part to play in the act of giving oneself to God.

Jacques Lacourt

No one has ever seen God. So much the better. So much the better, indeed, since otherwise the believer would be condemned to repeat this vision ceaselessly, with his or her vision riveted on the past. There would be nothing more to discover; this absence of God is the foundation of the freedom and responsibility of the believer. Without this absence there would be no possibility of history, or evolution, or true choice. If men and women are to become the agents of their future, they must be free from any presence which imposes itself upon them. So God is not behind us, consigned to books, expressed in well developed formulae, shut up in our once-for-all experiences. Faith can never be repose, a more or less invitation to sleep or to drugs. It is a quest, an initiative, an adventure.

A. Patin

account of them, whatever his or her philosophical and religious convictions, regardless of whether he or she is a believer or not.

What are these questions?

1. The cosmological proofs raise the question of the prime cause of the existence of the universe. Is it created or uncreated? Is it the result of chance, or the product of the creative act of God?

The 'teleological' proof directs us more towards evolution itself, that evolution which sees the appearance of life and the emergence of consciousness with human beings. Here again, is this evolution the result of chance or of the creative act of God?

2. The anthropological and moral arguments raise the question of human values, whether moral, spiritual or religious, which give us life, and the problem of the foundation of morality. Are there universal values which are more or less convincing to all men and women, or are values always relative to human beings and thus finally more or less subjective? If the former, what is it that justifies them and provides their basis?

3. The ontological proof leads us to ask about the idea of perfection. Does perfection exist somewhere, or is it merely the result of human projection, as Feuerbach thought?

These essential questions allow us to bring out what is involved in this debate on the problem of God and to explain in a particularly satisfying way the reasons which lead us to affirm God's existence.

2

Affirming God Today

'Does human life have a meaning, and do human beings have a destiny? Yes or no?'

Maurice Blondel, *Action*

An essential choice

It is a matter of justifying a choice, a very important choice, whether to accept God or to reject God. Here human beings are faced with a basic alternative, for on this choice will depend the meaning of their life and their destiny. That is why this choice is essential, no matter what the reply is.

So this is not a neutral or a secondary question. It is in fact an existential question, that is to say in the strictest sense of the term a question which is at the heart of existence, a question which involves human beings completely in all the most specific features of their lives. And precisely because it involves all existence, this question can only be resolved by intellectual arguments in favour of one theory or another. It presupposes a real human investment, and the response given to it can only be the consequence of a free and voluntary decision reflected on maturely.

It is in fact a question which demands a response, even if this response is a refusal to respond. For concretely, not to respond yes or

no, or to remain indefinitely in perpetual doubt without being able to decide, is another response, since in life, and in life at its most everyday, one necessarily has to make choices, if only, here again, to choose not to make a choice and to allow oneself to be tossed to and fro by life.

So this decision involves us completely, in our intelligence and in our sensitivity, in our material life and in our spiritual life in the broadest sense of the word. That is why intellectual or moral arguments, testimonies, or Christian revelation, by themselves and separately, cannot bring about the decision. It is a global choice made on the basis of the questions which we considered at the end of our study of the 'proofs' of the existence of God, and on the basis of our concrete experience.

In other words, if this choice, whatever it may be, can and must be justified by reason, it is also and inevitably a decision made voluntarily and with commitment. Believers know that they cannot totally justify the choice of God, as atheists know that they too cannot give a perfect account of their own position. This is an eminently free decision, but a decision which once again is far from being irrational.

So free choice does not mean arbitrary choice. And it is quite possible today for the believer, though unable to 'prove' that God exists, which, as we have seen, is impossible, to justify the choice in a reasonable and coherent way. How?

Here we come to the question of the meaning of the existence of the universe and the meaning of our own lives in this context.

The question of meaning

The questions we have been asking have brought us to raise the question of the meaning of existence. 'Does human life have a meaning, and do human beings have a destiny – yes or no?' asked the French philosopher Maurice Blondel at the beginning of his famous book *Action*. Whether we like it or not, he added, we are committed in practice. We cannot escape the demands of the real. In one way or another we are confronted with the question of meaning, consciously or unconsciously. It shapes our thoughts, our habits, our decisions. It is given practical expression in our affections, our relationships, our work, our political standpoint and the way in which we spend our leisure time. And if we pay no attention to it, and refuse to consider the basic questions which arise for us, we inevitably abandon ourselves to the hazards of irrational opinions.

This question is an essential one for everybody, and the reply is given from a complex of factors, an inextricable mixture of our experiences, our encounters, our education, our reading, our feelings, our most intimate personality, our temperament, our body and indeed our unconscious.

At the heart of this question we again discover God – and human beings. We can no longer talk of God without talking about humankind. These questions are now inseparable. To reflect on God is to reflect on humankind, and we cannot think of human beings without asking the question of God (even if it is to reject God). So the question is ultimately that of human beings faced with God.

Will God be a brake on our development, or help us to live our lives fully?

We shall explore the two aspects of this alternative with reference to the questions raised at the end of the previous chapter based on the 'proofs' of the existence of God.

The question of God is vital for men and women

In the present situation, marked by unbelief or at least a serious erosion of Christian truths, it is urgent for us to reintroduce the question of God as a vital question for men and women. To speak of God is identical with speaking of human beings, their destiny, the questions which torment them. That is why, if we are going to talk about God, we must do so by way of human beings, in two ways. First, by showing that the soil in which the idea of God can germinate is made up of human beings themselves; and then by showing that God only discloses his existence to authenticity. God, who is so often presented by atheism as a limit on human beings, should by contrast appear as the one who takes them out of their alienation by revealing infinite dimensions to them. That is the God of Jesus Christ. His word is not alienating, but liberating.

Marcel Neusch

The two alternatives

The vertigo of the infinite and the temptation to nihilism

What would happen first of all if one rejected the hypothesis of the existence of God? By denying the existence of God the atheist does not find the fundamental *raison d'être* of the world and of humankind. By rejecting God, atheists decide against an ultimate goal and meaning of reality (though that does not mean that from an atheistic perspective they cannot find some sense in reality and in their lives). There is nothing which really explains and justifies the existence of the world and their own existence. In that case, as Sartre says in *Being and Nothingness*, taking up the German existentialist philosopher Martin Heidegger, we are abandoned in a world in which, as Jacques Monod puts it, man exists 'in a world of icy solitude . . . like a gypsy, he lives on the boundary of an alien world; a world that is deaf to his music, and as indifferent to his hopes as it is to his suffering or his crimes' (*Chance and Necessity*, pp.158, 160).

The death of God is in fact an immense event with unimaginable consequences, since with it appears the eternal cold and night of nihilism, that is to say the conviction of total contradiction, of the non-sense and the non-value of reality. Nietzsche is beyond question the philosopher who has best demonstrated the suicidal aspect of this putting to death of God. When that happens nothing is any longer clear, evident, solid. Once their support disappears, customary values collapse. There is no answer to the question 'Why?' There is no purpose. The vertigo of nothingness appears.

God as the ultimate basis of reality

On the other hand, if we accept that God exists, what will happen to our understanding of the world and ourselves? We will find in God the ultimate meaning of reality and of ourselves. In this hypothesis God will be both the first origin of our life, the ultimate meaning of our life and the hope which encompasses our life. At the same time God will be the foundation, the origin, the support and the goal of all reality. In that case God will be the response to the essentially characteristic problem of reality. For all its difficulties, the affirmation of God gives coherence, value and meaning to life.

Maurice Blondel.
'Does human life have a meaning, and do human beings have a destiny?'

Is or is not the world sufficient in itself?

It seems to me that we must deliberately stop asking 'Does God exist?' and tackle the problem from the other end. It is not the hypothesis of 'God' that we must ask about but the reality of the world, the reality which surrounds us completely.

So the only question that we can legitimately ask is whether the world as it appears to us at this moment of our culture and our knowledge is sufficient in itself or whether it requires another Reality to make it exist and subsist? It is the reality around us which causes the problem. It is that that we must question, and do so ceaselessly.

Two kinds of answers can be given to this question. First, that the world is indeed self-sufficient and that we should not talk of other realities than it (that would essentially be the Marxist answer, for example). Secondly, no, the world is not sufficient in itself, and we have to seek to discover superior realities, and perhaps a supreme Reality, which make the world exist.

This is the quest in which both scientific thought and philosophical thought are engaged. We are all in search of 'meaning', of 'significance'.

Jean Milet

Why choose God?

Choosing God . . .

This choice of God seems more coherent and more satisfying in relation to the questions raised by reality because it seems to make more sense of reality, to the degree that we can see where it originates. That does not mean that unbelievers are incapable of giving coherence, value and meaning to their lives.

Atheists can make sense of their lives and have very lofty ideals, sometimes even loftier than those of many believers. Thus, to return to the French philosopher, Jean-Paul Sartre thought that human beings are constantly responsible to themselves and others, and must do everything to try to achieve the triumph of truth and justice. And whether or not one agrees with his ideas, it has to be recognized that he always defended the cause of the oppressed with courage and generosity, precisely because of his philosophical and moral options.

The basic problem here is to know why one

has thus to respect human beings, their freedom and their dignity. What is the ultimate foundation on which this affirmation rests? Sartre does not seem to have been able to find an answer to the question.

And it is clear that from this perspective atheists have had difficulty in finding answers to the great questions of the origin of life, the purpose of existence, the meaning of suffering and death, questions with which all men and women are confronted sooner or later.

That does not mean, of course, that things are easy for those who believe in God, for they too do not have ready-made answers to the questions raised by their existence. However, in God they do find someone who is meaning and who gives meaning, as well as reasons for living, struggling and dedicating themselves to others, along with elements for a solution to their basic questions.

. . . and the difficulties

Now while we can be very certain about trivial truths, certainty about an essential truth is that much more difficult to acquire. To be able to say 'God exists' presupposes a very strong commitment from us: nevertheless that commitment is always fragile, for very frequently doubt is never far away. Conversely, however, it is in the very act by which I cling to God that I acquire certainty about God's existence. So I have to take the plunge. At the beginning of this conviction there is necessarily an act of confidence.

This act of confidence cannot be purely rational, since there is no logical proof of the existence of God at this level. This act of confidence relates not only to human reason but to our whole selves, to our life as it is, with our spirits, our bodies, our intelligence, our desires, our unconscious, our cultural, social and religious environment.

However, as we have seen, this act of confidence is nevertheless not irrational. It is preceded by an activity of reflection which has its starting point in human experience and which makes an appeal to free human decision. For that reason we are not confronted with a blind and empty decision, but with a well-founded decision which relates to reality and which we can explain rationally.

So there is a kind of circular link, a certain reciprocity, between this act of confidence which one might call philosophical belief in God and its 'proof', so that without proof belief would be blind and without belief the proof would be empty and vain.

Yes to God

It is against this background of human questioning that we have the question of God, and only there can we find a solution. For the believer this solution is 'Yes to God', an affirmation of the existence of God which is lucid, coherent, rational and voluntary. This is the choice which seems to believers to allow them best to make sense of reality and their own existence.

So without being able to prove that God exists, Christians do not lack arguments to affirm and justify their conviction that he does. However, for them this God who is the object of the act of belief which I have just mentioned, this act which involves their whole being, is not only the 'God of philosophers and wise men'. Beyond this abstract and discarnate God they see the God of the Christian revelation, the God of Abraham, the God of Isaac, the God of Jacob, the God of Jesus Christ, to take up the fine words of Pascal in his Memorial: a God who is not only the organizing principle in the universe, but a living person.

Didier Decoin, writer.
'For me, God exists in the same way as daylight exists for other people.'

The God of the Christian revelation

So who is this God of the Christian revelation to whom I have just referred? I have already said a good deal about this God on previous pages, but my comments have necessarily been scattered. So here I shall bring them together from the specific point of view of the believer, stressing three points which seem to me to be basic. This God is first of all a personal God, then a God who liberates men and women and gives them hope in him, and finally a God whose image we must constantly purify.

A personal God

God is first of all a personal God, very different from the God of the Greek philosophers. God is not just a philosophical idea. God is a personal God with whom one can engage in dialogue, a God who is also creator of the world and who loves men and women like a father. Far from being totally separate from the world and completely indifferent to its fate, as for example Aristotle supposed, not thinking that God created the world, far less that he could be interested in it and bother about it, God is intimately present in the world.

For while God is indeed wholly other, at the same time God is deeply immersed in human history. Infinitely close to men and women but never imposing himself upon them, he fully respects their autonomy and their freedom and allows them to choose freely. This choice derives solely from human freedom and human responsibility.

A God who frees men and women and gives them hope in him

This God of Jesus Christ invites those who believe in him constantly to go forward. In an astonishing paradox, since he is 'all powerful', he refuses to be a haven for them, an 'opium' as Marx put it. God wants them always to be vigilant and watchful, for he puts his trust in them. That might seem strange, but if God created human beings to be creators and to be responsible for their own human creation, how could God not hope in human beings and leave them free to make their choices.

This confidence must be reciprocal, but God does not respond to human confidence by removing our difficulties or satisfying our needs. Rejecting all childishness, he wants men and women to be fully responsible for themselves and the world.

At this level this love of God for men and women is basically liberating. On the one hand because it gives them the possibility of finding the ultimate meaning of their existence and their destiny. On the other hand because human beings know that they can trust God who loves them completely, his respect for their freedom being the very sign of this love.

A God whose image we must constantly purify

Of one thing we can be sure, and that is that God is always other than our talk of God. We have kept coming back to this vital point, and constantly been reminded of it by all the theologians and philosophers.

In fact we are constantly invited to renew our views of God, since God is always other than we can imagine, think or speak of. If we are to do that, we must have the courage always to criticize our representations of God in order constantly to purify our idea of God and to drive out all idols.

In criticizing God and the images that religions – including the Christian religion – have of him, we need to move in this direction and to correct our errors of interpretation and presentation, which are often the source of ambiguities and errors which veil the authentic face of God. Paradoxically, in this way they help believers to rediscover the true face of God, the face presented to them in the Bible.

PART FIVE

God and the Problem of Evil

At the end of the day, in considering God, like everyone else believers find themselves confronted with the most terrible and most enigmatic of difficulties, the problem of evil. Unfortunately we have all come up against it in a quite specific way, and sometimes very painfully. It is a fact of experience which manifests itself in many forms, in particular those of suffering, physical or moral, and death caused by natural forces or by human evil. No matter what our philosophical or religious convictions, it is imposssible for us to escape this terrible and searing question (Chapter 1).

Since the origins of humankind, explanations have been sought, first through myths and then more rationally in a philosophical type of reflection. Experience shows that all these attempts are inevitably doomed to failure (Chapter 2). Finally it appears that we do not even find any more satisfactory explanations from religions, even from Christianity. We always keep coming up against the same apparently insurmountable contradictions.

These contradictions were summed up by Lactantius, a Christian philosopher of the third century AD, in terms which go back further, to the Latin orator Cicero: 'If God wants to suppress evil and cannot do so, it is because he is not omnipotent, and that is a contradiction. If he can do so and does not will to, it is because he does not love us, and that is equally a contradiction. If he cannot and does not will to do so, it is that he has neither power nor love and therefore is not God. And if he can do so and wills to do so, how is it that there is evil and why does he not suppress it?'

Does that not definitively put a question mark against the existence of God?

1

The Mystery of Evil

A terrifying silence

Irrational and scandalous, the mystery of evil quite legitimately provokes us to reject evil and rebel against it. We would like to do anything to avoid it, but are unable to. It encircles us inescapably. In his book *The Crucified God*, the German theologian Jürgen Moltmann has spoken of the vicious circles in which we are trapped, of poverty, violence, racial and cultural alienation, the destruction of nature by pollution of various kinds, and finally the vicious circle of absurdity in which we seem to be turning the world into a hell.

Numerous theories have been put forward in an attempt to resolve this mystery, but no explanation of any kind, mythological, philosophical, religious or other, has proved satisfactory. All these intellectual exercises always turn out to be sterile and derisory in the face of the actual experience of suffering. One cannot understand it, one cannot accept it and one cannot justify it.

Evil and suffering cannot be justified. We cannot find either purpose or function in them. They are inexplicable. These terrible questions seem to be met only with a no less terrible silence. It is a terrifying silence, because there seems to be no reply – and the problem seems to get even deeper, the more one tries to approach it by referring to God.

For a long time the objection to evil seems to have had a fairly limited influence on belief in God. Evil and suffering were far from damaging belief in God; they seemed to be more or less part of the natural order – though that did not prevent people from rebelling against them. This world was a valley of tears, and it did not seem very surprising that one suffered in it before knowing true happiness in the other world. Nowadays, rightly, such a perspective is seen by all, including believers, as quite intolerable and unjustifiable.

Why these manifold sufferings? Why this injustice in the face of them? Why are the good (or those who claim to be such) apparently affected more often than the evil? Why such inequality? Why these wars, this misery, these famines, these tyrannies, this violence? Why does something so manifestly inhuman, so revolting, enter into our life? And finally, why is there this obvious powerlessness, despite the efforts of many people and despite technological progress, to break these vicious circles in which humanity comes to grief?

In the face of this, a denial of God because of the existence of evil can be found through the ages, and it has become increasingly important in the modern period. The more human beings have advanced in their domination of nature, the more difficult they have found it to bear their existence and the intolerable limits that it imposes on them. Hence the growing movement of revolt against this apparently sadistic God, a movement of revolt based on the obvious reflection that if God really existed and was good and all-powerful, as believers affirm, he could not have allowed evil and suffering. Here lie the roots of many people's atheism. If God exists, why does he allow this curse which weighs so heavily on our lives and leads us to rebel?

The problem seems insoluble. As the French philosopher Paul Ricoeur asks in his book on evil, 'How can one affirm together, without contradiction, the following three propositions: God is all-powerful; God is absolutely good; yet evil exists . . . when only two of these propositions are compatible, never all three?'

Is there then nothing for believers and unbelievers alike to do, facing our helplessness in this situation, than face it with resignation?

Such an attitude of submission, worthy of respect though it may be, hardly seems satisfactory. For to the degree that evil imposes its terrible and unacceptable presence on all of us, precisely because it is unacceptable, it seems to demand that we should seek ceaselessly to abolish it. To do that we need to try to penetrate more deeply into its mystery, even though we are aware that we cannot pierce it completely.

A multitude of cries

Even more than in other spheres, when we come to reflect on the problem of evil we can see how difficult it is to provide logical and intelligent explanations, emerging ready-made from a well-constructed theological and philosophical system. This is because before being a problem for the intelligence, evil is a question raised by human distress, or more precisely by a series of questions, a multitude of cries. Why are our existences struck by the most savage and unexpected blows, the meaning of which often escapes us completely? Why are some lives constantly tortured by suffering?

All these questions, and others like them, which have always preoccupied men and women, but which pierce our times with renewed acuteness, derive from the drama of existence itself. They do not allow of easy answers.

Jean Bosc

What is evil?

Evil and consciousness

In the strict sense, it is only from the moment when there is consciousness that we can talk of evil and suffering. Matter and the vegetable world do not suffer, and we must reject our tendency to project our feelings on to nature and to use the term evil for what is in fact natural. Thus an earthquake is neither good nor bad in itself. It is a simple geological phenomenon. It only becomes evil when it costs human, or even animal, lives, because there we have suffering.

In fact, while suffering already appears in the animal world, the problem of evil appears only with human beings. They alone can actually think about their suffering, a suffering which, moreover, is not only physical but also moral. Human beings not only undergo all these sufferings directly, in the present, but encounter them from a past which they relive and a future which they dread – something which only intensifies suffering. And only human beings have the sharp awareness of a frustration which does not appear 'natural'.

Can one define evil?

It is extremely difficult to define evil, because while evil certainly exists in itself, one can only define it in relation to something which it diminishes or compromises. We can never give a positive definition of evil. It is always talked of as part of a pair of which good is the other term, and it is impossible to mention evil without reminding oneself of the good of which it is the privation.

However, the fact that we cannot define evil without referring to good does not prevent evil from existing. Evil is not just, as is sometimes said, the privation of some good. The famous French philosopher Henri Bergson remarked: 'The philosopher may enjoy speculations of this kind in the solitude of his study; but what does he think when confronted with a mother who has just seen her child die? No, suffering is a terrible reality, and those who define evil as a lack of good do so with untenable optimism.'

The evils of existence and evil arising from human freedom

Evil may be due either to nature (the evils of existence) or to human freedom. This distinction is not uninteresting, though in some cases it is of limited use – for example some illnesses (evils of existence) can be aggravated by bad living conditions: lack of sanitation or other forms of pollution (evil due to human freedom) – and it allows us to make certain discoveries.

The term 'evils of existence' is used to denote the evil which arises for human beings as a result of their 'natural' existence in this world. Men and women are subject to sickness, suffering, death, anxiety.

Though men and women cannot completely suppress suffering because of the limitations of their natural condition, they try to master it and remove it as far as possible. Here we have partly succeeded, thanks for example to the fantastic progress achieved in the medical sphere. However, we are well aware that we will never be able completely to eliminate suffering. We will never be able to escape all the natural phenomena which engender evil, suffering and death.

But in our world we do not encounter only natural suffering and evil. We also encounter evil as a result of the freedom human beings have for conscious and voluntary action, evil which results directly from their freedom. From concentration camps where human beings are so degraded, to our civilizations in which money corrupts everything, through wars, unemployment and famine, sometimes unimaginable and always scandalous sufferings are caused – scandalous because they are caused by human beings themselves.

The scandal lies in the perverse human use of freedom, as the French novelist Georges Bernanos pointed out: 'The scandal of the universe is not suffering. It is freedom. God made his creation free: that is the scandal of scandals, and all the others proceed from it.'

In both cases the question is the same. Why does evil exist? Who can explain metaphysical evil? Why do human beings so often use their freedom so badly?

Mass grave of World War II concentration camp victims.

And if God had not created men and women free?

Dostoievsky: 'The Legend of the Grand Inquisitor'

Against the sombre picture of misdeeds resulting from human freedom, one might ask whether a world of slaves were not preferable to a world in which freedom reigns.

Men and women would be happy because they were not free, whereas God, by creating them free, has taken the risk that they may misuse their freedom.

And unfortunately they do misuse it all too often.

Dostoievsky raised this problem in The Brothers Karamazov *in his famous 'Legend of the Grand Inquisitor'. Here are some passages from this great text:*

The action takes place in Spain, in Seville, during the most terrible time of the Inquisition, when fires were lighted every day throughout the land to the glory of God . . . (In the crowd Jesus) appeared quietly, inconspicuously, but everyone – and that is why it is so strange – recognizes him. The people are drawn to him by an irresistible force, they surround him, they throng about him, they follow him. He walks among them in silence with a gentle smile of infinite compassion. (He raises a little girl to life on the steps of the cathedral) . . . At that very moment the Cardinal himself, the Grand Inquisitor, passes by the cathedral in the square. He sees everything . . . and his face darkens. (He has Jesus arrested) . . . and so great is his power and so accustomed are the people to obey him, so humble and submissive are they to his will, that the crowd immediately makes way for the guards and, amid the death-like hush that descends upon the square they lay hands upon Jesus and lead him away . . .

(In the night the Grand Inquisitor pays a visit to Jesus in prison.) 'Why did you come to meddle with us? For you have come to meddle with us, and you know it. But tomorrow I shall condemn you and burn you at the stake as the vilest of heretics . . . You rejected the only way by which men might be made happy. You preached freedom which men in their simplicity and their innate lawlessness cannot even comprehend, which they fear and dread – for nothing has ever been more unendurable to man and to human society than freedom!

But in the end they will become obedient. They will marvel at us and they will regard us as gods because, having become their masters, we consented to endure freedom and rule over them – so dreadful will freedom become to them in the end. Man, so long as he remains free, has no more constant and agonizing anxiety than to find as quickly as possible someone to worship. But man seeks to worship only what is incontestable, so incontestable indeed that all men at once agree to worship it together. For the chief concern of these miserable creatures is not only to find something that I or someone else can worship, but to find something that all believe in and worship, and the absolutely essential thing is that they should do so all together. I tell you, man has no more agonizing anxiety than to find someone to whom he can hand over with all speed the gift of freedom with which the unhappy creature is born.

Instead of taking possession of men's freedom you multiplied it and burdened the spiritual kingdom of man with its sufferings for ever. But did it never occur to you that he would at last reject and call in question even your image and your truth, if he were weighed down by so fearful a burden as freedom of choice? But here too your judgment of men was too high, for they are slaves, though rebels by nature. I swear, man has been created a weaker and baser creature than you thought him to be.

We have corrected your great work and have based it on miracle, mystery, and authority. And men rejoiced that they were once more led like sheep and the terrible gift which had brought them so much suffering had at last been lifted from their hearts.

→

With us, however, all will be happy and will no longer rise in rebellion nor exterminate one another, as they do everywhere under your freedom. Oh, we will convince them that only then will they become free when they have resigned their freedom to us and have submitted to us. And what do you think? Shall we be right or shall we be lying? They will themselves be convinced that we are right, for they will remember the horrors of slavery and confusion to which your freedom brought them. Freedom, a free mind and science, will lead them into such a jungle and bring them face to face with such marvels and insoluble mysteries that some of them, the recalcitrant and the fierce, will destroy themselves, others, recalcitrant but weak, will destroy one another, and the rest, weak and unhappy, will come crawling to your feet and cry aloud, "Yes, you were right, you alone possessed his mystery, and we come back to you – save us from ourselves!"'

F. Dostoievsky, *The Brothers Karamazov*, Book 5, chapter 5

2

Attempted Explanations through Myths and Philosophy

Attempted explanations through myths

Contrary to what is all too often thought, myths are far from being little stories for children. Through the very different – sometimes very complex – forms that they can take, these fictional accounts try to provide an answer to the important questions which human beings ask about the existence of the world and their own existence, for example the mysteries of their origins, of creation, of the presence of evil in the world and themselves, and so on.

Though these stories – which come from all periods including our own (cf. Superman, Rambo) – may seem naive and infantile, they are in fact very interesting. Rather than providing a solution to the problems they touch on, they provide extremely important information about human beings themselves and their desires. That is particularly clear when it comes to this two-fold problem of creation and the existence of evil and suffering.

In the mythological stories about evil we always find the same elements. At one time, they say, human beings lived happily with God or the gods in an ideal and marvellous world, paradise,

where there was neither evil, nor suffering, nor death. Then for various reasons there was a rift between human beings and this God or gods. From then on the harmony has been broken. That happened at the fall, with the appearance of suffering, pain, evil, anxiety, time, death. Nostalgic for this lost paradise, human beings live in hope of finding it as a refuge from all that assails them and all the difficulties in their lives.

Etienne Borne, whose thought we have already encountered, has described myth like this: 'Myth posits a world outside the world and a time before time in which people live happily, protected from pain, guilt and death, i.e. from all forms of evil. Then, at a second stage, evil invades this superior sphere which precedes human existence. The gods make war; some angels turn into demons, and supernatural beings get involved in human passions and human affairs, giving evil the depths of the abyss. The two periods which form this antithesis in mythological narrative recur in the myths of lost paradise – and in the biblical creation stories in Genesis 1–3.'

However, important and rich in meaning though the mythological explanation may be, it is far from being satisfactory, since in fact it does not explain anything. In particular, it does not help us over the problem of evil. That is why we cannot stop there, following the Bible, which, after using myths to try to 'express the inexpressible', rapidly gives up this kind of approach to penetrate more deeply into these mysterious realities which form the framework of human life.

So, progressively other approaches have been adopted, particularly in the context of philosophical reflection.

The Garden of Eden.

Philosophical reflection on the problem of evil

Virtually all philosophers have concerned themselves with the problem of evil. They have approached it in very different ways, but leaving aside Manicheism, which is more a gnosticism than real philosophy, we can distinguish three major types of treatment. First, there are those who think that we must submit to all that happens, seeking always to remain serene in the face of evil and suffering (the Stoics). Then there are those who think that despite the presence of evil, suffering and death, the universe nevertheless ultimately forms a fairly harmonious whole, though evil and suffering are realities which attempts must be made to combat (those adopting this approach include the early Greek philosopher Heraclitus, in the fifth century BC, and the eighteenth-century German philosopher Leibniz). Lastly come those who are not content to combat evil, but who reject it and cry out their revolt against it, like Camus.

Put up with what does not depend on you: Stoicism

Aspiring above all to offer consolation in the face of evil, pain and suffering, the Stoic philosophers sought less to explain evil than to preach submission. Wisdom consists in cultivating what depends on us and bravely bearing the rest. This is clear from one of the greatest philosophers of this school, Epictetus: 'Do not ask that what happens should happen as you want it to, but want things to happen as they happen, and you will be happy.' We have to master our desires and passions and remain insensitive, particularly to evil and suffering, if we are to find true serenity. This attitude is summed up in a famous Stoic slogan. In Latin it is *Sustine et abstine*: 'Bear (anything that does not depend on you) and abstain (from all passion).'

Strangely, when confronted with evil, Stoicism can lead to two contrary attitudes. On the one hand there is a sometimes proud voluntarism in which people grit their teeth to show that they are above all suffering; on the other hand, there is sometimes a rather sad resignation.

This philosophical attitude of Stoicism is extremely important in the history of Western thought and above all that of Christianity, which has often had a tendency to take it over . . . sometimes forgetting rather quickly that Stoicism was basically opposed to the gospel in the sense that Jesus never preached submission or resignation in the face of evil and suffering, but rather active rebellion.

Despite appearances, the universe is a harmonious whole

This is an idea which goes a long way back in the history of Western philosophy, since it appeared with Heraclitus in the fifth century BC.

Heraclitus

Heraclitus stressed that we see only one aspect of things, but if we could see reality as a whole, in its totality, we would discover that it is in fact harmonious. He went on to say that the world constantly changes, and in this perpetual flux there is a constant confrontation between good and evil. However, in this confrontation, which is repeated again and again, good always wins in the end. 'Good and evil are both one,' he asserted.

If we contrast good and evil, it is because of our narrow and partial views. In reality they combine in a real harmony. In this perspective failure always heralds progress, injustice a new justice, death a renewal. Dusk is always recompensed with a dawn. And good will always win.

Manicheism

This doctrine was founded by Manes (or Mani) who was born and lived principally in Persia in the third century AD. Manes sought to explain evil by asserting the existence of two opposing principles constantly at war in the universe: good and evil. There is an absolute and constant opposition between two 'gods', the god of good and the god of evil, between the world of light and the world of darkness. Human souls are said to be fragments of light imprisoned in carnal matter, this latter expressing the original evil from which souls must try to free themselves.

Only gnosis, 'real knowledge', can provide illumination and lead to the truth. The way of liberation can only pass through asceticism and the practice of the virtues taught particularly by the divine messengers – who are for example Abraham, Buddha, Jesus and Manes himself.

Society is divided into two groups: the 'perfect', who renounce the world and live in chastity, purity and absolute asceticism, and the others. The supporters of this doctrine spread rapidly as far as Europe; there the best known of them were the Cathari (from a Greek word meaning 'pure'), who were active particularly in the twelfth and thirteenth centuries.

Manicheism has always been vigorously contested in the church as being contrary to Christian faith, since for Christianity there is only one God, the God of the Christian revelation.

Leibniz

These views of Heraclitus have regularly been taken up in very different ways over the course of history. In particular, they were adopted by Leibniz, who, in the eighteenth century, also tried to console humanity while seeking to acquit God. He thought the latter point more important than the former. That was to be the whole object of his 'theodicy', and in order to achieve it, he sought in turn to give a place to evil in the universal order. His thesis remained famous since it characterized the metaphysical optimism which Voltaire parodied in his *Candide*. This parody was somewhat unfair, because Voltaire very much caricatured the thought of Leibniz without seeing its depths.

To begin with, Leibniz never denied the tragic reality of evil. Quite the contrary. But he stressed that, if evil exists, it is because God could not create a perfect world. That would be a contradiction, for if God had created a perfect world, by virtue of its total perfection this world could not but be another God. That is unthinkable, because God is unique. So there cannot be two absolute perfections, in other words, two Gods.

Because the universe is created, it is necessarily limited, and consequently evil exists in it with equal necessity. But of all the worlds that God could have created, he created the best possible one. The world which he chose to create is definitely the one which contained the max-

Leibniz. God is innocent of evil.

imum of good and the minimum of evil. So God could certainly have created a world without Nero, the most famous Roman emperor, rightly described as a bloody tyrant, but a world without Nero would necessarily have contained other imperfections and other evils more serious than those which provoked his existence.

The problem, again according to Leibniz, ultimately taking up Heraclitus here, is that we can see only part of reality. If we saw reality as a whole we would see that it is all finally harmonious, and that in the end good always triumphs. Evil is necessary in the world, just as shadows are necessary in a picture to emphasize the light and bring it out, or dissonances are skilfully integrated into the overall harmony of a symphony. Evil is terrifying and terrible, but it always avoids even worse evils and always ends up in good.

It is superfluous to point out that this form of argument is utterly unsatisfactory. It is not only that it does not succeed in acquitting God, but it is also literally scandalous in the face of the specific suffering that evil causes. Evil is always evil, and we can never justify it in any way. So this kind of explanation must be ruled out.

'Theodicy'

Leibniz sought above all to justify God (acquit God from evil), hence the word 'theodicy' (from the Greek *theos*, god, and *dike*, justification), which he invented to express his thesis and to serve as the title of one of his main works on this problem: *Essays of Theodicy on the Goodness of God, Human Freedom and the Origin of Evil* (1710). From the nineteenth century, the word 'theodicy' has come to denote philosophical reflection on God in the light of reason and human experience alone.

Evil can never be reduced simply to the shadow side of good

'Evil has to be integrated into a plan or a wider design in which it plays the role of the mean or the necessary condition for a greater good . . .' This argument has been developed by very great philosophers, like St Augustine, St Thomas Aquinas and Descartes. Descartes writes: 'That which might perhaps seem, perhaps with good reason, to be very imperfect all on its own is very perfect if it is regarded as part of the universe.'

Leibniz, who pushed this idea furthest, thought that 'evil is no longer evil if it is a necessary element in progress'. Stalin said the same thing. So did Hitler. For him, the liquidation of six million Jews was a condition of human progress, just as, for Stalin, was the liquidation of all those who opposed his regime. Evil is said to lose its character as evil once it is set in the perspective of an overall development; suffering is no more than a crisis of growth; war is the travail of history; the sacrifice of present generations allows access to future society.

Such a justification of evil is not only superficial but unjust, and if it is unjust, it is also an evil. It is not a matter of making evil disappear, but of adding evil to evil. There are arguments which are not only ineffective but morally bad and literally scandalous. Such a philosophy is possible only if one counts the individual, the person, the particular man or woman as nothing.

François Varillon

The way of revolt

This normal and natural attitude of revolt is that of the great majority of philosophers, in particular numerous Christian philosophers. The revolt was particularly well expressed by an atheist philosopher, Albert Camus.

Camus

Camus' basic intuition is that of the tragedy of existence, which is expressed most painfully through the suffering of children, the most atrocious image of evil. That is his proof that God does not exist. Evil and God are contradictory.

However, for Camus this omnipresence of evil must never justify an attitude of submission, far less lead to suicide, even if the reality of suffering and death appears absurd, above all precisely because of evil. On the contrary, this omnipresence of evil cannot but stimulate the efforts of 'man the rebel' to try incessantly to suppress it.

Faced with evil, without ever being discouraged, men and women can only revolt and

Albert Camus.
Evil is absurd. One cannot but rebel against it.

Camus: Rebellion against Evil

In his novel The Plague, *Camus gives particularly dramatic expression to the problem of evil through the problem of the suffering of children.*

A terrible plague epidemic ravages Oran, claiming hundreds of victims every day. Among them are numerous children, and in particular one small boy who has just died. A priest, the Jesuit Paneloux, and a doctor, Rieux, are discussing in the courtyard, and Rieux explodes following the death of this child:

'Ah, that child, anyhow, was innocent – and you know it as well as I do!'

'I understand,' Paneloux said in a low voice. 'That sort of thing is revolting because it passes our human understanding. But perhaps we should love what we cannot understand.'

Rieux straightened up slowly. He gazed at Paneloux, summoning to his gaze all the strength and fervour he could muster against his weariness. Then he shook his head.

'No, Father, I've a very different idea of love. And until my dying day I shall refuse to love a scheme of things in which children are put to torture.'

Albert Camus, *The Plague*

constantly renew their efforts to reduce the injustice and sufferings around them. They must be like Sisyphus, the legendary figure in Greek mythology who was condemned by the gods constantly to push an enormous boulder up to the top of a mountain, only to have it roll back again as soon as he arrived at the summit. Camus wrote a book entitled *The Myth of Sisyphus*.

Camus certainly recognized that even if human beings succeeded in eliminating all the evils which they caused, there would always be suffering because of their limited and mortal condition. So despite the prodigious progress of medicine, human beings will never be totally invulnerable physically and psychologically. They will always inevitably be confronted with sickness and death. 'Man can master, in himself, everything that should be mastered. He should rectify in creation everything that can be rectified. And after he has done so, children will still die unjustly, even in a perfect society. The injustice and the suffering will remain, and no matter how limited they are, they will not cease to be an outrage' (Albert Camus, *The Rebel*).

That having been said, we must never give up this fight against suffering and evil. This fight, in particular this fight constantly to defend those who are most humiliated and most poor, presupposes a 'mad generosity' and a 'strange love'.

Praised be the name of the Lord!

Smitten with a cancer which no medical technique can treat, the narrator expresses his suffering in an overwhelming testimony. At one point he violently turns on God, parodying Job in the Bible:

The Eternal replied to Job from the midst of the tempest: 'Did I not create the crocodile which surpasses all the rest in abomination? Cannot the crocodile bite, slaughter, cripple, mutilate, destroy? How can you doubt my authority when I am the master of abominations?'

The Job replied to the Eternal and said: 'You are right. I recognize that you are the most ignoble, the most repugnant, the most brutal, the most perverse, the most sadistic and the most nauseating being in the world. I recognize that you are a despot and a tyrant and a potentate who obliterates and kills everything . . . You invented the Gestapo, the concentration camp and torture; so I recognize that you are the greatest and the strongest. Praised be the name of the Lord!'

F. Zorn

The Christian attitude

Camus rightly thinks that Christians have a role in this fight against evil. Even if the convictions of Christians and atheists differ, in the face of evil there is nothing that could justify anyone opting out. Speaking to Dominicans in Paris, Camus pointed out that while honestly recognizing that he did not share their hope, 'I share with you the same horror of evil.' Then he asserted that by very reason of their faith, Christians cannot fail to take part in this conflict: 'If you do not help us, then who in the world can?'

The great majority of Christians, in complete conformity to the gospel (and fortunately they are not the only ones), do not cease to respond to this dramatic appeal of Camus, in the name of their hope, to collaborate as effectively as possible in the constant struggle against evil. Faced with this scandal of evil, they feel that the only positive attitude is to engage in active revolt in an attempt to suppress evil.

They differ from Camus only when he affirms that because of this the world is absurd and that God does not exist. Certainly, for them, as for Camus, the mystery remains with all its tragedy and incomprehensibility, despite all attempts to explain it, but it does not lead them to reject God.

3

Christian Reflection on Evil

A different perspective

Though the mystery of evil remains insoluble from a strictly philosophical perspective, the believer often hesitates to recognize that the same is true of religions. But it is clear that no religion, including Christianity, provides a really satisfactory solution.

Certainly Christianity appeals to the idea of 'original sin', but though in so doing it asserts that evil is in every human being, that does not explain *why* they have evil in them . . . far less explain the evils of existence.

Why does not this observation that they are unable to give a valid explanation of the existence of evil and suffering lead Christians to reject God? Why does it not lead them to think that the world is ultimately absurd?

First of all because Christians have an 'other' image of God, particularly, as we have seen in previous chapters, in that they reject the omnipotent image of God in traditional theism and atheism, that of the real potentate or tyrant manipulating human beings at will, in favour of a God who is close to human beings and respects their freedom, the God who is conceived of in the Christian revelation.

Then it introduces other elements which relate more to the sphere of faith and theological reflection, elements which we must now take into account in order to understand the Christian attitude, even if this takes us to some degree beyond the strict framework of philosophical reflection.

Evil is always evil and has to be fought against constantly

As we shall see, believers agree with Camus when he asserts that we must struggle constantly against evil. It is worth stressing this position, since it is in fact the starting point for Christian reflection on evil.

Believers do not claim to provide 'the' solution to the problem of evil (which they do not explain any better than unbelievers). Rather, they call for a practical attitude which is essentially one of rebellion and active combat against all evil and all suffering, even if it is true that unfortunately this attitude has not always been that of all Christians, many of whom have sometimes tended more to cultivate Stoicism than active revolt.

As the theologian François Varillon has put it:

'Christians are invited to turn away from an explanation of evil which can only be sterile and inadequate towards the specific attitude which men and women must take in the face of evil. They must once and for all stop trying to find an explanation, a function, a purpose in evil and suffering. Even within faith, there is no explanation of evil . . . Faith is not there to explain things (that is for science or philosophy). God does not explain the problem of evil; he is not a teacher who gives us academic answers to questions which we put to him. He does not respond to our intellectual curiosity. Evil is not there to be understood but to be fought against.'

However – and here there is all the difference in the world from Camus – this attitude of rebellion and resistance to evil and suffering is based on convictions which ultimately lead us not to reject God but, despite evil and suffering, on the contrary to affirm God's existence.

For believers, this attitude of rejection of evil and suffering and constant struggle against them is in fact based on two certainties:

1. Human beings are made for happiness, and God never wills evil or suffering.

2. Though apparently powerless in the face of evil, God is nevertheless in solidarity with men and women in suffering.

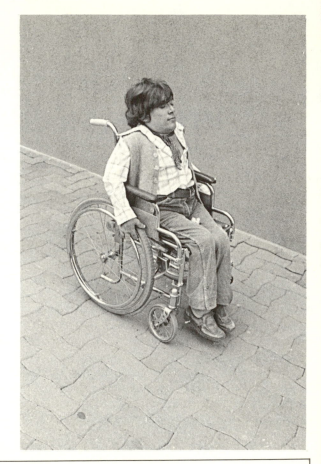

Original sin

This expression cannot denote the sin of Adam and Eve since these figures never existed – not to mention the fact that had this been the case, it would have been profoundly unjust for all their descendants to undergo indefinitely the consequences of their possible 'original' mistake. If God had created someone for whom sin was lurking round the first corner which would entail a death that was to last throughout the existence of humankind, then God would be to blame. We now think it iniquitous that death and finitude should originate in a single individual and a single sin. Such a belief can only lead to atheism.

It looks as if the creation stories unhesitatingly attribute the existence of thorns and weeds, weariness resulting from work, and the pains of childbirth to Adam's initial fault. But that kind of interpretation of the creation stories does not work, and we need to be bold enough to say so.

That does not mean, however, that we have to reject the Bible completely at this point. In fact the story of original sin in Genesis 3 is a mythological and symbolic story. As such it is a very rich account which stresses that evil, sin, this famous original sin, is in human beings – all of them. But the story does not tell us *why* sin is there: it does not explain the origin of evil.

Some scandalous suggestions

Unfortunately, in theological books which appeared before the Second Vatican Council it is possible to find numerous examples of scandalous suggestions that God 'willed' evil . . . for the good of humankind.

Thus among a great many others, a Dominican, Fr Deman, in a work of 1943, could write:

'Speaking of the evils with which we are afflicted, we often tend to call them trials. The name is well chosen. It signifies that our ills have this effect of testing or controlling what we are. Thanks to them we know how much our virtues are worth. There is no substitute for evil in this testing power . . . Indeed in all the evil that God permits or causes, he is in pursuit of good; I say that and proclaim that forcefully . . .

Not only is it better once a person has sinned, for him to be punished than to remain unpunished, but thanks to these guilty ones a special beauty appears in God's work which would have remained hidden had human beings only been innocent . . .'

And to end the discussion, Fr Deman makes this unimaginable comment:

'Let us bow down before the avenging arm . . . In every case, even in this form, we must be capable of admiring the invincible providence of God.'

This kind of suggestion has unfortunately been very frequent, as is witnessed by a more recent book by F. Petit published in 1958 on the problem of evil in which one could still read:

'God has allowed evil in order to be able to show his love for us in a tragic way which one could not contradict, by accepting our punishment and our suffering.'

God never wills evil or suffering

Human beings are made for happiness. No matter what form it may take, evil is *always* evil and is never willed by God. All Christian theologians and philosophers are in fact in agreement in asserting this very clearly, even if unfortunately for a long time people thought not only that God allowed evil but that he actually provoked it for the good of the faithful. And even that he rejoiced in it!

And as if it were not enough to have to pay for an alleged sin committed by Adam, human beings were thought to have to pay for the sins of others, past and to come.

For example, a person was born blind because his or her parents had sinned. It would be instructive to have an opinion poll on this among the parents of handicapped children. Think of the ravages that religion has committed among them! And as for paying for the future; in this perspective suffering becomes the great currency, the dollar of the heavenly bank. God loves suffering infinitely. The more we give him, the more he likes it.

It goes without saying that along with contemporary Christian theologians and philosophers we must firmly condemn suggestions which ultimately make God the greatest of sadists and perverts. How dare we talk like that and at the same time assert that God is wholly love? That is quite scandalous.

Indeed it is blasphemous. How could we imagine an indifferent God leaving the world to plunge into the abyss and suffer, or, even worse, a supreme spectator who puts us to the test to see

how we stand up to it, whether we fail, and savours this experimentation with a strange kind of delight? A calculating God who invents enticement and then torture in order to educate people? Can we accept that the true God would have such a horrible technique? We could not call anyone good who acted so treacherously with his friends and submitted them to such indignity. Whatever the solution to our enigmas, it cannot lie there.

Evil and suffering always remain terrible realities against which we must never cease to fight . . .

To repeat it again and again: evil and suffering do not have and cannot have any value in themselves. (They cannot even be said to be a warning for illnesses to come: serious illnesses like cancer can develop over a long period without causing any pain, while minor ailments like toothache can be extremely painful!) Evil can never be justified, and we must reject absolutely any philosophy or theology which seeks to find any meaning in it at all.

Evil is something terrible, terrifying, against which we must always rebel constantly, whether we are Christians or not. Christians – like everyone else – can certainly accept evil when they are its unfortunate victims, but they can never look for it or desire it in any way.

. . . even if they can be the occasion for deepening personality

There are those who point out that suffering can provide the occasion for deepening our personalities. However, it has to be said that in such instances suffering is not absolutely the cause of this human and spiritual deepening; it is only the occasion for it. Everything in fact depends on the way in which suffering is received and experienced. Here we are faced with the unfathomable mystery of suffering, and the equally unfathomable mystery of its rejection, or the effort of will by which a person can or cannot surmount trials, the way in which suffering can either be a source of the purging and deepening of the personality or, on the contrary, overwhelm and consume those who endure it.

104

Men and women are made for happiness

That having been said, it nevertheless remains that human beings are made first and foremost for happiness. And that is so true that this quest for happiness is the goad which constantly drives men and women to fight against evil and suffering: their desire for happiness is stronger than evil.

François Varillon, whom we have met earlier, writes:

'The rebellion of conscience in the face of evil would be an absurdity were it not rooted in a certainty. Unless we resign ourselves to the absurdity of our most basic aspirations to justice, good, love, brotherhood; unless we accept that all this is an illusion, we have to accept behind the rejection or scandal of evil an aspiration which in a way already assures us that evil has been overcome. Is it not because we are made for joy, because happiness is our vocation, that we protest against evil and suffering? I assert that if our vocation were not a vocation to joy, our indignation against evil and suffering would not be what it is.'

A God who is apparently powerless, but who shows solidarity with human beings in their suffering

So if it is impossible and unthinkable that God should provoke evil and suffering, the mystery nevertheless remains, to the degree that God would himself seem impotent in the face of these terrible realities. Here we come up against something as paradoxical as it is inexplicable: the apparent weakness of God.

This strange and quite disconcerting paradox seems to be specific to the Christian God: a good and omnipotent God who proves impotent before evil. So impotent is God that theologians have even been able to speak of the humility of God and his suffering in the face of his creation. Why? Why does God not do something, and above all can he do nothing against suffering and evil? As Alexandre Dumas pointed out, 'Even in the agony of the Berlin bunker, Hitler had more destructive power than God has liberating power. Why?'

To some extent we can understand this powerlessness over evil when the evil is caused by human beings: since men and women are free,

Suffering and death are part of our human condition

Who would think of blaming parents for having wanted the suffering, the sin and the death to which their children will be subject on the pretext that they wanted their children to exist? They know that since their children will be human, they will be the subjects of suffering, sin and death. Either they do not have these children, or the beings that they produce will be subject to suffering for the same reason that they will be subject to happiness, subject to sin for the same reason that they will be subject to good, subject to life. And that relates not only to the imperfection of their procreation or their own imperfection (far less that of their children!) but to the nature of their condition. Now it is the same with God.

Jacques Pohier, *Quand je dis Dieu*

God makes them responsible for their actions and refuses to intervene to clear things up.

But that does not apply to the evils of existence (disease, suffering, 'natural' death, etc.). Certainly they seem to be part of the nature of our human condition and its imperfection. But why did God not make nature less destructive of human beings if God wished their happiness?

Once again we come up against a terrible and dark mystery, and the only certainty for the believer is that God stands beside men and women both in their suffering and in their fight against it and against evil.

In Christian theology, this point is essential, since it brings the believer to the mystery of the cross.

It is despite the non-sense of evil, suffering and death that the believer affirms the existence of God

Faced with this mystery of evil and suffering, the believer is as powerless as the unbeliever. The Christian revelation does not contribute any satisfactory solution to these terrible realities which seem to escape all explanation and all justification. Is that a reason for rejecting God? For some people it is, and we have also seen, with Camus, that there is a consistency about this choice, just as there is a consistency in the choice of the believer who, *despite* evil and suffering, nevertheless affirms the opposite, that God exists.

This choice is not an easy one to make. It does not amount to a refusal to seek to understand reality or to look it in the face. Nor is it a desire to seek a sterile and passive refuge in a more or less mythological, capricious and perverse deity whom one then tries to cajole in order to avoid the worst. Far from seeking to escape reality, believers in fact try, rather, to take it on and do everything possible to change it, since it is full of evil and suffering.

Nor is this a naive choice. Certainly it does not lie in the direct line of strict philosophical rationality, which brings out the real basic contradiction between God and evil . . . without being able to go any further. But this choice which consists in holding together two apparently contradictory realities – the existence of God and the very real existence of evil and suffering – is rooted in the two-fold conviction of which I have just spoken. On the one hand God can never will evil and suffering for human beings, who are made for happiness. On the other hand God stands alongside us in these terrible realities, in the face of which, for mysterious reasons which escape us, he in fact seems powerless.

This presence of God in solidarity is essential for believers, since it is on that that they base the consistency of their choice, and it is always that which finally justifies their hope. But it is true that this solidarity is not an explanation, and that in inviting us to hold together the two apparently contradictory facts of the goodness of God and the actual presence of evil and suffering in the world and in ourselves, the Christian revelation does not in any way resolve this tragic mystery.

So like everyone else, the believer is still confronted with a terrible and unsurmountable contradiction. The reason for this is that it is always despite evil and despite the non-sense of suffering and death that Christians definitively affirm the existence of God.

106

Where is your God?

(There was in the camp) a young boy, a *pipel* as they were called . . . One day when we came back from work we saw three gallows rearing up in the assembly place, three black crows. Roll call. SS all around us, machine guns trained: the traditional ceremony. Three victims in chains and one of them the little *pipel* . . . The head of the camp read the verdict. All eyes were on the child. He was lividly pale, almost calm, biting his lips. The gallows threw its shadow over him . . . The three victims mounted together on the chairs . . . The three necks were placed at the same time in the nooses . . .

'Where is God? Where is he?', someone behind me asked . . .

At a sign from the head of the camp the three chairs tipped over . . .

The two adults were no longer alive . . . But the third rope was still moving. Being so light the child was still alive. For more than half an hour he stayed there, struggling between life and death, dying in slow agony before our eyes. And we had to look him full in the face.

Behind me I heard the same man asking.

'Where is God now?'

And I heard a voice within me answer him:

'Where is he? Here he is – he is hanging here on the gallows.'

Elie Wiesel, *Night*, p.75

Albert Gleizes,
Contemplation.
Photo P. Migeat.

108

Conclusion

At the end of these reflections on the problem of God, where are we? Having stressed the importance that I attached to approaching this question of God from a philosophical perspective, that is to say, essentially from our experience at its most concrete and most profoundly existential, I deliberately set the discussion in the modern world, precisely because I wanted to begin from present-day reality. Taking this reality into account has led us to ask about the contemporary phenomena of secularization and atheism. But in order to understand better the roots of this new perspective, we had to analyse in more depth the development of the underlying philosophical reflection, particularly since Descartes and Kant.

With them a shift takes place. And what a shift! From now on human beings are at the centre of everything, human beings with their basic questions which are timeless: the questions of the meaning of life and the meaning of the universe and our own existence within it. Now if one raises these questions – and we have seen that for a variety of reasons one can refuse to take them into account and life in what Pascal called 'diversions' – one is necessarily led also to ask questions about the existence and nature of God. These questions are there, whether we answer them in the positive or in the negative.

Now in fact we can no longer talk about God without talking about human beings. For the effect of modernity is to shift the question of God, so that the problem is no longer that of God as such, but of God in his relationship to men and women. Thus human beings find themselves at the heart of this debate about God – and that is an excellent thing, since they are the ones most concerned.

It is precisely by taking very careful account of this new perspective that we have touched on a certain number of important problems bound up with this two-fold question of human beings and God: the relationship between science and faith, the problems of the creation of the world, of human freedom in the face of God and divine providence, the mystery of evil. It seemed vital to clarify matters here, since for many people it is here that atheism has its roots. So I wanted to show that although these questions need not lead us to deny God, because of the importance that we attach to human beings and their legitimate demands they can lead us to take into account the hypothesis of his experience and eventually transform this hypothesis into a certainty.

Do we transform this hypothesis into a certainty and affirm God? That is the choice that I have made. It is certainly not an easy one, for any choice in this sphere cannot be evident or completely obvious. But it is legitimate for us in that in our eyes our universe and even we ourselves only make sense if we appeal to someone who transcends us, i.e. God.

That does not amount to seeking refuge in an imaginary absolute, as Feuerbach and Marx thought, or in keeping an infantile and irresponsible attitude, as Freud affirmed. Nor is it a matter of evading our strictly human responsibilities and denying our freedom, as Sartre thought. Believers are confronted with the same difficulties as other people, and if they live out their faith authentically, they know that they must take their own lives in hand, that they are free and responsible for what they do and cannot use God to provide facile excuses. God is the basis of human freedom, but God never comes as if by a miracle to resolve the problems of those who believe in him. Life is as beautiful and as hard for believers as it is for anyone else.

So why choose God if God is not there to smoothe out our difficulties and come directly to our help when everything is going badly? In my view it is because only the acknowledgment of God can allow us to find the ultimate meaning of the existence of the universe and our own existence.

This is not a 'proof' in the strict sense of the term. The affirmation of God, like the negation of God, is a reality which is more the result of a joint act of intelligence and will than the conclusion of a definitive and irrefutable demonstration. In fact we should speak here of 'reasons for believing' rather than 'proofs'. These 'reasons for believing' seem to me to be sufficiently important and decisive for us to make a firm, free and clear choice for God.

For Further Reading

Anselm, 'Proslogion', in *A Scholastic Miscellany: Anselm to Ockham*, ed. E. R. Fairweather, LCC X, SCM Press and Westminster Press 1956

D. Bartholomew, *God of Chance*, SCM Press 1984

Martin Buber, *The Eclipse of God*, Gollancz 1953

Albert Camus, *The Plague*, Hamish Hamilton 1948; Penguin Books 1960

Albert Camus, *The Rebel*, Hamish Hamilton 1953; Penguin Books 1962

Jean Delumeau, *Ce que je crois*, Grasset, Paris 1985

René Descartes, *Discourse on Method and the Meditations*, translated by F. E. Sutcliffe, Penguin Books 1968

Ludwig Feuerbach, *The Essence of Christianity*, translated by George Eliot, reissued Harper 1957

Sigmund Freud, *The Future of an Illusion*, The Pelican Freud Library Vol.12, Penguin Books 1985

John Hick, *Evil and the God of Love*, Macmillan ²1977

Immanuel Kant, *Critique of Pure Reason*, translated by Norman Kemp Smith, Macmillan ²1933

Walter Kasper, *The God of Jesus Christ*, SCM Press and Crossroad Publishing Company 1984

Hans Küng, *Does God Exist?*, Collins and Doubleday 1980

Jürgen Moltmann, *The Crucified God*, SCM Press and Harper and Row 1974

Jacques Monod, *Chance and Necessity*, Collins 1972

Hugh Montefiore, *The Probability of God*, SCM Press 1985

Christian Montenat, Luc Plateaux and Pascal Roux, *How to Read the World: Creation in Evolution*, SCM Press and Crossroad Publishing Company 1985

Blaise Pascal, *Pensées*, Everyman edition, Dent 1908

Jacques Pohier, *Quand je dis dieu*, Editions du Seuil 1977

Jacques Pohier, *God – in Fragments*, SCM Press and Crossroad Publishing Company 1985

Alan Richardson and John Bowden (eds), *A New Dictionary of Christian Theology*, SCM Press and Westminster Press 1983

Jean-Paul Sartre, 'The Flies', in *Three Plays*, Hamish Hamilton 1949

Pierre Teilhard de Chardin, *The Phenomenon of Man*, Collins and Harper and Row 1965

Thomas Aquinas, *Summa Theologiae*, edited by Thomas Gilby OP, Eyre and Spottiswoode and McGraw Hill, especially Vol.II, 1964

Elie Wiesel, *Night*, Penguin Books 1981

Heinz Zahrnt, *What Kind of God?*, SCM Press 1971

Index of Names

Index of Subjects

Illustration Credits

GARDEN CENTRE MANAGER

Chris Snook
Ken Crafer

Grower Manual No 4

Grower Books

Nexus Media Limited, Kent

Grower Books
Nexus Media Limited
Nexus House
Azalea Drive
Swanley
Kent BR8 8HU

First published 1999
© Grower Books 1999

ISBN 1 899372 15 6

Series editor Peter Rogers   Production Jayne Hewish
Publisher Tony Salter

Typeset by Kate Williams, Abergavenny
Printed in Great Britain

Contents

1 Garden centre location

Choice of location.

The public interest in gardening and leisure certainly does not seem to be diminishing and with an increasingly ageing population, all the indications are that there will be an increase in spend on gardening and related products. As a result of this the industry has experienced a considerable increase in outlets, possibly reaching saturation point in the UK.

The rapid growth in demand had meant that it was relatively easy to make money but the situation has now changed. The industry is now seeing the development of chains, often purchasing sites from independents and certainly taking market share. It is likely that the DIY stores will have the largest market share by early into the millennium.

Garden retailing still represents a profitable sector with margins far higher than in many others. It is a simply a question that modern garden retailers must become more professional in their outlook – those who fail to respond will not survive.

Let us consider the various aspects of the garden centre in more detail, and address some of the more important issues.

CHOICE OF LOCATION

The person who said that the three most important factors relating to retailing were location, location and ... location had it about right! The choice of a site should be determined primarily by the potential customer numbers and not purely the cost of the land. The first move is to do your homework. Basic research should include the following.

What is the competition?

Rarely will a business be trading in complete isolation – other companies within the area will be trading in similar merchandise and offering similar services. In the early stages it is important to analyse the strength and weaknesses of existing operators offering similar services. Compile a dossier giving an overall view of their whole trading set-up.

A study of the competition in such a way will give an indication of your likelihood of success. It would also be worth carrying out an (honest) assessment on the type of outlet you wish to introduce by way of comparison. This may be difficult as once you have a business idea (particularly if it your first business) there is a tendency to see the whole project through rose-tinted spectacles and gloss over potential problems. Sometimes a study of the cars in the car park gives a good idea of the customer base of a competitor (both numbers and type). In certain countries the licence plate will also give some indication of where the customer base is being drawn from but unfortunately this information source will not work in Britain.

Aspects to include in competitor analysis	
Layout	Cleanliness
Stock range	Stock quality
Staffing	Information offered
Ability to expand	Current size
Profitability	Pricing structure
Promotional strategies	Customer facilities
Delivery service	General ambience

How many people are within the catchment area?

Published garden centre research within this particular subject area is particularly scant. There is a general assumption in the UK that the majority of customers will be drawn from within a 10-mile radius. While this may be a useful starting point there may be many other factors that play a part including:

Image and facilities: *special attractions draw people further, as does a good reputation.*

Population density: *a centre in the country will need to attract people from greater distance compared to a similar turnover centre in a city.*

Conurbations: *often a centre has difficulty drawing custom from the opposite side of a major town.*

Road infrastructure: *easy access roads may mean that customers tend to visit from along this axis.*

In many situations rather than purely looking at the distance element it may be useful to consider the time it takes to travel to a centre. Indeed one garden centre chain based in London has stated that increased road congestion is actually increasing sales since customers are not willing to travel as far to find competition!

Calculation of the customer potential in the neighbouring population also has other difficulties since not all people are keen gardeners. The **demographic** segmentation of the population needs to be analysed in greater detail. Aspects such as age, family status, housing and income all will have a bearing on the potential demand for your proposed product range – indeed the product range and style of the centre will probably be shaped by it. A number of different classification systems exist to help define these issues, often classified by either social grouping or residential neighbourhoods. Computer modelling is also available to help project the outcome of siting a business in a particular position.

The attitude to gardening

A factor forgotten by many garden centre managers is that other people may not be as committed to gardening as they are. Some people positively hate it, so there is little point in allocating resources to specifically target this group. Mintel research has revealed three main types of consumer with the garden market:

Horticultural hobbyists

Serious amateur gardeners who often devote a lot of time to gardening. Whilst new varieties may be of interest to them, they are often well settled in their homes and consequently may already possess the essential buildings and equipment. They already have a mature garden and will propagate most of their own plants from seeds and cuttings at low cost.

They may in fact spend less money in the garden centre than other groupings.

Leisure gardeners

Often 'fair weather' gardeners, perhaps with a large area down to lawn and shrubs/perennials to minimise the labour input. They potentially spend more than the hobbyist above, but this may be lavishly in one or two spending sprees (i.e. in spring and autumn). They may be especially keen on container gardening, water gardening and other 'fashionable' aspects and are likely to spend heavily on furniture, watering equipment and ornamentation.

Investors

Spend less time in the garden with highest expenditure in the first few years or prior to putting the house on the market for sale. Expenditure may be on evergreen shrubs and hard paving as these are low maintenance. Larger investment may result in the loss of part of the garden for car parking areas or a conservatory, designed to increase the value of their property.

Profile of Horticultural Hobbyists	
	%
Men	38
Women	62
Under 45	27
Over 44	73
15–19	1
20–24	2
25–34	8
35–44	16
45–54	19
55–64	20
65+	34
Working	39
Not working	37
Retired	24

Source : Mintel 1997

Of these three main purchasing groups, the horticultural hobbyists tend to visit the specialist garden centre (although more specialist seeds etc may be purchased mail order). The investors are drawn to the DIY stores with the lure of competitive prices and the ability to pick up items along with other home improvement materials.

As for the leisure gardeners, this may be the key battleground. They are a core market for the specialist garden centre but are being wooed by the DIY stores and perhaps even the emerging product ranges of many supermarkets.

Clearly the above is an oversimplification of the UK gardening market and many exceptions exist. The key aspect is however to identify who your customer base is. The centre that claims to attract all groups is probably lying!

Whilst at this moment in time it is also fair to say that there is a tendency for younger people to visit DIY stores whereas the older generation usually prefer the specialist garden centre, there is no certainty that the specialist site will continue to inherit this customer base. Younger customers are used to the style and facilities of the DIY store and may continue to demonstrate their loyalty there.

Accessibility

Up to 60% of new customers may discover the centre when simply passing by. It is therefore quite important for the centre to be sited on a main road, or at the very least, be easily visible, a fact which may be at odds with the local planning authority. The romantic notion that customers will search down country lanes to find a centre is a little far-fetched. If you prove too difficult to find they will 'stumble' across somebody else.

Approaching traffic needs ample warning that the centre is ahead so that entry is safely achieved. Once again when assessing a potential site it is far too simplistic to stand at the side of the road and count how many cars pass during a specified time. The speed of traffic

Cars moving at higher speeds need more warning!

30mph

Thinking distance	9m
Braking distance	14m
Total stopping distance	23m

60mph

Thinking distance	18m
Braking distance	55m
Total stopping distance	73m

Source: Department of Transport

is also vitally important, as drivers need enough time to react if they are going to make an unplanned stop. This was a fact ignored by a small chain of centres which purchased a site only to discover that drivers travelled too fast to make an impulse call.

Many local authorities may also require the centre to fund changes to the road layout, such as acceleration/deceleration lanes as part of the planning permission to help prevent mishaps by cars slowing suddenly.

Clearly signage is vitally important if the traveller is to be warned adequately of the centre's presence. This may also be covered by the planning permission. The sign will also give that all-important initial impression of your centre so the choice of a suitable format and font is vital. Research shows that lower case letters are easier to read than a sign purely composed of upper case (capital) letters. Letters at least a fifth as wide as they are high are also considered to be preferable.

Many centres also include ornamental beds to help mark the entrance and to give an appropriate horticultural feel (provided they are well cared for). Safety still needs to considered here though, as they may cause blind spots for incoming and outgoing traffic. Likewise it is preferable to separate the entrance route from the exit to help reduce bottle-necks in peak periods.

Green field or existing sites?

There is no one ideal solution for everyone. Every case needs to analysed separately, with all the pros and cons put down on paper. The implications in both the short and long term need to be considered.

Local and central government planning policies will affect the availability of certain sites. Indeed at this present time planning policy in many areas actively discourages the development of new out-of-town shopping complexes. Garden centres are considered to be retail outlets for this purpose. Planners are seeing the link to growing and production as being far more tenuous in many centres. In many cases where planning is allowed there may be the requirement for the centre to fund changes to the road network (new roundabouts etc) to facilitate ease of movement on and off the site.

The route favoured by many developing chains is to purchase existing sites and redevelop to their own requirements. This approach often leads to less planning problems as a

Buying an existing site

Advantages:

- Existing customer throughput will ensure a level of initial customer loyalty
- Records already exist to help calculate business viability
- Infrastructure already in place allowing trading to happen from day one

Disadvantages:

- Site typically not laid out to your requirements
- Buildings may be dated and need significant investment
- Premium needs to be paid to vendor for 'goodwill'
- Reputation and image may not be compatible with that you intend to convey
- Layout of site may hinder future planned developments (i.e. car park size)

Buying a green field site

Advantages:

- Design tailored to fit precise needs
- Modern building design will increase customer perception of the operation
- Future development may be planned for in the initial building work

Disadvantages:

- All infrastructure needs to be installed leading to increased development costs
- Planning consent needs to be obtained (and currently this is difficult!)
- Low initial awareness within the area may lead to longer pay-back on investment
- Less precise information as to the potential viability of the business

business already exists. Some organisations have gone as far as to build a new centre adjacent to the existing outlet, in this way retaining income and customer loyalty during this interim period. The old store is subsequently demolished and returned to car park use once the new unit is 'on-line'.

The acquisition of existing sites may be the way forward for many operators. In the UK the industry is currently at the stage where many 'first generation' garden centres have proprietors who are looking to retire. In the absence of a family member wishing to take over selling may be the best solution.

One major chain readily admits that it receives a number of offers to buy garden centres but has set criteria to which it works. The chain states its criteria to be "A catchment of at least 40,000 people within a 10-mile radius. A site of at least 3 acres in size with good road frontage. The site must accommodate at least 120 car parking spaces".

Another group less precisely states that it is interested in large, well recognised independent centres with high quality customer profiles, situated in prime locations and stocking full ranges of garden leisure goods.

Car parking
Some garden centres hold the view that the quality of the product they sell will act as sufficient stimulus for repeat visits and sales. This notion neglects to take into account that

consumers are creatures of impulse and consequently tend to act on first impressions. A poorly surfaced, untidy car park gives an unfavourable view of your centre before they even set foot in the door to make a judgement on the merchandise. If a centre is being developed on a limited budget (and let's face it which one is not?) there could be a lot to be said for ensuring that the external features are up to standard and look to make savings elsewhere. Remember that your potential customer sees your business from the outside in!

Car parks need to be large enough to facilitate easy parking. After all this is one of the attractions for customers to visit your premises instead of shopping for the same goods in the high street. Painting lines on the car park actually increases parking space efficiency by up to 40% in addition to looking more professional. Allow sufficient space between the lines – if cars cannot manoeuvre easily there is a high risk of a minor accident occurring. Whilst centres may disclaim any responsibility it does not improve customer relations.

One of the biggest complaints at peak times in garden centres is the lack of parking. Overflow grassed areas are fine as long as the weather has been dry. Cars take up a lot more space than many operators first imagine. Expansive car parks may have their disadvantages too – in quieter periods the centre may actually be moderately busy but only appear part full due to the cars looking 'lost' in the car park. Some managers get around this problem by encouraging staff to park their cars in strategic places during these times to make the centre appear busier.

Movement around the centre

There are many specialist designers and consultants available to help in the detailed planning and layout of the centre. Before employing such help the owner must have a good idea of the style of centre he wishes to run and what he feels he wishes to offer.

Clearly those items in the first two sections need to provide sufficient revenue to help fund the attractions at the centre. This may cause a quandary in that the presence of the attraction is the reason that many people visit the centre in the first place. After all gardening is a leisure activity and many perceive therefore that our job is to entertain. The logical progression to this line of thought is that the centre should actually charge for such facilities. If this is indeed the case there needs to be a far greater focus upon the quality of these attractions and the 'cheerful amateurism' approach will not suffice.

Ranges of possible activities with a garden centre

Sales:

Plants, sundries, houseplants, lawn mowers, swimming pools, water gardening, stoneware and ornamentation, fencing & paving, pets, gifts, Christmas decorations, toys, furniture, BBQs etc.

Services:

Gift tokens, refreshments, planting up containers, landscaping, machinery repair, machinery hire, pest & disease diagnostic services, Gift wrapping, plant finding service, garden design schools etc.

Attractions:

Play areas, children's zoos, display gardens, water features, demonstrations, butterfly house, museums, working nurseries etc.

Paths and walkways

Wide paths encourage customers to explore more of the sales area as space gives a relaxed feeling. Wider pathways also encourage people to browse for longer. All pathways must (at the very minimum) allow two people (with trolleys) to pass comfortably. In practice this means a minimum width of two metres for most paths with major thoroughfares being a minimum of three metres. Boxes, plants or trolleys left in the pathways will instantly affect

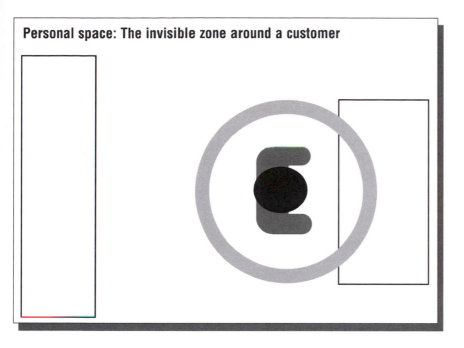

Personal space: The invisible zone around a customer

the width of affected routes (if you work in a garden centre, test these criteria against your centre – it's amazing what you will discover!).

In order for customers to feel relaxed enough to spend time within a certain part of a centre they must not feel that they are in the way or that there is any violation of their own personal space. Everybody has a distance at which they feel happy to converse with a stranger, an invisible circle around them (or 'ring of confidence' to borrow from an old toothpaste advert). Infringement of your personal space causes you to feel ill at ease with the consequence that you move. The extent of this zone varies from person to person and from culture to culture (people who stand too close to you in conversations have a smaller personal space than you do).

Unless sufficient space is left for passing in pathways, browsing activities will diminish with a consequent decrease in sales. This is one of the main reasons why specifically 'browse' products are not sited in the main thoroughfares. The temptation to squeeze in another row of shelves should be avoided.

Under cover?

No customer likes to be exposed to the worst of the weather. Research clearly shows that the greater the sales area a customer can reach with ease, the more they are exposed to products and the more they buy. The development of covered walkways and sales areas is a must in modern garden centres, although planning permission may be a problem.

Polythene clad structures are typically the cheapest to install and the indications are that in many centres the investment will be recouped in one year alone with the increase in sales (and the better care of stock).

The current trend in the UK is to move to more substantial glasshouse-based modules. Whilst having a longer pay-back period these structures raise the image of the centre further and may be more flexible in terms of usage. Similar structures have been in use in mainland Europe for some years.

This evolution has been clearly demonstrated in a recent garden centre redevelopment of a site in Widnes, Cheshire which has included a large plant sales area under glass which merges into the sundries sales area. This design not only means that customers meet plants first on entry, but there is a far more subtle demarcation between what has been classed as indoor or outdoor sales goods. The opportunity to develop linked sales within this shopping environment is far greater.

Displaying outdoor plants under cover has distinct advantages particularly in protection from the weather. The plant manager has to learn a whole new set of skills to make the best of this new environment. Covered sales areas may increase the possibility of disease such as botrytis and the reduced light levels (which may be up to 40%) may not suit all grey-leaved plants. Some golden-leaved plants may fade under these conditions too. Perhaps the solution is to have a structure with a retractable roof such as those starting to appear on certain sporting stadiums?

Goods inwards

Despite all the care and attention that is lavished by owners on store layout, utilising the latest retailing theories and techniques (much of which will be tackled in later chapters), scant regard has often been made to the goods inwards element of the operation. Just think about it for a moment ... all the stock that is sold from a garden centre has to be delivered to it too!

How many customers see packages of sundries or boxes of plants in the pathways and not on display when they visit the centre? Far too many! Even visits to those enterprises which are considered to be more efficient in their materials handling show that they are still guilty of leaving loaded Danish trolleys full of plants in gangways, obstructing customer flow and preventing access to stock.

Compare the scene with the typical high street retailer. The customer does not have to put up with the same inconveniences, so why should they have to just because it is a garden centre? Unmerchandised stock should be well out of sight and be prepared for sale before reaching the shop floor. On a recent visit to a major garden centre we saw a (sizeable) range of specimen stock imported from Italy. This stock was in the plant sales area, obstructing some of the main pathways. It was a Friday morning and we learned that the stock had been in that position since Monday, still wrapped and unpriced. Not only were these plants unavailable for sale during the whole of this period but they were actually preventing access to other plants which were also ready (not taking into account of the image given to customers all week too).

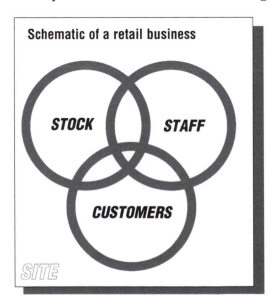

Schematic of a retail business

STOCK STAFF CUSTOMERS SITE

When designing (or redesigning) a centre the good inwards system needs close investigation as do the requirements for different types of goods. At the very least goods vehicles must be separated from the vehicular traffic generated by the visitor to the site. There are numerous safety implications of having members of the public wandering in unloading areas. Unfortunately the arrival of new goods (especially plants) acts like a magnet to interested customers looking for a bargain so access must be restricted. Forklifts and customers do not mix!

SUMMARY

Whilst it is impossible to design the definitive garden centre there are many things that can be learned from the mistakes of others! It is strongly advised before embarking upon a project to visit as many similar sites in operation around the country so that you get a good feel for the new enterprise. Even so, mistakes will still be made but be prepared to learn from these mistakes and to adapt the 'master plan' in the light of new discoveries. Despite the initial cost the best approach is clearly to employ an expert who can aid in the planning and the initial set-up – this will certainly help to avoid many of the potential mistakes. Be prepared for a steep learning curve!

2 Display and merchandising

Layout. Merchandising. Atmospherics. Use of colour. Display.

For many people the concepts of display and merchandising contain a significant over lap, and producing a widely accepted definition is very difficult – indeed the definition varies either side of the Atlantic too! For some the scope of the term merchandising may be almost as wide as that for retailing itself, but for the purposes of this book we will take a far narrower definition. Both activities aim to expose the product so that it is in 'danger' of being sold to the customer, but the term display is used for particular store features fulfilling this function whereas merchandising is more concerned with the general layout and replenishment of stock in the site.

LAYOUT

The layout of a garden centre is a careful balance between shop fittings, stock for sale, pathways, and non-selling areas such as storerooms, checkouts, workrooms etc. All of these aspects need to be balanced in order to make the optimum use of the space available.

When a centre is first designed, there is often a clear idea view as to the layout and its relationship to customer flow around the site. As the centre 'matures' the often-resultant increase in stock range and addition of extra display units frequently confuses this initial vision. If we are to accept the adage that the more a consumer sees the more they buy, many centres are lacking.

Most centres start off with good intentions concerning path width, allowing customers to pass each other with ease. Changing stock pressures often mean that a temporary display is added, which ultimately becomes a permanent feature, encroaching into the path. If customers feel that they are in the way they will spend less time browsing a particular product range.

The aim of the layout is to encourage customers to visit as much of the centre as possible, giving the maximum opportunity to pick up additional 'impulse items'. Layout has a great influence on this – not purely in the physical positioning of units but also of siting of particular stock lines. If items of great demand are positioned farther back in the centre, customers will have to make more effort to get them.

Most textbooks on the subject speak about three main layout types; a brief summary of the pros and cons of each is listed below:

Layout styles

Grid

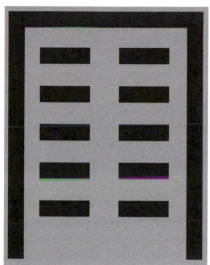

Comments:
Little waste of space
Economical in use
Good circulation

Boring
Not all areas shopped
'Utility' feel

Boutique

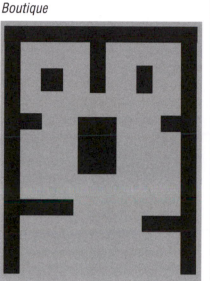

Comments:
'Shop within a shop'
Products in departments
'Relaxed' feel

Poorer space utilisation
Not all areas shopped
Security problems

Free-flow

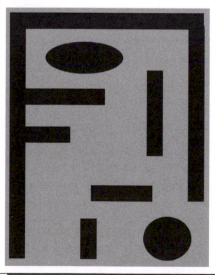

Comments:
Visually appealing
Flexible for displays
Potentially good flow

May look disordered
Path width problems
Difficult to retain the original vision for layout

In reality the typical centre will contain elements of all three layout theories, the more utilitarian product ranges such as garden chemicals being arranged for maximum space utilisation in a grid layout. Items such as seeds or bulbs may use a boutique layout giving the product range a specific identity and bringing together related items. This layout gives ample opportunity for customers to browse through the range to make their selections. The free-flow arrangement is typically more suited to gift-oriented items where there is a lower stocking density of product, giving a feeling of greater exclusivity and the ability to browse at the customer's leisure.

The choice of a layout style may also affect the price perception of a particular product grouping too. Merchandising houseplants in a grid type layout, using straight uniform rows helps to emphasise the quantity of product on display (implying a high volume, lower cost item). A more mixed display where the customer is expected to browse signals a more expensive (and exclusive) range, as in the case of specimen plants.

MERCHANDISING

There is more than meets the eye to shelf stacking. Attention to detail is important – do all your staff know the in-house rules which operate concerning shelf layout? What may seem obvious to you may not always be so to a member of staff in a hurry. Why not run a quiz or questionnaire in a staff training session to check their understanding or get them to criticise the quality of merchandising? (Beware it doesn't get too personal.)

Below is a summary of issues that need to be answered for your centre.

(1) *Is there a shelf plan?*

Is shelf allocation and facings based upon 'hard' sales information or is it based upon the amount of items still held within the stock room? The implementation of the 'facings theory' helps to ensure that in-demand items are readily available to the customer, increasing sales. It is easy to have an apparently full shelf that is only holding slow moving items. Note: whilst many people adhere to the facings theory there is evidence that it only really applies to volume lines. Application to slower selling, prestige items may actually be counter-productive, taking away a level of exclusivity and making the item look cheap.

(2) *Are the correct sizes on the correct shelves?*

Most people have heard of the adage 'eye level is buy level' but in reality it does actually work. Positioning volume-selling items in positions where the customer has to bend or stretch will reduce sales.

(3) *Are the products in the right order?*

Some customers will truly take the first item they see (the 'first seen, first sold' theory) so check that if this is the case this is working to your advantage. Many centres also arrange the different sizes of a product in the same order. The theory is that arranging sizes small to extra large encourages the right-handed person to buy a larger size (or indeed the size or product which makes you the most profit). Whilst results from this theory may be somewhat debatable, the adoption of a common format certain is more pleasing visually.

(4) *Is the space sufficient?*

The nature of the garden centre business is such that there is a considerable difference between the stock holding of a centre between high and low seasons. Both eventualities create their own challenges. Too much stock on shelves hampers accessibility and lowers the perceived quality of the centre. It may also make re-ordering and stock management more difficult. Conversely, in the low season centres are faced with too little stock. If this is displayed merely 'facing thick' whilst it may look acceptable from a distance, it gives a message to the potential customer that the centre is about to close down! Taking display equipment out of service during this time allows the stock that is available to have a far greater impact.

(5) *Is the stock attended to?*

Putting the stock onto the shelf or onto the bench is not enough. Time will also be needed to re-face shelves as stock is sold. Few customers will buy the last few plants on a bench if there are large gaps between them ("after all, the best must have already gone and there must be something wrong with these"). Re-gapping and blocking up helps to change the complete appearance (this point may seem abundantly obvious but the authors have numerous photographs where this has been overlooked). One of the most effective tools a manager has in this respect is a camera. Choose a day at random, and simply shoot a roll of film of what you see walking through the centre. You will be amazed at what the pictures will show you! We can all justify why the particular problem has occurred but in truth we don't have this same opportunity to justify it to a customer!

(6) *Is stock well signposted?*

As a person almost living within our own retail environment it is very easy to take the positioning of stock for granted. Indeed working within a garden centre trains us also where to expect to find stock in other centres too but such is not the case for our customers. Good clear signs marking the location of departments are a must. Many centres do use them, but what is less well managed is the repositioning once stock is moved. Do the signs in your centre really help the customer in this respect? Within the section attention must also be paid to ensuring that customers get the information they need easily. Remember 'BPBP' – band, products, benefits, price – which not only helps the customer to find where the product group is, but also to identify the benefits of the product and price to aid in easy selection.

(7) *Is the layout customer friendly?*

This is mainly directed at the layout within the plant area. Look critically at the choice of grouping. Many centres, whilst putting great effort into ensuring that impulse displays are easily accessible and vibrant, still use a form of alphabetical layout for the other less impulse-based items (the A-Z beds). This form of layout favours few customers – only those who know that they require a specific plant. Bench layouts based closer to providing customer solutions (i.e. plants for shady areas, plants for tubs) may encourage easier selection and extra sales. Such a layout does require a greater level of knowledge by staff however!

ATMOSPHERICS

It is often said that there are three principal ways to increase the sales and subsequent profit of a garden centre namely:

- Get larger customer numbers
- Encourage customers to visit more frequently
- Encourage them to spend more in each visit

In certain ways the 'feel' of the centre will have an effect on all three! Like it or not we are all affected by our environment. When we shop a number of our senses are called into play when we make a judgement about the store. An inappropriate sensory experience may have a significant effect on our willingness to buy.

Most of the above factors are under the control of the retailer (albeit within certain parameters). Temperature control of buildings is clearly identified, but what of the barrier to purchasing large bags of compost if they are situated outside and it is raining heavily?

Smells also are important; they often trigger memories (for one of the authors, a favourite smell is bone meal!). Whilst the association may be positive, it is not always the case: the smell of bacon cooking in the coffee shop may be irresistible if you are hungry, but the smell of bacon fat cooking when you are full is most unpleasant. Our industry is blessed with a great number of attractive fragrances – perhaps it is something we should take more advantage of?

Shopping and the senses	
Sight	• Colour
	• Light intensity
	• Size and space
	• Aesthetics
Sound	• Pitch
	• Volume
Touch	• Temperature
	• Flooring materials
	• Humidity
Smell	• Scent
	• Odours

USE OF COLOUR

Of the senses mentioned above, sight is the most powerful and it therefore seems appropriate to briefly investigate colour theory. As with many topics within this book we can only hope to scratch the surface here and if you wish to dig deeper there are many books which cover this subject in great depth. For the average garden centre manager a broad working knowledge is all that is required. (See the colour wheel in colour plates.)

Firstly, how many colours are there? The answer is truly an infinite number (your computer screen will probably handle millions!). The big problem is that we do not actually have enough names for them all. Try this test among your friends. Ask them to point to an object of the following colours: purple, lilac, violet and mauve. The argument could last for hours!

In reality colours are all built up from three basic colours, the **primaries**. These pure colours cannot be made by the mixing of others. By mixing these primaries, it is possible to make a range of colours classed as **secondaries**. Further mixing produces **tertiary** colours, building up a complete palette. The addition of extra lightness or darkness (black and white) creates **hues** and **tints** of these pure colours. In colour theory, black and white are not colours, merely the absence or presence of light.

Whilst the above information may be familiar to many people (the fundamentals may have been taught to us when we first started school), it is the way in which we use it which makes the difference.

Our environment and culture have given us a 'language of colour'; a rulebook that may be bent at times but is typically adhered to. Listed below are some of the normal connotations associated with common colours.

The use of colour may help to convey a message about a product by the environment it is contained within long before a customer can read the details on the label. Some colours are clearly very evocative of a season. The use of red in a display can conjure up a very

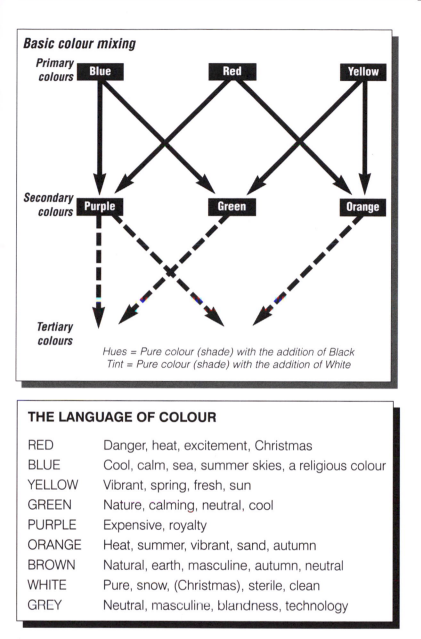

Basic colour mixing

Primary colours: Blue · Red · Yellow

Secondary colours: Purple · Green · Orange

Tertiary colours

Hues = Pure colour (shade) with the addition of Black
Tint = Pure colour (shade) with the addition of White

THE LANGUAGE OF COLOUR

RED	Danger, heat, excitement, Christmas
BLUE	Cool, calm, sea, summer skies, a religious colour
YELLOW	Vibrant, spring, fresh, sun
GREEN	Nature, calming, neutral, cool
PURPLE	Expensive, royalty
ORANGE	Heat, summer, vibrant, sand, autumn
BROWN	Natural, earth, masculine, autumn, neutral
WHITE	Pure, snow, (Christmas), sterile, clean
GREY	Neutral, masculine, blandness, technology

clear association with Christmas (particularly if linked to silver, gold or green), so much so that it is a colour to be completely avoided in January or February when people may be suffering from festive overkill. Selective use with other colours may also make it suitable for a display of barbecues where heat is to be suggested (particularly in a wet British spring).

In addition to background colours, it may also be possible to extend this to plant foliage in certain situations. People respond well to cool blues as the temperature rises. Why not feature steely blue conifers and white flowered plants?

Colour combinations

Our brains, in addition to associating certain colours with events or seasons, also work to a set of rules concerning colour combinations. Those skilled in the use of colour often have an almost innate awareness of this, but for many others it has to be learned. By far the easiest way for the beginner to get to grips with this concept is to use a colour wheel. Within this tool colours have been matched with others of similar hues and tints, and positioned on the wheel accordingly. Likewise colours which are formed by the mixing of two others are positioned between them.

Close colours	Distant colours
Violet	Blue
Brown	Green
Yellow	
Orange	
Red	

Once it has been possible to ascertain the main colours within a product or background you can start to find other colour combinations that will enhance the visual quality. Colour clashes normally result from completely ignoring the key principles. (See colour plate section for illustration showing easy colour combinations.)

More advanced practitioners may use three or more colours in a display, often splitting the colour wheel into three.

The use of particular colours in backgrounds may also affect the visual depth of the display so colours are perceived to be closer whilst others do the opposite.

DISPLAY

If merchandising is more about maximising the effectiveness of shelving space, display has a far greater range. The main aim is to help inspire the customer or to educate them in the use of products. The typical garden centre stocks so many products in certain ranges that it actually confuses the non-gardener so the use of display here may be to help simplify the situation.

The typical householder is perhaps far less aware of the seasons than their predecessors; supermarkets are now able to offer fresh produce throughout much of the year. Something like soft fruit was only available to our grandparents for a few weeks a year whereas now it is available much of the year. Therefore it is quite understandable that we find customers looking for daffodil bulbs when they are in flower in the spring, or asking for seed potatoes once new potatoes appear in the shops!

The real test for the garden retailer is do we make the message clear? True, a display has a great impact when it is first put into place but there will also be a need to keep the display fresh with new ideas throughout the year. Do we actually clearly identify, for example, which seed varieties are ready to sow now from the many hundreds on display?

When setting up a display we must be certain as to its function. What is the main aim of the display? Possible answers could include:

- Extra impulse sales – a direct selling display
- Awareness of a new product range (bulbs now in!)
- Lifestyle displays – co-ordination of display to include linked items within the store
- Education – how to, now is the time to
- Ambience – total immersion of the visitor to a product range or a concept (as with the Christmas theme)

Display checklist

Whatever the reason for building a display, there are a number of issues which need to be addressed:

Accessibility If consumers are expected to shop from a display, can they reach the products?

Space The common adage 'less is more' certainly is true here. If a prestige product is the focus of attention its perceived value is higher if there appears to be a level of exclusivity. Conversely an item piled high helps to convey the message that it is excellent value.

Focus Is there a real focal point within the display? Otherwise the display will lack impact, as the eye will tend to wander.

Balance Does the display look pleasing to the eye? This does not mean the use solely of symmetrical displays – some of the most effective are asymmetric.

Complexity If a display is intended to be shopped does it encourage the customer to do so, or is it so perfect that any purchase will spoil the effect?

Signage The silent salesman! Are customers provided with everything they need to make the purchase? Conversely they will not stand and read a book! Encourage the customer to buy now – deferred sales do not happen! Beware jargon too.

Safe and secure Does the display comply with all the relevant Health & Safety regulations? This is not just the positioning of heavy items but also accessibility of pesticides or poisonous plants. Likewise, does the display cause a greater security risk? (Research from a seed company who have just started installing tags in their packets, suggests that up to 15% of seed stock may be stolen from a centre.)

Use props Many customers need inspiration or education: bringing products together helps to tell the whole story and encourages the consumer to 'buy the kit'. They are less likely to visit the whole of the centre looking for the component parts.

Show stopping! Probably the final word on the subject. Does it look good? The aim of a display is to stop people in their tracks. To quote Walt Disney "You never get a second chance to make a first impression". Display is probably one of the most fun aspects of managing a garden centre – let your enthusiasm show through and make your customers smile too.

3 Advertising and promotion

Key questions to ask. Layout of newspaper adverts. Direct mail. Sales promotion methods. Advertising v publicity.

Advertising is a topic which may cause a wide variety of reactions in garden centre managers. Some see the real benefits while others feel that it is a waste of time or at best a necessary evil. The fact is however that we are all affected by it. Whenever we switch on the television, open the newspaper, or even walk down the street we are subconsciously being informed as to the benefits of certain products or our views are being influenced on other subjects. Just think for a moment the number of TV commercials you can remember!

The fact is, no matter how much you may dislike the thought of advertising, a company will not succeed unless people know what it has to offer or even the fact that it exists at all.

The main objection to spending money on advertising is the inability to quantify the true advertising response leading to the feeling that much of the effort is wasted. Indeed a leading industrialist when tackled on this subject admitted that he thought that probably half of his company's advertising spend was wasted – the problem was he did not know which half!

KEY QUESTIONS TO ASK

Advertising by itself does not sell anything; it only acts as a link between the retailer and the consumer and must be backed up by a good sales strategy. There would be little point a manufacturer launching a major TV promotion if goods were not also available in the shops for the consumer to purchase.

Below are the points to be considered.

A sobering thought

WHY IS IT?

A man wakes up in the morning after sleeping in an advertised bed, in advertised pyjamas. He will bathe in an advertised bath using advertised soap, shave with an advertised razor, eat a breakfast of advertised cereal and toast (from an advertised toaster), put on advertised clothing and glance at his advertised watch.

He will ride to work in an advertised car, sit at an advertised desk and write with an advertised pen.

Yet he hesitates to advertise, saying that advertising does not pay ... until finally, when his unadvertised business goes under, he will ADVERTISE IT FOR SALE!

Author unknown

What is your target market?

Not everyone in an area will come flocking through your door for your service. Decide who you are aiming at and what benefits you offer over the opposition. Not all of your rival's customers will be tempted to shop at your establishment, but there may be a considerable area of overlap.

There are many texts devoted to the study and analysis of customer types together with copious data available for purchase on demographic groupings within your catchment area. In addition to this demographic data (household type, income etc) psychographic (lifestyle) issues must also be taken into account. For example people interested in caravanning or boating are likely to spend more weekends away from home so are less likely to spend money on plants for the garden. Having an outdoor lifestyle may make them a potentially bigger customer for barbecues and related leisure items however.

Your target market

Total population

Your clients

Rival's clients

Direct competition

What are you trying to achieve with the advert?

Never advertise without a clear objective. Much advertising money is wasted because people haven't clearly considered what the advert is setting out to achieve.
Examples of objectives include:

- A new product or service launch
- Announcing changes to premises or location
- Increasing customer numbers in quiet periods
- Bringing your company to the attention of new residents in the area
- Or simply to achieve extra sales!

In any of the above cases the message to be transmitted and the tactics employed may be quite different. Whatever the case, after an advertising campaign has been run, a review should be carried out to evaluate how well the objectives were met.

Where to advertise?

Advertisements appear everywhere! Every company will sell you the benefits of their particular communications medium. Comparing different media is not particularly easy. Figures from newspapers about distribution, radio listening figures, or the 'opportunities to see' a poster give no real indication as to what proportion of these people are likely to visit a garden centre. Clearly a garden centre advert in a gardening magazine is likely to have a greater response that that in a general publication with similar circulation figures. The costs associated with its effectiveness often reflect this too however!

Type of media	Number of companies
Newspaper	15
Radio	2
Demonstrations	2
Yellow Pages/trade directories	11
Exhibitions/shows	1
Direct mail	2
Other promotions	1
None at all	5
Sample size: 30 independent garden centres	

19

A small-scale private study of garden centres in Kent revealed some interesting information about their advertising habits.

You could draw the conclusion from this sample that one-sixth of the centres must feel that they either have enough trade or that everyone knows who they are!

How much should I spend?

A good question and a difficult one to answer. You would assume that with increased outlay a greater response should be seen (eventually reaching a saturation point). There is no set rule that must be adhered to but one marketing group budgets for a figure based at 2% of the retail turnover. This figure seems to be a good aim with the provision that 2% of very little is very little indeed! Value for money must form part of the consideration, and maybe a smaller centre will need to exceed this figure if they are to see a real impact.

When the financial situation is tight, the advertising budget is one of the first expenses to be lined up for reduction ("...after all its benefit is hard to quantify anyway ...") but just one thought – if your business is in need of new customers, how will they find out about you if you cease to tell them?

Is it worth employing a professional?

If a manager is to allocate the time a co-ordinated advertising and marketing campaign requires, there may not be time for him to fulfil some of his other functions. Given the value of the manager within the business it may well be cost effective to allocate this responsibility to an advertising agency. True, they do cost money, but they will probably be able to negotiate rate discounts on your behalf, and are expert in their field – how many owners or managers have training in advertising?

One way to make this aspect more cost effective is to participate in joint marketing activity with other similar centres in a buying and marketing group. One set of design and origination costs will then be shared amongst all the participants rather than a centre bearing all the costs alone.

LAYOUT OF NEWSPAPER ADVERTS

Even though there are many different media available to help communicate your message to the potential customer, local newspaper advertising is considered by many to be the most effective (and it does seem to be the most common). The problem is that the average householder is subjected to hundreds of different advertising messages each week. In order for your advert to be noticed it must stand out from the rest. It is a very useful exercise to pick up a copy of the local paper and see which adverts do just that. Remember if the advert has not caught someone's attention in the first couple of seconds then it will be passed over. Looking at a newspaper critically shows that the local garden centre has some very stiff competition for the consumer's attention. One marketing expert speaking at a conference summarised the problem in the following way "...if funeral directors promoted their product as aggressively as do the vendors of fridges and washing machines, they would instantly be referred to the European Court of Human Rights!". Returning to the local newspaper for a moment, if you have ever placed an advert in the paper for your centre can you truthfully say that you have never had to search through the publication more than once to find it?

So what makes a good advert? Whilst not a definitive list, these may be a few useful ideas:

- **Headline**

  Try using an action title – Act now!

  Let customers know what is in it for them.

  Get the offer over simply and quickly.

  Challenge the customer – Have you seen better value?

  Avoid vulgarity and puns; these appear downmarket and people don't always get the joke.

  Try to be original. During a football World Cup for example, many manufacturers include a football theme in their communication with the result that with so many similar messages they tend to blend into each other and none of them remain particularly memorable.

- **Body copy (main text)**

  Use short paragraphs, or even better short phrases.

  Avoid complicated words and jargon (people won't read any further).

  If the text needs to be long, use sub-headings.

  Try not to cram in too much information – people like empty space.

  Encourage the person to act now.

  Copy set in a curved shape will stand out from the rest of the newspaper page which is column set.

  Repeat the main offer (perhaps twice or more).

- **Advert frame**

  Attractive border may stand out from the crowd.

  Printing in reverse colours to the rest of the paper (dark background/light text) may give more impact.

  Logo and slogan should be included to help build customer recognition and perception of the centre.

  Address, telephone number and map ensure they will come to your store.

- **Position**

  Adverts on the odd number pages have greater impact than even numbers.

  Front and back pages are best (but the price reflects this).

  Regularly referred-to pages such as TV listings are more desirable.

  Pages with news are preferable to those which are fully advertising.

A common acronym used to help good advertising and sales promotion is AIDA

attract	**A**ttention
gain	**I**nterest
generate	**D**esire
take	**A**ction

A potential customer's first contact with your business may be through some form of advertising. It is therefore very important that the image you project is the correct one.

DIRECT MAIL

The development of computer databases has had a considerable effect upon promotion targeting giving an opportunity to communicate regularly with established customers thereby enhancing image and loyalty. The response is significantly greater than is achieved by newspaper adverts although the execution is far more complex. The key is to ensure that the target audience is well focused. This can be achieved by either compiling your own database or using the services of companies who have already collated the data.

> **The average UK consumer's letter box in four weeks receives:**
>
> 4.3 Free newspapers
>
> 8.7 Leaflets and coupons
>
> 19.6 Items of personal mail
>
> 7.3 Items of direct mail
>
> Source : Royal Mail Consumer Panel

The advent of loyalty cards also provide a valuable tool in assessing which parts of the database are active allowing communication mainly with those who are visiting and purchasing regularly, or contacting those who have not visited for a while.

Once again as above it is important to ensure that your communication stands out as you are not the only one vying for the consumer's attention.

Under these conditions, whatever you design does not have long to catch the potential customer's interest before it reaches the rubbish bin. Despite the protests from householders about the level of junk mail they receive, a surprisingly high proportion is read.

SALES PROMOTION METHODS TO ENCOURAGE BUYING

Getting action is one of the essentials of advertising. Promotional activities are designed to do just this and greatly enhance the returns on the investment. This action may be initiated simply by a price reduction special offer or by more sophisticated schemes. Below are just a few examples:

Games and contests

Few people can resist the chance of winning something for nothing. There are numerous public relations possibilities too, heightening the profile and perception of your company within its customer base. All entries received may form the basis of a mailing list for improved targeting in future promotional campaigns. This tactic has obviously proved successful if the number of such promotions received via junk mail is any indication. The centre must ensure that they comply with the terms of the Data Protection Act in the storage and subsequent use of the household information gleaned including allowing the participant the opportunity to decline future communications.

For this type of initiative to work well it needs to appeal to as wide an audience as possible, providing prizes that people want to win. A producer of a concentrated organic fertiliser ran a consumer promotion offering a ride in a hot air balloon (with their logo on the side of course). This prize seemed to be far more attractive than a year's supply of their product!

In the UK the law dictates that competition requiring a purchase to enter must be designed with an element of skill needed to win. Clearly a simple prize draw does not fit the bill (although this is perfectly suitable if the competition is free to enter). A series of questions to be answered by the contestant would fulfil this criteria but must not be so difficult as to prevent entries (and the resultant purchasing of the product). A tie breaker question often in the form of a slogan is, in effect, the way the competition is decided.

Coupons

Another commonly used method of stimulating action from the potential customer. A coupon will often be carried around by the consumer reminding them of your presence and utilising a closing date on the voucher should help to encourage a swift response. They are also a very useful tool to use to assess the effectiveness of a particular advertising medium or to identify penetration into neighbourhoods if the redemption also requires the customer to add their name and address.

It is certainly very interesting to see the significant level in response between the more targeted approaches (direct mail and on-pack promotion) compared with the more 'scatter gun' approach.

Effectiveness of coupons (1996)	
Type of media	*Redemption rate*
Newspaper	1.1%
Magazine	1.5%
Door-to door	4.3%
In/on pack	20.2%
In store	9.0%
Direct mail	21.7%
Average redemption	5.8%

Source: NCH Promotional Services

The value of having a reliable database of existing and potential customers cannot be emphasised too strongly. These results also help to put into context the level of response which is nationally achieved by even very professional companies from more random drops. It takes a tremendous amount of effort to make a consumer try something new or to change their shopping habits!

Free samples

As identified above, people are creatures of habit, normally continuing to use the same product and shopping at the same store unless something dramatic causes them to change. Large companies are well aware of this phenomenon and see this technique as a way of encouraging use of their products or services. Often the trial product is linked to a coupon to encourage repeat buying hence starting a new purchasing habit. Garden centre products are, in many ways, harder to distribute by this method. The use of promotional postcards or empty bags encouraging the customer to visit the centre to redeem their free item seems far more preferable, as the customer may also buy other items on their initial visit. A free cup of coffee may also prove a popular promotion, particularly if aimed at increasing midweek trade when the centre's facilities have spare capacity.

Loyalty bonuses

As has already been stated, it takes a lot of effort to gain new customers – your voice is just one amongst many others. It may prove to be more beneficial to allocate some of these resources to rewarding your existing customer base. A number of different systems have been used by centres to achieve this, and whilst there is no one ideal system, there are a number of lessons to be learnt:

a) **Nature of the bonus** A straight discount off goods at the time of purchase may be popular with the customer at the time but does not do much to increase the number of visits. A system whereby customers work towards a bonus, either a product or voucher, may prove more effective. The system used must be easily understood by the customer and perceived to be easy to achieve otherwise they may feel it not worth bothering.

b) **How much discount?** Look critically at the discount levels being given away. Can you afford it? Remember, even though you may be achieving a healthy gross profit, there are still the running costs of the business to take into account (wages, power, rates, overdraft etc). The true profit being made by the garden centre is far less – are you giving away all this profit? A good solution may be to offer a bonus off future product purchases. The customer still feels that they are getting good value for money but in reality it costs the centre far less.

c) **How will it be managed?** The true cost of running a scheme is not purely the discounts being given away but the amount of resources it takes to operate the scheme, both in clear monetary terms and also in time, perhaps management time which could be used more effectively in some other way. Understandably the costs of operating a scheme for large numbers is proportionately less than those with a smaller database. Indeed for many smaller businesses it is financially not viable to offer a comparable scheme to a large retailer on their own. Organisations such as HART with their Garden Card may indeed be the solution for the independent centre. The day-to-day management and organisation of the scheme is run centrally taking the responsibility away from the centre with the added benefit of the cost savings which are possible by being involved in a larger initiative.

Special events and demonstrations

Garden centres are perceived by many as being a good (free) afternoon out for the family. Many centres actively encourage this by the addition of attractions such as play areas and pets' corners which in themselves do not bring in any revenue. The view is that if people spend longer in the centre they are likely to buy more and visit more often. Talks and demonstrations may also help in this respect but have the added bonus of helping to educate the visitor, creating ideas for further purchases. Events such as hanging basket planting, barbecue cooking demonstrations and fruit tasting are well established, but there are many other opportunities. Why not have a rose sniffing weekend to promote summer rose sales or stage the local horticultural show on site? Some centres have diversified into coach trips to famous gardens and flower shows too. All this helps to integrate the garden centre into the community as well as encouraging the best form of advertising ever discovered – word of mouth.

As previously stated, working in the garden centre industry it is very easy to forget that the majority of the population are not as enthusiastic about gardening as we are. They are often prevented from purchasing goods by fear of buying the wrong item and are too embarrassed to ask for help. Communicating advice in these more innovative ways may help to stimulate sales enormously by broadening the consumer's horizons. They will thank you for it.

Depending upon the activity, it may well be worthwhile to consider getting the event covered in the local media. Publicity should not be shunned – some garden centre owners seem to get more than their fair share. Newspapers are constantly looking for stories with local interest so effort should be directed at helping them as much as possible. The advantages of this type of publicity are great since the costs are often minimal. Get to know your local newspaper personally.

Case study

THE REALLY GREEN CHRISTMAS TREE SCHEME

Hadlow College Plant Centre perceived itself to be at a considerable disadvantage at Christmas. Situated outside a main population area, people tended to purchase their live trees closer to home in the busy run up to Christmas. The centre was selling only containerised trees from its own nursery, a more expensive product. People purchasing the trees came back for more however since they remained very fresh, losing few needles since the tree was potted immediately after being lifted from the ground. (Other containerised trees may have their roots exposed to cold before being potted.)

It was decided to try to make a special selling feature of the tree's greater viability and offer to replant the tree again after Christmas. The customer returning their tree in January got a reward voucher to spend on bedding plants in the centre in May. Everybody in the supply chain had something to gain from the scheme:

Customer
- Less needle drop from their traditional tree
- Feel that they are doing something 'green' by taking their tree back for replanting
- Gains a reward voucher for returning their tree

Plant Centre
- Able to sell trees at a viable price
- Brings extra customers in to purchase their special tree
- Customer visits again in January (a quiet period) for voucher, giving a chance to increase sales.
- Customer must return in May to use their voucher on bedding, typically buying far more than its face value during this key time.

Production Nursery

- Sells more trees
- Christmas tree pots are expensive, those returned may be re-used next year, reducing costs.
- Replanted trees, whilst not all surviving, gives a good opportunity to resell the tree for a second time!

Contacts were informed on the local newspaper about the initiative who wrote a good article, bringing in more customers who had read it.

Other sectors of the media read it too, prompting coverage by two TV stations, three local radio stations and even an article in *The Times*!

Sales went through the roof, so much so that it was impossible to supply the full demand. The benefit had been achieved, the centre was now in a position the following year again to sell large quantities of trees at a price which made the product line profitable to it.

ADVERTISING V PUBLICITY

Publicity has an obvious cost advantage, but what are the other issues?

1) **Control of message** – not all publicity is good. Advertising gives full control over the information given to the public.
2) **Use of sponsored events** – the name of a product or company may reach audiences by another newsworthy event in a more subtle way than traditional advertising. The company is then associated with the qualities and values of the event.
3) **Credibility** – messages received on news reports are believed far more than the traditional advert. Try to make some item newsworthy even if it is relatively light-hearted.

Publicity still costs money and should be budgeted for. The biggest problem is how to assess its effectiveness. At least with adverts it may be possible to include some sort of direct response such as a coupon (tactical advertising). Publicity work is often longer term with little immediate effect. This is commonly known as the strategic approach, aiming for a long-term relationship with the customer through an improving perception of your business. In the short term the only way of assessing the effectiveness of the publicity is to keep a scrapbook of all the media coverage and evaluate the amount of media exposure, in column centimetres of newsprint, to 'x' circulation and minutes of air time to 'y' numbers of viewers and listeners.

Whatever you choose to do, SHOUT ABOUT IT! Create the situation whereby when the local media want a comment on some horticultural (or even weather) matter, your name instantly springs to mind.

A final thought

The codfish lays a thousand eggs,
The homely hen lays one.
The codfish never cackles
To tell you what she's done.
And so we scorn the codfish,
While the humble hen we prize –
Which only goes to show you
THAT IT PAYS TO ADVERTISE!

Anon.

4 Security

Store layout. Security equipment. Changes to layout. Pricing. Payment fraud. Refunds. Internal use. Goods inwards.

Garden centres are designed very much with leisure in mind. Indeed one of the main aims is to encourage people to take the time to browse using innovative layout designs, often resulting in secluded areas away from the main traffic flows. Unfortunately such an environment has the tendency to tempt the more unscrupulous elements of the population with resultant security problems. Research shows that such theft is still on the increase, both by the opportunistic amateur and the sophisticated professional, often stealing to order.

It is a sad fact that many garden centres have little idea of the scale of such activities at their centre, preferring to think that only other centres have a major problem and that their customers are far too nice for that! Research suggests that given the opportunity, over 7 out of 10 people would be dishonest. The manager's job is not to give them this chance.

Whilst it is subject to great speculation, the average garden centre may lose 5% of its annual turnover as 'shrinkage'. Therefore in the case of a centre with a turnover of £1,000,000 this would equate to a sum in the region of £50,000! Just think of the

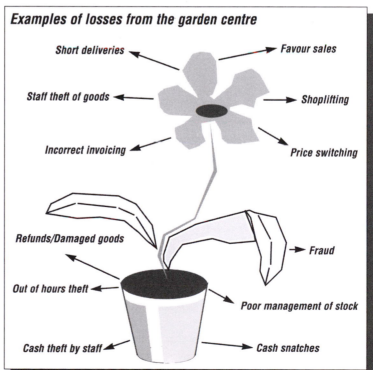

Examples of losses from the garden centre

- Short deliveries
- Favour sales
- Staff theft of goods
- Shoplifting
- Incorrect invoicing
- Price switching
- Refunds/Damaged goods
- Fraud
- Out of hours theft
- Poor management of stock
- Cash theft by staff
- Cash snatches

other uses such a sum could be used for such as extra staffing at the centre (or even your dream car!).

Attention to security matters can help develop a 'virtuous cycle' as follows:

Garden centre revolution – control of shrinkage

Better store security

Investment in security measures

Less shrinkage

Greater profits

STORE LAYOUT

As is already apparent the primary aim of a store layout is to encourage the customer to shop in as much of the store as possible, so that the maximum amount of stock is exposed. Such designs often are to the detriment of store security however.

Take a walk around the garden centre, as if you were a thief. Look for places where you would have the opportunity to conceal items e.g. far corners, secluded browse areas, rarely visited areas etc. High shelving units inhibit the view of customers as well as hindering security operations.

In most centres the till area is constantly manned (it would be nice if the same could be said about information desks), therefore it is prudent to ensure that the till operator has a good commanding view along the aisles of the shop. Ideally payment points should be positioned between the merchandise and the exit, with no goods for sale beyond this point which once again might be the cause of temptation. Provision also needs to be made for bulky goods – not only can things be concealed under these in trolleys but if loaded directly into the car elsewhere, staff should be involved in all such activities.

Entrances and exits need to be clearly marked to prevent embarrassing mistakes being made by customers. Despite the staff's perception to the contrary, customers *do* read signs and a regular sign audit will ensure that they are still performing their intended function and are not hidden by subsequent displays.

Automatic door systems may only respond to one way traffic and will help to encourage the correct customer flow within the centre. It must be added at this point though, that the determined customer will simply wait until the door is operated from the other direction before moving through. Just because someone leaves by the entrance door does not instantly make him or her a thief however – some customers feel intimidated about walking through the tills if they have not purchased anything so will look for another route for escape.

Turnstiles are sometimes used to ensure departure by the correct exit, and whilst very effective need to be carefully designed if they are to encourage the 'leisure feel' about the centre and not that of a football match. The centre also needs to be very mindful of push-chairs and wheelchairs with such an arrangement too.

SECURITY EQUIPMENT

What about the other security equipment which may be used to cut down on theft? Many centres use mirrors or camera systems to help cover inaccessible areas. It should be remembered however that this equipment is only as good as the staff using it. Personal experience has shown that after a few months staff forget to check security mirrors for example. Likewise video surveillance needs someone to monitor it if a thief is be caught red-handed. The reliance on video recording may mean that the offence is only really identified once the thief has left the premises. (It is also surprising how often when the video recording is actually needed, that the resultant image is not discernible due to poor maintenance.) Some centres with camera systems philosophically consider that the system may actually be of greater benefit in determining customer flow than catching criminals.

Replica or dummy cameras may offer a cheaper alternative to the real thing, simply plugging into an electric socket to 'operate'. This can work well, as long as staff keep the secret to themselves and that all the wires are seen to disappear in the regular manner rather than simply being left to hang under the device, as has been seen on more than one occasion.

The security tagging of goods is becoming far more routine within centres, particularly on high value and small concealable items. The difficulty at this present time is that there are three different systems all commonly in use within the retail sector. This is proving a barrier to the routine source tagging of goods by the manufacturer, as currently the 'winning' system is not clear. Unwins Seeds now source tag their products in each of the three systems to ensure compatibility with the centre's system. As you can imagine this means that the company has to hold four different variants for each product in its range. A non-tagged version is needed by centres without a system to prevent embarrassment if a customer subsequently goes into another shop and their tags have not been de-activated.

Some centres feel that the use of security equipment detracts from the leisure atmosphere and consider that more physical approaches to the problem are needed.

CHANGES TO LAYOUT

Favourite areas for shoplifting include all those quiet areas in the store where the customer flow is very limited. It is not just items displayed within this area that are vulnerable since goods may be carried from high traffic areas into these spots for concealment. Apart from the obvious bid to increase sales from these dead areas, if the area is more actively shopped the opportunity to steal is less likely to occur. The customer toilets are an area of particular danger, giving thieves a chance to hide goods around their body. If you wish to get an indication of the scale of the problem, look at the amount of packaging that has collected in the toilet cistern. (These are only the items that would not have flushed easily!) Ideally such areas should not be directly accessible from the main sales floor, or failing that, no goods allowed to be taken into such areas.

Despite the best-laid plans, the theft of goods will still occur. What practical steps can be taken? Despite the polite words, shoplifting is theft and should be treated as such. Even so, unless a correct procedure is followed, the manager or assistant may find themselves fac-

Sensible, cost-effective security measures

A) Increase lighting in dark areas

B) Displays should not be placed too low (pocket height is most prone)

C) Avoid putting small, 'collectable' items in under shopped areas or near the exit

D) Signs announcing Shoplifters will be Prosecuted in theft-prone areas of the store

E) Do not display items beyond the checkouts

F) Supply adequate trolleys and baskets

G) Discourage customers from entering storerooms and goods inwards areas

H) Staff must load bulky items that bypass the checkouts into the customer's car

I) All payments must be made through a checkout and a receipt given

J) TRAIN STAFF TO BE VIGILANT AT ALL TIMES

ing legal proceedings. This is a point that the professional shoplifter is only too aware of. Before a suspected shoplifter is apprehended, the garden centre must be absolutely certain that they are right. Indeed depriving someone of his or her liberty may actually be classed as kidnapping!

For many centres the best approach may be to follow the suspect and actually ask them if they need assistance. An innocent customer will not take exception to this approach but a thief will realise that they are being watched and may feel that it is advisable to 'shop' elsewhere. Another technique which has been employed by certain centres is to make a call over the public address system for the store detective – this is often enough to put a level of doubt in the thief's mind. An even more extreme solution is the case of the British garden centre owner who takes Polaroid photos of suspects for future identification.

It is actually very surprising to many managers to find that many of those who are caught thieving are those whom they would least suspect. Some of your most regular customers may also be your best shoplifters. They evade suspicion by being on good, even first name, terms with the staff. (Just think of the number of visits they make!) Seeds seem particularly vulnerable to this type of 'browsing' customer.

If a centre is tight on security matters then its reputation will spread through the criminal element who will go elsewhere for easier pickings. Town centres that have installed closed circuit television systems to monitor criminal activity are often very pleased with the results but neighbouring areas may report an increase in crime over the same period. Whilst we may never be able to completely eradicate customer theft, ensure that you do not get more than your fair share.

PRICING

Although shoplifting is a major source of loss to the garden centre, another factor of large proportions is that of price changing. The substitution of a lower price label onto a higher priced item sometimes is only perceived as being as serious as cheating the taxman. The assumption is that the company can afford it since they must be making such huge profits (" ... just look at those queues at the tills in the spring!"). The advent of EPOS till systems has significantly cut down on the incidence of this as the packaging often contains the bar code. Even so unless checkout operators are vigilant and knowledgeable they will not detect the difference between a plant in a 3-litre pot and that in a 10-litre for example.

Less sophisticated till systems obviously do not have this backup so the store is entirely dependent on the experience of cashiers. Is your centre guilty of employing mature, experienced till staff during the week but younger, inexperienced till staff at weekends when it is at its busiest?

Many customers also have learnt that damaged bags of compost are sold off at a reduction in certain centres. Whilst it is commendable to get some revenue back from a damaged product, what is to stop a customer purposely damaging bags to get a bigger discount?

PAYMENT FRAUD

This may be the largest potential loss within the business. There is a considerable trade in stolen cards and cheque books so identification needs to be always sought and thoroughly examined. Banks offer a range of training materials to help in this area but the onus is on the centre to ensure that procedures are maintained and regular updating is carried out as 'shortcuts' will creep into the cash handling process. Unless a strict training manual is adhered to it is very likely the same 'shortcuts' will also be passed onto new staff very quickly.

Not convinced of the size of the problem? As a study, look closely at the way your own cheques and plastic cards are handled in retail outlets you visit over the next two weeks. The difference between the best practice and the worst will amaze you! Now look critically at the procedure within your own establishment.

Whilst many customers focus on customer fraud at the checkout, a considerable threat may also be posed by staff themselves. How can you be sure that *all* your staff are trustworthy? Indeed how many businesses fail to research fully the employment history and references of new employees?

A simple procedure should be implemented and adhered to by all staff (including the manager) for all aspects of cash handling to reduce some of the potential problems. Implementation of more rigid policies may be interpreted as a threat by some staff who perceive that you do not trust them. The implementation of such policies is in fact for their protection in situations where discrepancies arise. (If money were missing from the takings, would your system be sufficient to eliminate staff from suspicion?)

The quest for many checkouts is for greater speed. Customers perceive the checkout system to be slow (particularly compared to the supermarket). This desire for increased throughput must not be achieved by the loss of accuracy and vigilance. After all if you were using a fraudulent payment system when would you use it, when a centre is at its quietest or busiest?

TEN RULES TO REDUCE CASH HANDLING FRAUD

1) Ensure all till staff are trained and competent
2) Refunds should not be allowed without authorisation
3) Ensure transactions recorded under correct transaction type (not under one common button – it's easier to make unauthorised adjustments)
4) Each till float to be used by a single operator (new operator – new float)
5) Refunds and other 'higher function' activities assigned to the supervisor and not handled by junior staff
6) Money should not be exchanged between tills
7) Till operators should not have their own money on their person
8) All till errors should be accounted for
9) Discounts to be authorised by the manager/supervisor
10) Till operators must not serve their own family/friends

REFUNDS

Whilst it is a legal requirement in many instances to give a refund, there are many other situations where such an act will create goodwill between customers and the centre.

The retailer in many ways is relying upon the honesty of the customer. Firstly in the fact that the item was faulty in the first place and secondly that the item was actually purchased from them. Although receipts are generally given, they are rarely retained for any length of time (how many receipts do you retain as a private customer?). Therefore, despite any signs stating the requirement for a receipt to be produced for a refund to be given this is rarely enforceable. In the main, the general public is honest in such respects and will be more loyal to those companies who give them the least hassle in such situations. Remember, those people who actually bother to bring their problems to your attention are actually your company's best friend and should be treated as such. At least with these people you have a chance to satisfy them. Those that do not return do not give you the same opportunity.

The method of initial payment may raise some issues however. Credit card payment refunds should be made by debiting the cardholder's account rather than giving cash (a useful way of profiting from a stolen card). Likewise cheques may also pose a problem. If the bank has not cleared a cheque the retailer may find that in addition to giving a cash refund the cheque actually bounces too. One way of dealing with such a potential problem is by offering to mail a cheque for the amount to the customer's home address, thereby reducing the likelihood of fraud, as the retailer would have an address on file. Cash customers have a right to a cash refund.

If the authority to give refunds is limited to selected staff then there is also a greater chance of spotting those people who are regularly requiring them. Such a system will also limit the potential for staff to make their own false refunds.

INTERNAL USE

A great source of irritation for many garden centre managers! The fact is that the more staff see a plentiful supply of an item on the shelves displayed for the public the less they respect that item. One garden centre manager found 52 pairs of used gardening gloves in his staff room! The problem was that rather than look for an existing pair, staff found it easier to simply write off another set from stock. The system had no way of checking what was going on. Similar stories abound at most centres as to the use of certain commodities. On an item such as gloves, for example, it may be a solution to issue all staff with their own pair; if they lose them they have to purchase a replacement set. On the other hand, if they happen to wear them out they will be entitled to another pair (and receive plenty of praise for working so hard in the process). Clearly if this is be adopted, the borrowing of gloves is to be discouraged too.

In a similar vein, close monitoring of stock disposal has to take place. The problem with using some form of dustbin system is the fact that people may be able to retrieve these thrown away items. In fact it is not unheard of for a centre to refund or replace a plant which has previously been consigned to the skip! Such a system also gives an opportunity for staff to hide goods amongst the rubbish for collection after work. Many companies make it a dismissable offence to take home any stock that has not been purchased. This may mean that certain goods are purchased by staff for small nominal sums but such a ruling will prevent any misinterpretation of more lax systems.

Goods consigned to the skip should not be retrievable, even if this does mean spending time on destroying stock which has no value to the company (including removing plant labels). The risk of having 'rescued' substandard plants on display in people's gardens is not worth the time savings. With the sheer volume of waste materials being produced by a centre the use of a compactor will make more efficient use of skip space plus get rid of some of the above problems.

Once again it cannot be emphasised too strongly that accurate documentation is important, not only as a record of the value of goods that have been thrown away but as to the type of goods to help prevent such occurrences again in the future.

Sample document for monitoring internal use

ABC GARDEN CENTRE
Internal use of stock

Quantity	Description	Retail Price	Reason for use

Signed ....

Countersigned ....(supervisor)

GOODS INWARDS

The designs of many goods inward areas are poor (that is assuming they exist at all!). Obviously the more space allocated to this then the less space there may be for selling. Certainly customers should have no access to the stock until it has been assessed as being of a suitable quality and all present! One manager explained that he did not have sufficient time to check off the goods so expects to be delivered the correct amount because he is a valuable customer! Whilst his supplier may indeed treat him as such, no account has been taken of the trustworthiness of the delivery driver, whom on discovering such a lax system, may well take advantage of it. 'Spare' stock is sometimes available from such drivers who will sell it on to other owners and managers. Unless good documentation is in place to monitor deliveries, invoices, goods to be returned and items short on deliveries, considerable amounts of money may be lost.

SUMMARY

The problem of security is complex and will not go away just by simply throwing plenty of money at the problem. Whilst no hard recommendations can be made in a single book, there are some important principles that can be established. The key to the whole problem of security is staff. Vigilant, honest, experienced, tactful and trained staff are a very valuable resource. Despite all the physical adaptations that can be made to prevent loss either during opening hours or out of hours, the success or otherwise depends upon the people operating the systems. It is important that they remain motivated and keen, accepting the problem as a challenge to overcome. If they do achieve targets in such areas, let them know that their efforts are appreciated. It is not possible to wipe out theft completely; it has to be looked upon in a similar way to animal repellents within the garden. As soon as you give the issue less attention the problem will return. All that happens in the meantime is that the problem tends to be diverted elsewhere. There are many consultants willing to give advice in this field, so it may be worth getting their opinion. Certainly the local police force will only be too happy to advise you on ways of making your premises and stock more secure.

Lastly the table below gives an indication as to where the losses are allocated. The implementation of secure systems will also safeguard staff too. For those who are innocent it will help take away the level of suspicion associated with staff investigations.

Retail losses – where it goes

44%	Customer theft
11%	Burglary
2%	Fraud
5%	Damage
4%	Robbery & till snatch
27%	Staff theft
7%	Unidentified

Source: British Retail Consortium
Retail Crime Survey 1997

5 Finance

Financial and management accounting. Working capital. Final accounts. Simple and EPOS documentation. Cash flow. Summary.

Finance is the subject which seems to make the blood of most business people run cold. In the garden centre industry it is no different. Those who have come from a retail background may have more idea of cash handling routines and systems, but they may not have any greater idea of the underlying principles than those coming from a plant production or other discipline.

The most important single thing to understand is that business and personal finances must be kept *separate*. The diagram overleaf illustrates this point and also introduces many of the concepts we shall deal with in this chapter.

Some terms used in business accounts

The **Trading and Profit and Loss Account** is a statutory document detailing how the business ran throughout the year. It includes concepts like:

- **Sales** Income, receipts, revenue
- **Cost of goods sold** Actual sale price minus purchase price of goods
- **Gross profit** Sales minus cost of goods sold
- **Overheads** Other expenses of running the business
- **Net profit** Gross profit minus overheads
- **Stock** Goods for resale, inventory
- **Rate of stock turn** How quickly stock is sold and replaced by new (usually stated as number of times per year)

The **Balance Sheet** is the other main statutory document. It gives a snapshot view of all aspects of the business at that one date. It includes concepts like:

- **Assets** What you own
- **Fixed assets** Generally permanent items whose value does not change from day to day, comprising:
- **Fixed capital** Fixed assets such as land and buildings

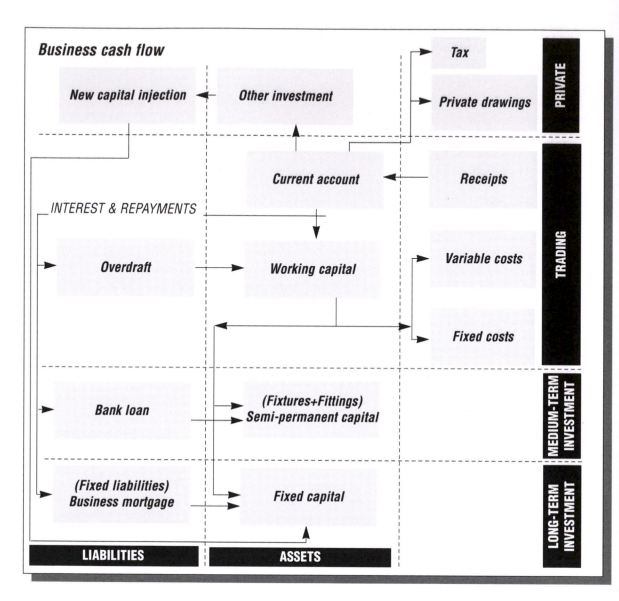

Business cash flow

- **Fixtures and fittings**   Fixed assets of a relatively short life (e.g. tills)
- **Current assets**   Continuously changing and being used up in trading (e.g. stock, debtors)
- **Liabilities**   What you owe
- **Fixed liabilities**   Long-term loans, business mortgages etc.
- **Current liabilities**   Have to be repaid in the short term (e.g. creditors)
- **Working capital**   Current assets minus current liabilities (the quick test for financial solvency of a business)

FINANCIAL AND MANAGEMENT ACCOUNTING

Many garden centre owners were previously nursery owners before moving to the retail side of the business and a good number in fact run a number of businesses from one site, of which growing plants, retailing them and planting and maintaining customers' gardens is the most usual combination. To this may be added catering on the retail site. From a financial point of view this can be rather a curate's egg if not handled properly. Some positive aspects about a range of enterprises include:

- **Diversity**   Spreading the risk among a range of offers to the public.
- **Compatible seasonality**   The highs of one part of the business may cancel out the lows of another part at any time of the year.
- **Increasing sales**   More turnover may help cash flow in turn leading to advantages of scale.

The negative aspects may include:

- **Dilution**   Of management skills and attention to each part of the business which it deserves.
- **Blurring of boundaries**   A nursery and a garden retail outlet are very different in their financial demands and controls. Each component should be treated separately at least for management accounting purposes.
- **Incompatible seasonalities**   If all the sectors have closely related high and low periods, there will be great strains on staff, assets, stocks and cashflows on a regular basis.

Financial accounting

At the end of each financial year, all businesses are required by law to report their activities and results in financial terms. It is up to each business to decide the start and end of its financial year. This may be in terms of a natural break in the year's activities (e.g. Christmas tree wholesaler) or for ease of stocktaking, or to align with the national tax year end (5 April in the UK).

The basic financial statements required are the Trading and Profit and Loss Account and Balance Sheet. In the case of partnerships and public limited companies, there are additional statutory requirements.

Management accounting

This includes concepts such as costing, budgeting, and break-even calculations. The financial management of a business includes all the above as well as the control of the business finances on a day-to-day basis, as shown in the table overleaf.

The idea of two different concepts (financial and management accounting) sounds to some people like keeping two sets of books – one for the tax man and one for personal use. This is not the case. The financial accounts are an artificial format designed to allow even-handed assessment of every business's potential tax liabilities and to provide transparent financial information for the shareholders in PLCs.

Management accounts and records are practical tools for the successful running of a business on a daily basis. They can be customised to suit you and your business advisors. In any business, the type of information required as well as the format it is presented in requires regular review. To have consistency of information is important, as a series of figures or results calculated in the same way allows a long-term picture of the business to be observed. However, new functions or departments will need new or extra systems. New technology such as Electronic Point of Sale (EPOS) systems may demand a complete overhaul of the presentation of management accounts within the business.

EPOS is now being implemented in many garden centres. The size of centre is not a

Financial needs	In conjunction with	Information typically required
(a) Short term (less than 1 year)		
Change for tills	Local bank	Weekly till schedule
Paying-in to bank	Local bank, security co.	Agreed schedule
Overdraft	Local bank/bank business centre	Quarterly or annual cashflow forecasts
Supplier credit terms and offers	Suppliers	Purchase records and forecasts
Customer credit terms	Trade customers	Sales records and forecasts
(b) Medium term (1 to 3 years)		
Loans for working capital	Bank business centre, owners, outside sources of finance	Cash flow forecasts, strategic plan, 3 years' final accounts
Debt factoring	Factoring company	Debtor records, cashflow forecast
(c) Long term (5 years +)		
Loans for fixed assets (e.g. land/ buildings)	Bank, building society, owners	Cashflow forecasts, investment appraisal, 3 years' final accounts
Setting up/restructuring the business	Owners/shareholders/venture capitalists/banks	Business plan + others as relevant

Tax issues

In the opinion of the authors, one of whom observed many businesses while working for a major bank at one time, it is never worth the effort of trying to defraud the tax authorities. Not only is it illegal (and you may consider it immoral), you always get caught in the end. Additionally, you may damage the ongoing success of your business and its eventual sale value. Consider the effect of under-declaring cash sales by £10,000 per year over 5 years. You may feel you have saved tax, but as you will see, there are very few things you can do with your ill-gotten gains.

Event	Penalties
Cash removal: £10,000 × 5 = £50,000	The money can only be spent on trivia. The purchase of annuities or capital assets will trigger investigation from the tax authorities.
Your business will show a reduced gross and net profit	Both VAT and tax authorities have statistical profiles of all types of business. If yours deviates too much, that will trigger an investigation.
	If you wish to obtain finance for the business, or to sell it, the relatively low margins will work against you.
You wish to purchase capital items	This may now have to be done on borrowed money (see above!) and will almost certainly cost more in the long run.

For a supposed saving of at most, £20,000, there will be a long-term legacy of perceived inferior performance by your business and personal worry about the consequences. As the widow of one garden centre owner remarked after her husband's death and a subsequent tax investigation of his affairs, "I don't know which got him in the end; the tax man or the Hamlets".

particularly good predictor of whether EPOS has been installed. Confidence and understanding of computer systems, or exposure to large organisations on the part of the owner or manager may result in an EPOS system being used in almost any size of operation.

The perceived benefits of such a system and the results gained from it are also variable and may depend on the knowledge, enthusiasm and attitude of the management as much as the technical specification and capacity of the system. Some financial systems are easier to automate than others. However, all systems, manual or computerised, require updating, analysis and ACTION. This is best ensured by keeping everything clear and simple for the users. It is also critical that *all* users know what part of the system they are responsible for, to whom they report and when. It must be an absolute requirement to present all information of a financial nature when requested WITHOUT FAIL. This alone will overcome one of the main reasons for financial difficulties in many businesses – out-of-date information.

Examples of computerised and manual documentation used for financial control

The human brain does not react well to large quantities of abstract concepts such as numbers; even less to derivative numbers, such as percentages. What it is very good at is assessing patterns and changes. Even those people (including one of the authors) who seem to have a strange knack of evaluating large blocks of numbers at a glance, are only looking for variations and trying to assess their significance. Almost everyone can see the important changes and trends more easily when they are prepared in graphic rather than numerical style. A PC with relevant, simple programs is now a necessity, not a luxury, for even the smallest business. As with everything, practice makes better, if not always perfect!

All the systems in the world will not help if information is not updated and acted upon. The cashflow forecast is probably the best known and most commonly used tool of garden centre financial management, if only because the bank asks for one every year. It is possible to spend an hour on a cold autumn afternoon, with no customers around, and create a complete work of fiction dignified with the title of Cashflow Forecast just to keep the bank manager at bay. At the other extreme, one can try to

Daily takings analysis – simple one-till operation

Date	£	pence
Credit card		
Cheque		
HTA voucher		
Other vouchers/coupons		
Accounts		
£50		
£20		
£10		
£5		
£1		
50p		
20p		
10p		
5p		
2p		
1p		
Total		

Weekly analysis: sales and customers

Day	Date	Takings excl. VAT £	Takings incl. VAT £	No. of customers £	Average sale £
Monday	July 21st	279.87	326.21	36	9.06
Tuesday	July 22nd	540.11	614.61	82	7.50
Wednesday	July 23rd	742.92	829.18	67	12.38
Thursday	July 24th	640.90	734.81	82	8.96
Friday	July 25th	838.18	970.00	91	10.66
Saturday	July 26th	1320.78	1379.76	49	28.16
Week's Total		4362.76	4854.57	507	11.93

Daily takings analysis – multi-till operation

ABC Garden Centre

Takings Analysis Sheet

Date		Time		Till Nos.	1	2	3	4	Supervisor's initials
					5	6	7	8	

	Totals			Totals
CASH		**CHEQUES etc**		
Notes		Cheques	£	
£50	£	Credit/Debit Cards	£	
£20	£	HTA Tokens	£	
£10	£	Other vouchers/tokens	£	
£5	£	Customer Accounts	£	
Total Notes	£	Total Cheques etc	£	
Coins		Total Cash	£	
£2	£	GRAND TOTAL	£	
£1	£	Till Reading	£	
50p		[x] or [z] – tick		
20p		Difference	£	
10p		[+] or [–] – tick		
5p				
2p				
1p				
Total Coins	£			
TOTAL CASH	£			

EPOS information: Till sales report for week ending 26/7/97

No.	Group description	Qty	Gross value (£)	Net value (£)	Cost (£)	Profit (£)	Margin %
01	SHRUBS	77.0	521.40	443.81	223.59	228.22	49.6
02	CLIMBERS	20.0	178.22	151.68	65.28	86.40	57.0
04	RHODODENDRONS	7.0	49.50	42.13	37.35	20.88	11.3
05	BEDDING PLANTS	111.0	243.78	207.49	106.06	104.02	48.9
	FRUIT	6.0	29.66	29.66	15.15	14.51	48.9
08	ROSES	25.0	126.71	107.80	49.25	58.55	54.3
09	HERBACEOUS PERENNIALS	115.0	490.25	417.14	215.43	201.94	48.4
10	ALPINES	6.0	23.54	20.06	10.20	9.86	49.2
11	HERBS & VEGETABLES	30.0	35.75	35.75	16.70	19.05	53.3
12	CONIFERS	1.0	6.79	5.78	2.55	3.23	55.9
13	HEATHERS	36.0	41.00	34.88	17.82	17.06	48.9
14	FLOWER SEEDS	46.0	56.02	47.72	24.59	23.13	48.5
15	VEGETABLE & GRASS SEED	28.0	32.21	32.21	17.45	14.76	45.8
19	CHEMICALS	55.0	279.04	237.45	133.91	103.54	43.6
	FERTILISERS	30.0	91.14	77.51	43.39	34.12	44.0
21	PEAT & COMPOST	45.0	151.25	128.78	70.97	57.81	44.9
22	CLOTHING	1.0	5.00	4.26	2.13	2.13	50.0
24	HOUSEPLANTS	97.0	246.03	209.35	106.55	102.80	49.1
25	POTS, TRAYS, CONTAINERS	42.0	171.66	146.10	86.16	59.94	41.0
26	FLORIST SUNDRIES	3.0	4.01	3.42	1.61	1.81	52.9
27	GIFTS	50.0	84.06	71.50	44.88	28.95	37.2
29	TOOLS	22.0	122.69	105.27	61.48	43.79	41.6
30	BOOKS	36.0	380.50	380.05	290.08	90.02	23.7
31	FOOD & CONFECTIONERY	30.0	58.85	58.85	34.18	24.67	41.9
49	RECEPTIONS	153.0	1281.00	1241.14	924.73	351.81	25.5
50	HARDWARE/GDN SUNDRIES	57.0	144.51	122.97	77.62	45.35	36.9
	Report totals	1129.0	4854.57	4362.76	2679.10	1748.35	38.6

predict next year's business in terms of weather, fashion trends, local population shift, competitor businesses, new product lines, national and international economic forecasts and the sunspot activity cycle.

Commonsense would seem to predict a middle course! The example shows a number of factors used in the construction of a cashflow forecast for a mythical, but not unrealistic garden centre. Regardless of the degree of care or sophistication present in the original analysis it is only useful to management when it is kept up to date. This means that the actual cashflow (broadly, takings) must be entered into the spreadsheet or other format AS IT OCCURS. Without this check, the whole exercise is totally wasted and worse, the bank (who do monitor your actual cash flow against your predictions) may well demand explanations from you if performance is adverse and you reach borrowing limits!

Exceeding your predictions by a wide margin is as dangerous as not achieving them. In either case you can use up all your working capital and even end up in bankruptcy.

CASHFLOW CHART

Parameters for inclusion

(1) Last year's figures

(2) Amendments to last year's figures for known anomalies (e.g. date of Easter, unseasonal weather, unplanned closures etc.)

(3) Internal changes for next year, including:
- hours of opening
- departments opening/closing
- infrastructure changes (e.g. car park spaces)
- new/additional customer payment methods

(4) Estimate of growth for next year (like-for-like basis)

(5) External changes for next year
- change to public road layouts
- opening/closing of competitors
- new housing/businesses in the area
- new legislation (e.g. Sunday Trading Act)

(6) Demographic changes
- age and status of customer base
- catchment area and transport requirements
- frequency of, and reasons for, customer visits

(7) Economic changes
- domestic interest rates
- reported consumer confidence
- state of the housing market
- exchange rate of sterling
- international economic cycles

Items (1), (2) and (3) can be estimated with some degree of certainty. Item (4) may be a summary of your feelings about items (5), (6) and (7), as well as other market research, but without any hard data.

It is probably easier to predict higher growth rates in the first few years of a business' life than when it reaches maturity.

More research to try to quantify items (5), (6) and (7) may be purchased – often at considerable cost from specialist publications.

WORKING CAPITAL

This is a crucial concept which any business misunderstands or ignores at its peril! The technical definition is simple (the so-called quick or acid test for solvency):

Working capital = current assets – current liabilities

Only part of the capital of a business is available for working capital; the rest is represented by fixed capital. (See Balance Sheet, p 45.) The working capital from that example would be:

Current assets	£	£
Stock	106,000	
Debtors	7,000	
Cash in hand	2,000	
		115,000
Current liabilities		
Creditors	81,000	
Overdraft	24,000	
		105,000
Working capital		10,000
(Net current assets)		

The problem arises in several ways. The stock figure represents capital tied up and released into cash when it is sold. A garden centre has such strong seasonality built into its various product groups that much of the stock value may be effectively unsaleable at any particular time of the year. The proportion of stock that is selling at the moment has to turn over that much faster, with an increased likelihood of stock-outs and lost sales.

If debtors take an excessive time to pay, working capital is reduced by that amount.

If trade increases dramatically, either seasonally or because of an unprecedented surge, purchases will have to increase, causing increases in creditors and a decrease in cash (increase in overdraft) if most of the extra stock is not sold.

This could lead to a situation as below:

Current assets	£	£
Stock	115,000	
Debtors	10,000	
Cash in hand	1,000	
		127,000
Current liabilities		
Creditors	94,000	
Overdraft	30,000	
		124,000
Working capital		3,000

The examples have shown the overdraft rising but if this is not possible, the only other way of remaining liquid (i.e. solvent) until some excess stock is sold, or debtors pay up, is to slow down payment to creditors.

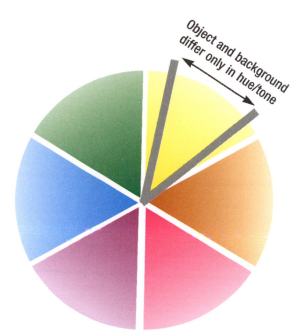

Easy colour combinations

The safe option – No chance of clashing
Object may blend into background

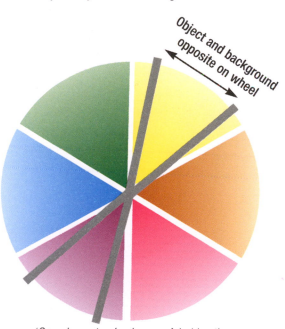

'Complementary' colours – A bold option
Object will stand out from background

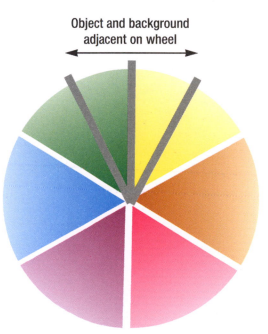

Colour harmony – Object distinct from background
Ideal for beginners!

Signage: useful plant information encourages purchases

A good example of clear signage [courtesy Snowhill Garden Centre]

Poor spelling reflects on the business and while many might not know how to spell 'osteospermum' some will – and so should the staff

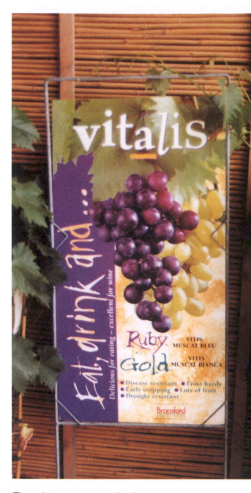

*The picture creates the image,
the image creates the sale
[Bransford Garden Plants]*

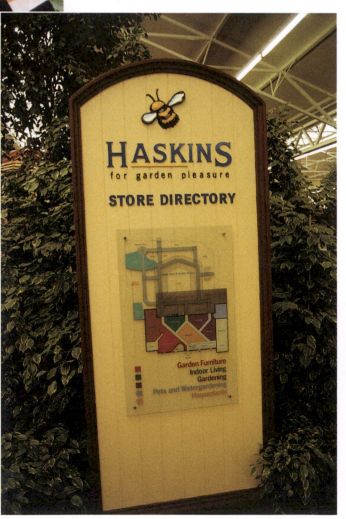

*A well-designed store directory can be useful
for customers as well as creating the
impression of a comprehensive service
[courtesy Haskins Garden Centre]*

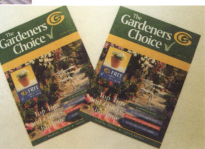

Some say it is overdone, but Correx POS can help to sell plants, particularly out of season, as can good literature support

Good, clear directional signs help customers to orientate themselves [courtesy Millbrook Garden Centre]

Reassurance for buyers – a bedding plant information desk [courtesy Redfields Garden Centre]

Don't spoil things: here what is clearly good quality stock is unfortunately blocking the path to the information centre

Destocking: empty and half-empty beds are lost sales opportunities

But too much stock can be a barrier to sales

And useful as they are, trolleys can be a barrier to sales

The vertical option, demonstrating a good use of space [picture courtesy Millbrook, Crowborough, Sussex]

This cheery entrance display sets out to create a positive impression on customers [courtesy Haskins Garden Centre]

An attractive entrance creates a good welcome [courtesy Coolings Garden Centre]

Whatever the source of working capital shortage (= bad control of cashflow) the temptation is to buy time by slowing down payment to creditors. This is the starting point for many long-term problems. Creditors whose patience is too often tested may:

- impose surcharges
- refuse to do business
- sue for all outstanding sums
- spread rumours in the trade about your financial position

All of these can be embarrassing and some can be potentially disastrous.

Inadequate control of cashflow, leading to shortage of working capital, typically comes home to roost one or two months after peak trading periods and lasts for one or two months. For garden centres this means that difficulties are usually experienced in July, August, January and February.

What can be done to influence this situation? A brief glance at the example above shows that three items – stock, debtors and creditors – are sufficiently large to take effective action about. Stock control is such a major issue that a whole chapter is devoted to it later on in the book and the others are considered below.

Debtors

These are the people who owe you money in the course of trade. Although retail sales are predominantly cash in the sense of immediate payment, very few businesses operate with no credit sales at all. Local government, schools, other local businesses, family friends and members may all wish to operate some form of account system with your business. If this is truly a minuscule portion of your annual turnover (say 1% or less) it is probably not worth setting up formal systems to deal with debtor accounts. The moment it becomes more than a notional part of your turnover, however, it is a real risk and must be handled as such.

Creditors

These are the people you owe money to in the course of trade. The debts you incur can be for immediate trading items (stock) or for capital purchases (vehicles, shop fittings etc.). One of the problems for many businesses is trying to satisfy all the cash needs from one pot. The most regular creditors are those from whom you buy stock for resale. These are the people on whom you rely to keep you supplied and able to trade. It is vital to maintain good relationships with them, as illustrated above. One way to avoid longer term debts (capital purchases) from impacting on your trading cashflow is to pay them as regular amounts from a separate account. If you can see cashflow problems looming and you are not willing or able to go to your bank for help, the following checklist may prove useful.

(1) Analyse your trading creditors by:
- future payment dates and amounts
- how critical their goods are to the next week/month's trading
- the quality of your present relationship with them.

(2) Rank the creditors from the above into categories:
- must pay under all circumstances
- could fall into arrears briefly
- may have to extend payment times and risk damaging the relationship.

(3) Contact *all* creditors who you might not be able to pay on time to advise them of your problems and seek their help. Like anyone else, they may not want to hear bad news, but they will be much more inclined to be positive and not take drastic action if they are kept informed. One of the authors was overwhelmed by the positive reaction of the major suppliers to a company he worked for when there was a devastating fire one day. The company had had a difficult trading period prior to the fire and relationships with creditors were not all that great. Nonetheless, when told of the news, all without exception offered not only new stock, but also staff, vehicles and anything else they could think of to help us start trading again.

(4) As well as information, give creditors an action plan for paying the outstanding debts. This will have a number of benefits:
- your problems may impact on their cashflow. Their bankers will want figures too but this may enable them to help you.
- if they agree a payment programme with you, that differs from the contractual terms originally agreed, it will help protect you from demands for instant payment in full.
- it will help to restore/maintain confidence and the flow of goods to you.

(5) Once you agree something, STICK TO IT. The experience is not pleasant and can even be very humbling. It does however happen to most businesses at some time and if properly handled will cause no lasting damage; even to the manager's ego!

Sources of help

Financial matters are not difficult to deal with as such. Most people manage their personal affairs tolerably well. It is rather like riding a bike or playing chess. There are a few basic skills to be mastered but it is mostly a matter of practice. For many people, it is the fear of being shown up that really worries them. Here are a few possible ways of acquiring the habit of relating to financial data, depending on whether you prefer to work on your own or with others.

- Read the quality papers, particularly the *Financial Times*. If you compare the FT with your favourite paper, you will find the same news coverage but with an extra layer of reporting which specifically looks at the financial implications of the news. You will also find a surprising amount of articles and information relevant to the trade.
- Any public library will have a wide range of management textbooks, including quite a few in the 'teach yourself' style.
- If you are an HTA member, you can join the Retail Business Improvement Scheme which is a forum for members to share trading data confidentially with other RBIS members. If you wish, you can also take part in meetings where RBIS members discuss the meanings of their figures and talk about future plans.
- There is a wide range of courses available both locally and nationally covering both finance and all aspects of business. Many lead to specific qualifications as discussed in the chapter on training. They can be undertaken locally, or at specialist colleges such as Hadlow College, where the emphasis will be on examples relevant to the garden centre industry.

SUMMARY

Financial decisions and implications permeate every part of business life. If your financial information is sound and timely, you can make firm and accurate decisions for the profitability of your business. If it is out of date and based on guesses or assumptions you will lack the information to *know* whether your business is profitable or if and when changes may be necessary.

In the final analysis, systems do not make or keep a business profitable; rather it is the people who do that. The systems are there as guidance and tools to be used. The users of those systems must be selected, trained and motivated with care and skill.

This chapter has taken a glimpse at the more technical issues surrounding business finance. It does not aim to be more than an overview. How to use these and other concepts explored in the book to control improve profitability is the task of Chapter 9.

If in doubt, always seek the advice of properly qualified advisers before making any major financial decisions.

Blooming Awful Garden Centre Ltd: Balance Sheet as at 31 August 1998

Fixed assets	Cost	Depreciation	Net Book Value
Freehold premises	£	£	£
– land	200,000		200,000
– buildings	50,000	42,000	8,000
Fixtures and fittings	18,000	14,000	4,000
Forklift truck	7,000	1,400	5,600
Renault Master van	12,400	8,600	3,800
Office equipment	6,500	5,800	700
	293,900	71,800	222,100
Current assets			
Stock		106,000	
Debtors		7,000	
Cash-in-hand		2,000	
		115,000	
Creditors (Amounts falling due within one year)			
Creditors		81,000	
Overdraft		24,000	
		105,000	
Net current assets			10,000
Total assets less current liabilities			232,100
Creditors (Amounts falling due after more than one year)			
Mortgage on freehold premises			24,000
			208,100
Capital and reserves			
Share capital			180,000
Reserves at 1/9/97		25,100	
Profit for year ended 31/8/98		3,000	
		28,100	28,100
			208,100

Blooming Awful Garden Centre Ltd:
Trading and Profit and Loss a/c for the year ended 31 Aug 1998

	£	£
Sales		356,000
Less: cost of goods sold		
Opening stock	98,000	
Add: purchases	238,000	
Less: Closing stock	106,000	230,000
Gross profit (35%)		126,000
Less: Expenses		
Director's remuneration	20,000	
Wages and salaries (+ employers NI)	45,000	
Mortgage repayments	20,000	
Rates	9,000	
Services (including phone)	3,000	
Printing and stationery	2,000	
Advertising	3,000	
Van expenses	2,500	
Insurance	1,500	
Professional fees and bank charges	2,500	
Credit card charges	2,000	
Training	500	
Depreciation	8,000	119,000
Net profit (before interest and tax) (2%)		7,000
Less: interest charges		4,000
Net profit before tax		3,000

6 Purchasing

Purchase planning systems. Control of stock flows. The Pareto Principle. Visual and diagrammatic techniques. Just-in-time stock control systems. Standards and targets. Training to be a buyer. Suppliers and the distribution chain. Purchasing for sustained profit.

Purchasing is the choice of **range** and **quantity** of goods bought for resale by a business. Pricing is the **value added** to those purchases to create a **sales price**. The considerations involved in purchasing and pricing decisions are critical to the success of all businesses.

In his book *Pricing for profit*, John Winkler states that the three most important indicators of business health are, in order: **GROSS PROFIT MARGIN; NET PROFIT MARGIN; RATE OF GROWTH.**
This observation is apparently valid for almost all kinds and sizes of business, operating within most economic systems.

Purchasing, stock control and pricing policies are closely linked but will be considered separately. Strategic marketing decisions about the nature and positioning of the business will determine the broad targets for both purchasing and pricing policies (see diagram). The tactics for each business will depend on seasonality, cashflow and specific price offers or availability of certain kinds of goods. In many ways the role of buyer can be the most interesting part of the general management of the garden centre.

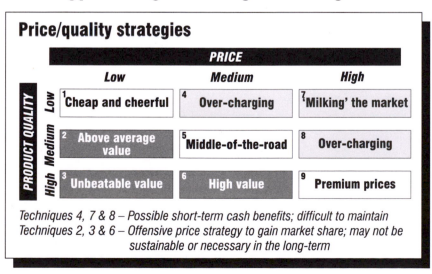

Price/quality strategies

PRODUCT QUALITY	PRICE		
	Low	*Medium*	*High*
Low	1 Cheap and cheerful	4 Over-charging	7 'Milking' the market
Medium	2 Above average value	5 Middle-of-the-road	8 Over-charging
High	3 Unbeatable value	6 High value	9 Premium prices

Techniques 4, 7 & 8 – Possible short-term cash benefits; difficult to maintain
Techniques 2, 3 & 6 – Offensive price strategy to gain market share; may not be sustainable or necessary in the long-term

PURCHASE PLANNING SYSTEMS

Stock is commonly considered in terms of three parameters: value, seasonality and space. Analysis and action in each of these areas is vital to link purchasing and stock control for effective use of resources. Systems for monitoring and control of purchases can include:

Cash limited purchasing

In this type of system the choice of goods is left up to the manager or buyer. However there is a periodic purchasing cycle which has cash limits on how much may be spent. This system requires a good knowledge on the part of the buyer, to ensure that all product groups are fairly catered for in each purchasing period. It also requires fairly simple financial management information and is probably, in one form or another, the most commonly used control system in garden centres.

Open-to-buy

This concept links seasonality and value. A particular category of goods is designated open-to-buy only during its high trading period, plus an initial delivery phase. If six weeks' stock is normally carried, the open-to-buy window may close three or four weeks before the expected date of sales falling off. Sophisticated support systems are needed for managers to operate this kind of system.

Space utilisation

Parkinson's Law states that work expands to fill the time available. In retail terms, stock expands to fill the space available. When the multiples first came into the garden centre market, the rest of the trade commented on how small their outdoor plant areas were. Despite this they have gained understanding and professionalism in this key area of plant sales.

CONTROL OF STOCK FLOWS

When purchasing any goods for resale, part of the contract will involve the time taken from order to delivery, known as the **lead time**. This may be relatively certain, as in the case of routine weekly deliveries from a sundries wholesaler, but it may also be far less certain, as might be the case with importing plants from Holland. If you are convinced you can accurately predict both the rate of sale of stock and the lead time for delivery of the next batch of stock, then it would be possible to operate a perfect **just-in-time** stock system. In practice this seldom happens and a quantity of **safety stock** has to be allowed for in the reorder calculation.

A final complication is the **economic order quantity** (EOQ). This is a calculation of the balance between costs and benefits of a larger or smaller order for a particular product or range of products. The diagram below summarises all of the above but does not indicate whether the reorder quantity is the same as the EOQ.

While the example opposite is an accurate technical statement of the flow of stock in a sys-

> **Stock purchase flow chart**
>
> Know present stock levels, rate of stock-turn, safety levels and lead times
>
> Evaluate present and other possible suppliers
>
> Decide on levels of delegation for:
> (a) routine (b) new stock lines
>
> Ensure all information is circulated as necessary
>
> Take feedback and action as appropriate

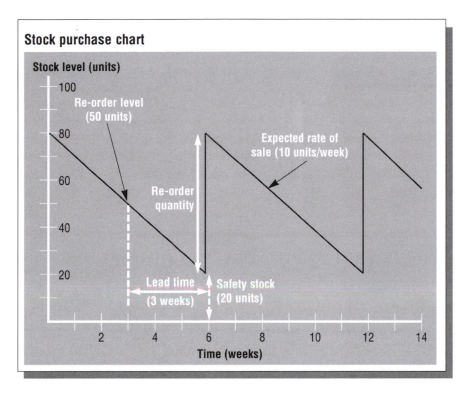

Stock purchase chart

Stock level (units)

- 100
- Re-order level (50 units)
- 80
- Expected rate of sale (10 units/week)
- 60
- Re-order quantity
- 40
- 20
- Lead time (3 weeks)
- Safety stock (20 units)

2   4   6   8   10   12   14

Time (weeks)

tem, it is too neat and too abstract to be much use on a day-to-day basis. A system similar to the one below was used by both the authors in their respective garden centres and as a training aid in their courses at Hadlow College.

It is not possible to carry out these calculations and procedures for each individual stock line, unless each represents a significant proportion of sales in a particular department or sales period. It is more usual to group product lines into categories (e.g. strimmers, 9cm herbaceous) to make calculating and ordering more manageable. It is unfortunately still possible to overlook the really key selling lines, so a further technique is introduced below.

THE PARETO PRINCIPLE

Otherwise known as the **80:20 Rule**, it is a general observation that in any system, roughly 80% of the work, output or problems are caused by roughly 20% of the stock, machinery or whatever. In retail terms, it is generally recognised that about 20% of stock lines represent 80% of stock value and hopefully, of sales.

Any good stock control system, whether manual or EPOS driven, should enable the manager to focus on the crucial 20% of stock lines that represent such a critical financial burden. This is the only sure way to maximise purchasing (and consequently, financial) efficiency.

Because of the pronounced seasonality of garden centre trade, the 80:20 analysis will focus on widely varying stock groups from month to month. As an example, Christmas tree purchases will probably be worthy of very careful analysis from late November to Christmas Eve, but not at all the following week!

As mentioned above, individual stock lines are often placed into groups (e.g. herbaceous perennials). It is easy with EPOS systems, but quite difficult manually, to evaluate all such major product groups for the 80:20 spread present within each one. This permits a fine tuning of the purchasing process. Such techniques are common in larger companies with dedicated purchasing staff but are still seen as difficult in smaller organisations.

VISUAL AND DIAGRAMMATIC TECHNIQUES

A way of visualising the space available for stock is by means of a map of the area in question or of the whole centre. An example is given in the chapter on stock control. To cope with the problems of forward planning of orders, a diagram similar to the one below may be a good aide memoire for the skilled manager and a training aid for their assistant.

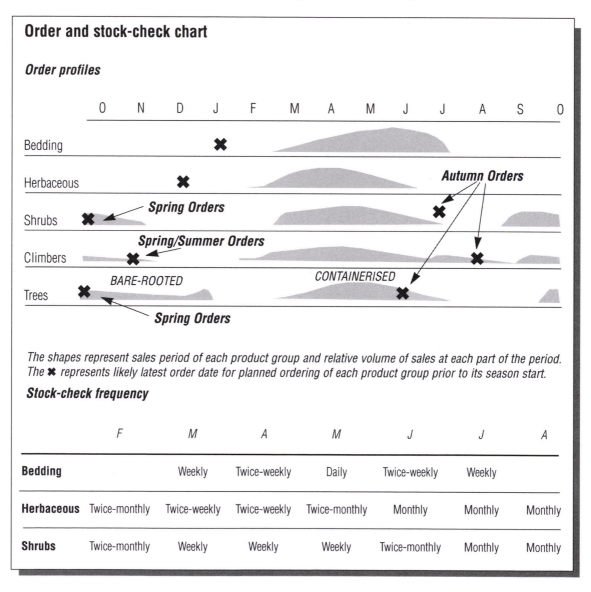

Order and stock-check chart

Order profiles

The shapes represent sales period of each product group and relative volume of sales at each part of the period. The ✖ represents likely latest order date for planned ordering of each product group prior to its season start.

Stock-check frequency

	F	M	A	M	J	J	A
Bedding		Weekly	Twice-weekly	Daily	Twice-weekly	Weekly	
Herbaceous	Twice-monthly	Twice-weekly	Twice-weekly	Twice-monthly	Monthly	Monthly	Monthly
Shrubs	Twice-monthly	Weekly	Weekly	Weekly	Twice-monthly	Monthly	Monthly

JUST-IN-TIME STOCK CONTROL SYSTEMS

This is an American concept from the 1940s, now famously associated with the amazing recovery of the Japanese economy after the Second World War. In essence, it is concerned with the creation and implementation of systems designed to minimise the holding of stock or inventory in a manufacturing plant. It requires both uninterrupted infrastructure and transport systems and an almost symbiotic relationship between the manufacturer and its suppliers. Such systems reach the news headlines when they break down. In Japan, this is usually infrastructure failures, such as after the Kobe earthquake in 1996; in Europe it is typically a breakdown in industrial or business relationships within or between manufacturers and their suppliers.

In its purest form, the notion is that stock holding could be so low that a worker could take the last component from a bin to use in an assembly, at the same moment that the next batch of that item arrives at the bin. In retail terms it is not possible to operate in such a way for the reasons shown below.

Uncertainty of supply

The weather in this latest season (1998) has been so at odds with normal patterns that goods, particularly plants, have not been available when required. Either the nurseries have been unable to bring stock on at the right time; or have done so and found no retail demand, causing them losses; or have been overwhelmed by demand when it did occur, causing shortages and stock-outs all down the distribution chain.

Customer demand

'Stack it high and sell it cheap' is famously supposed to have been the motto of the founder of Tesco. Retail customers want to have choice. In garden centre terms the ultimate example is probably Christmas trees. Which of us has not stopped at least one potential punch-up between disgruntled customers each wanting the same tree – in a yard with two hundred others to be chosen from?

Substitution

It is not possible to fit a car with three wheels of one size and one of another (despite cynical feelings to the contrary on occasions!). However, customers may be able to change variety or have an order filled from a range of plants not originally specified by them.

STANDARDS AND TARGETS

Regardless of size, every garden centre can make a major improvement in its stock control and purchasing decisions by setting some basic standards and targets. Crucially, these must then be monitored for the ability to achieve them.

Every centre should evaluate and choose its most important stock control and purchasing issues for such a system.

Detailed information on the theoretical models and formulae associated with stock

---

For example:

Standards	Targets
Out-of-stocks will not exceed 5% of sales	Stocks will not exceed, on average, 12% of the last period's turnover
Bedding plant markdowns will not exceed 3% of bedding sales	Lead times for purchases will fall by two days on average this year
No purchases will be made of out-of-season lines without the express consent of the owner	The purchase ledger will reduce from 200 to 180 accounts before next season

control systems may be found in management accounting and operations management textbooks. However, these tend to be very abstract and academic and the diagrams below seek to summarise the key issues in practical terms.

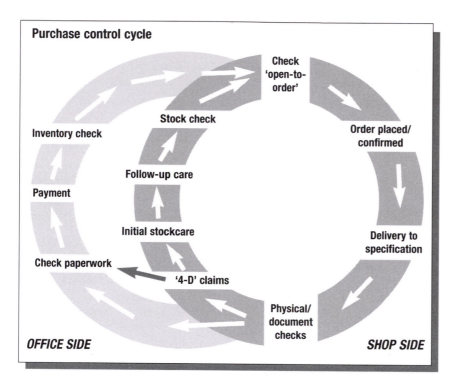

Purchase control cycle

Check 'open-to-order'

Order placed/confirmed

Stock check

Inventory check

Follow-up care

Payment

Initial stockcare

Delivery to specification

Check paperwork

'4-D' claims

Physical/document checks

OFFICE SIDE

SHOP SIDE

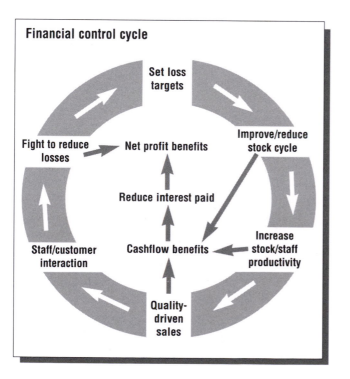

Financial control cycle

Set loss targets

Fight to reduce losses

Net profit benefits

Improve/reduce stock cycle

Reduce interest paid

Staff/customer interaction

Cashflow benefits

Increase stock/staff productivity

Quality-driven sales

TRAINING TO BE A BUYER

Very few people come into the garden centre trade with a retail qualification, although an increasing number are now available. Most people acquire their buying skills by watching their managers. Unfortunately this leads to a very variable approach and some distinctly dubious methods are perpetuated in this manner. Not many buyers in the trade have any real objective measurement of the efficiency or effectiveness of their buying systems and techniques. Some of the problem areas are shown here.

Skill area	Qualitative	Quantitative
Marketing analysis of business	* *	* *
Choice of stock range	* *	* *
Selection of dry goods for:		
• quality	* *	*
• quantity		* * *
• availability	* *	* *
Selection of plants for:		
• quality	* *	* *
• quantity		* * *
• hardiness	*	* *
• shelf-life	*	* *
• availability	* * *	*
Fashion trends in gardening	* * *	
Weather forecasting:		
• short term	* *	* *
• long term	* * * *	

SUPPLIERS AND THE DISTRIBUTION CHAIN

Any business that buys and sells goods is said to be part of the distribution chain. This concept is useful in placing a garden centre in its correct relationship with both its customers and its suppliers. For buyers to be professionally competent, they must have a good knowledge of all the links in the distribution chain that can influence their business and also of the distribution channels, the physical means by which the goods will arrive at the garden centre.

The distribution chains for our industry are manifold, due to the very wide range of goods sold by most garden centres. The example shown overleaf is a simplified one for the distribution of hardy plants.

It can be seen that garden centres are far from being the heart of the distribution chain! Indeed, the worrying thing from a retailer's point of view is to consider how many different ways the final customer has of getting their plants (or indeed anything else they may need).

Several points emerge from a brief study of this diagram:

- The greater the number of links in the distribution chain, the more likely the plants are to be (a) expensive (b) tired and (c) not traceable to their original source. This has implications for the consumer and the retailer who finally supplied them.
- A greater number of links in the chain can relate to a small scale of trading by the retailer. To buy direct from major auctions or nurseries can involve a larger scale of stock or financial risk than a small retailer can handle individually. Such considerations have led to the formation of co-operative groups such as HART.
- There are risks for the grower in each method of distribution. These relate to the proportion of the nursery's production that is committed to forward sales under contract, sales from catalogue or 'over-the-gate' direct retail sales. In virtually any business, it is considered undesirable to commit more than 20% of total sales or output to one customer, due to the power they may acquire over the provider.

By having a clearer understanding of the challenges and preoccupations of your suppliers (as you do with your customers) you can build a better relationship with them. While

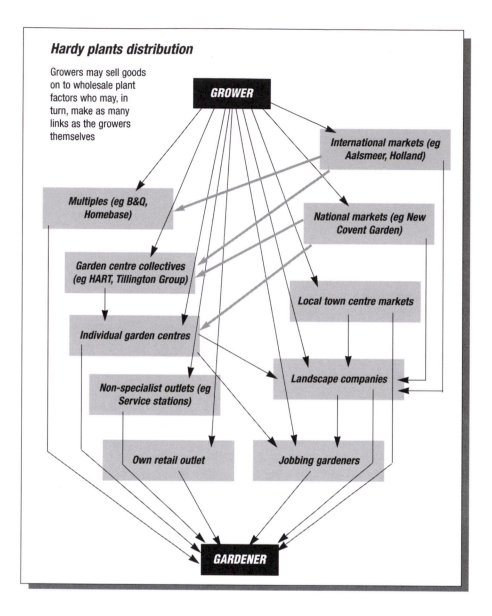

Hardy plants distribution

Growers may sell goods on to wholesale plant factors who may, in turn, make as many links as the growers themselves

GROWER

International markets (eg Aalsmeer, Holland)

Multiples (eg B&Q, Homebase)

National markets (eg New Covent Garden)

Garden centre collectives (eg HART, Tillington Group)

Local town centre markets

Individual garden centres

Non-specialist outlets (eg Service stations)

Landscape companies

Own retail outlet

Jobbing gardeners

GARDENER

What retailers need from suppliers

More professional sales calls

Flexible marketing programmes with easy administration

Plants pre-labelled and priced to spec

Consumer pull-through ads

Train retailers' staff

What suppliers need from retailers

Improve marketing skills

Improve buying skills

Improve merchandising skills

New marketing techniques

Develop strong inter-relationship

Source: US Garden Trade Survey 1987

quality, returns and payments are still the major source of conflict with suppliers, there is a whole range of other areas, as shown on the previous page, where better mutual understanding will be most helpful.

Another way of looking at the problem is to consider the whole life cycle of a plant from the grower to the final customer. Each link in the chain performs seemingly similar functions – but ponder on the differences.

Complete plant life history

Nursery

Grow	Hold	Sell
Self-grown	Outside	On contract
Bought-in	Inside	Off catalogue
Sexual	Quality	Into HONS trade
Asexual	Quantity	To auction
Range	Time	Direct to public

Garden centre

Grow	Hold	Sell
Quantity	Breadth	To whom
Quality	Depth	Quantity
Range	Time	Seasonality
Price	Losses	Price/discounts
Timing	Seasonality	

Gardener

Buy	Nurture	Replace
Quantity	Good	Early death
Quality	Average	Delayed death
Seasonality	Poor	Oversized
Perceived purpose	Not at all	Changed plans/owner

PURCHASING FOR SUSTAINED PROFIT

By now it will be clear that the buyer's role is far more wide ranging and subtle than perhaps at first appears. Ultimately, the buyer has to be able to repeat the purchase cycle on a regular basis to maintain the smooth flow of trading. This is why the concept of sustained profit is not necessarily the same as maximum profit – at least in the short term.

Consider the situation in the price wars among many of the DIY multiples in the early 1990s. The boom housing market of the late 1980s had turned into negative equity for many people. This not only reduced the number of house moves but knocked the confidence of house owners generally. The result was a double whammy against DIY and gardening retail sales. The multiples were in a weak position (see The pricing paradox in Chapter 8) and the response of all except Homebase was to offer ever greater discounts to their retail customers. The authors were only two among millions who 'cruised' the retail parks looking for the ever-lower prices on key lines.

To try to recoup some of the profits given away so freely, the suppliers and manufacturers were invited to lower their prices to the retail giants. After two years or so, a number of (inevitable?) results occurred. Firstly, manufacturers rebelled. Many articles in the trade press made their feelings very clear. Then followed a period of 'de-listing' when major groups on both sides declined to trade with each other.

At the start of this chapter, it was made clear that gross profit margin was the key performance indicator for long-term survival prospects. The following thoughts on margins are followed by the most consistently successful businesses in all sectors.

Protecting your margins

- Know your required average gross profit percentage
- For every low margin line, have a balancing high margin line
- Rigid, high unit price = limited sales. Volume at any price = trouble!!!
- Work your product mix; price flexibly; use price changes to your best advantage
- Go for steady *profitable* growth; keep the business tight; keep unit costs under pressure

After: Winkler, Pricing for Results

SUMMARY

The major skill areas underpinning all the above are financial and negotiating skills. To this may be added an appreciation of the market in which we operate, often referred to as 'scanning the environment'. Success in purchasing is both an art and a science, where personal taste and intuition are tempered by understanding budgets and other financial forecasts.

This diagram summarises the whole process of buying, holding and selling stock for retailing in general. It has particular relevance to perishable goods, such as plants, where control is all important, and it also provides the link to the next two chapters.

Stock management cycle

BUY	HOLD	SELL
Timing	Time	Who to
Quality	Depth	When
Quantity	Breadth	How much
Source	Location	Price
Price	Losses	Added value

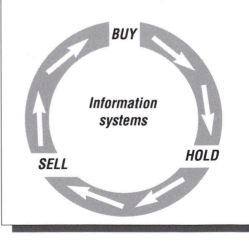

7 Stock control

Stock control. Basic definitions. The Virtuous Cycle. Stock losses. Reductions.

Purchasing impacts heavily on stock control. A quick glance into any management accounting textbook will show a sizeable chapter on stock control issues. This is due both to the strong financial implications of stock control and its relationship to other key business areas as shown below. All of these relationships are examined in this or related chapters.

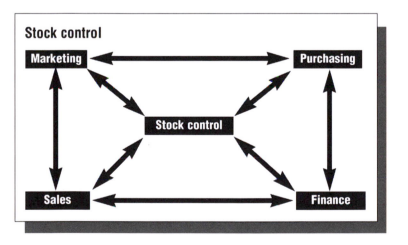

STOCK CONTROL

Stock control is a largely quantitative technique (how many bales of peat in stock?) but with some qualitative aspects (how soon will those flowering shrubs 'go over' and by how much should they be marked down?).

Unlike a manufacturing concern, a retail outlet usually only has one type of stock or inventory, which is goods for sale. Without adequate levels of the appropriate kinds of stock, a retail outlet will very soon cease to trade. However, as stock is at risk in one way or another all the time it is on the retailer's premises – and as it represents the bulk of their working capital – it has to be monitored with great care, as shown below.

Reasons for holding stock

These can include planned choices such as:

- Seasonal variations in demand
- Extra discounts for sizeable purchases
- To anticipate future shortages
- To minimise out-of stocks
- As an investment policy

Other, generally unplanned factors can also come into play:

- Obsolete or imperfect stock remains on sale
- Poor purchasing records lead to excess buying
- Buyers' personal likes or preferences overriding logical choices

Associated stock costs

These can be divided into:

Holding costs:

- Interest on working capital tied up in stock
- Opportunity costs
- Handling costs
- Losses (death, damage, theft, obsolescence etc.)
- Insurance

Out-of-stock costs:

- Direct loss of profit from lost sales
- Loss of customers to other outlets
- Additional cost of emergency purchases

Purchasing costs:

- Researching and sourcing stock
- Staff costs of ordering, goods in and book-keeping
- Goods-in delivery costs (carriage inwards)

All garden centres should have a system that recognises and minimises all the above costs for maximum profit. A useful stock control system will accurately inform the buyer what to order, when and in what quantity. The diagram at the end of the previous chapter will set the scene.

BASIC DEFINITIONS

Stock can be considered in terms of **breadth** and **depth**. Breadth is the number of different **lines** held and depth is the **quantity** of each line. A line is a uniquely identified type of stock. For example, 'garden spade' may not be a single line – each size, type, manufacturer and range of spades stock will give rise to another line. The number of lines represented by garden spades may be in double figures! A simple example would be the Shape Shop, as below.

Stockholding for the Shape Shop

Depth of stock – two to six items

Breadth of stock – five lines

The total quantity of stock can be expressed as numbers of items, financial value, or physical space taken up. Even quite a small garden centre may have over 10,000 lines in its stock profile, even if not all are in stock at the same time. A large retail operation, like a major supermarket, may have in excess of 30,000 lines. With plants, every cultivar, in every size, from every source, may be treated as a different line. On this basis one of the most famous plant centres in the country has had over 1,000 lines of rhododendron alone listed on its computer stock system. It can become a real nightmare to control a stock system with vast numbers of lines, all with different seasonalities, risks and profit margins associated with them. Computer-based buying systems, linked to EPOS sales systems, can give management precise and timely answers. The trick is to ask the right questions.

The same questions are asked and answered by managers who have a manual stock control system and no EPOS. This includes at least one of the top single-site garden centres in England. The owner remains to be convinced about the need for EPOS and quotes many problems encountered by friends and rivals in the trade. Some of the pros and cons of computer-controlled purchasing/stock control/sales systems are shown below.

PROS AND CONS OF EPOS

Like the Internet and personal computers, EPOS was once a mystery which very quickly became crystal clear with familiarity and so it is tempting to assume that every garden centre must have it.

It eliminated the individual pricing of goods, of course, but its big breakthrough was speed at the checkout. In a well-organised retail outlet it is at the till that its great benefit to the customer emerges (provided steps are taken to avoid the potential log-jam a slow shopper/packer can cause).

For some however, the most important aspect of EPOS is as a management tool. The information available from the electronic processing of itemised sales should be invaluable to the

The changing space demands of stock groups in a garden centre, at different times of the year (representational only).

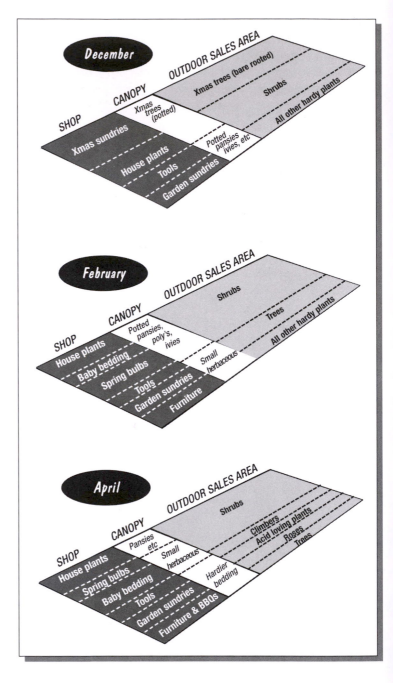

garden centre manager, provided it is used properly. There is little point in collecting mountains of data if it is not analysed on a regular basis.

However EPOS is not an unmitigated blessing – it has its downside. It is costly, not only to install but also to maintain, and in addition you have to make provision for breakdown. Remember: an EPOS-reliant checkout that goes down can take that day's business with it if there is no back-up system!

The problem of total stock quantities can be made more understandable and manageable by breaking it down into sections. This can be in terms of the product group and/or its

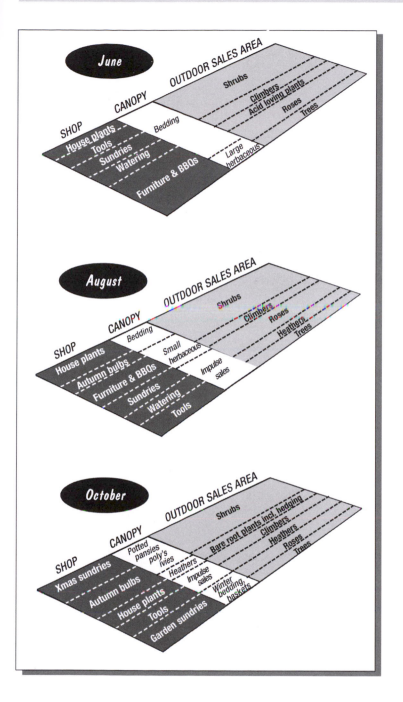

relationship to other sections. The map can be diagrammatic or an accurate representation of the areas occupied by stock. Each section can then be considered in terms of stock value, space occupied and seasonality. The example overleaf shows in simplified terms how this might work.

Each section can then be subdivided into categories. Taking the example of autumn bulbs, the main categories might include:

(1) Autumn flowering crocus

(2) Prepared hyacinths and narcissus

(3) Untreated hyacinths

(4) Crocus

(5) Narcissi

(6) Tulips

(7) Minor bulbs

(8) Amaryllis and other gift packs

(9) Bulb compost, bowls and sundries

There will be a space allocation, varying from mid-August (quite small, only items (1), (2) and (9) on show) through September and mid-October (large, items (2) to (9) on sale), reducing again as lines sell out and space is needed for Christmas items. With each major product group, a similar movement of space will be noticed, and seasonalities within the seasonality may also exist. Sources of information about these complexities may be sought from suppliers of the goods as well as previous sales, purchases and space allocation records. Photos of previous displays and long-term members of staff can all help the process.

Another relatively easy technique is to plot the sales of key lines within product groups over their maximum sales period. An example relating to cell-grown bedding plants is shown below. This kind of data can be assembled from manual sales or purchase records but is much easier from an EPOS-type system. Some typical EPOS records are shown in the Appendix.

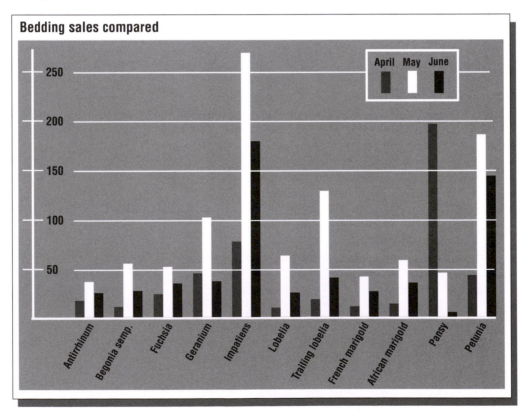

Allocation of space can also be critical in terms of financial control. While Sainsbury's Homebase is considered to be the most plant-oriented of the DIY sheds, it still has outdoor plant sales areas typical of its sector. They can look very small compared with most traditional garden centres. This is deliberate policy aimed at matching expected plant sales to the number of lines stocked. The benefits are that only a limited amount of cash can be tied up in stock at any one time, rate of stock turn is maintained at a high level and the manager is forced to consider each purchase very carefully.

Comparisons of outside plant sales areas		
Factor	*Typical multiple*	*Typical independent*
Area:	100–400 sq m (120–480 sq yd)	400–3,000 sq m (480–3,600 sq yd)
Outdoor plant sales as % of g/c turnover	10–20%	20–70%
Stock layout	100% benching 60–80% multi-tier	20–80% benching 0–30% multi-tier
Stock density	Very high	Low to high
Seasonal variation	Reduce/expand no. of sales units	Increase/decrease plant spacing
Rate of stock turn (p.a.)	10–15	2–6
No. of lines sold	500–2,000	3,000–15,000
Types of lines sold	Bestsellers in all major plant gps	Generalised (all plant gps) and/or specialised (rare and 'difficult' plants in one or more major gps)
	Small amount of opportunistic purchasing	Small to large amounts of opportunistic purchasing
	Very small stocks of ornamental/ fruit trees	Small to large stocks of trees
Reasons for lines stocked	Detailed analysis of: • previous sales • market trends • local/regional competition • stock availability in v. large quantities • profitability • pre-planned marketing targets Plus specialist judgement of full-time buyers	Detailed analysis as for multiples (some garden centres) plus experience/intuition. Own production (if linked to a nursery). Own plant likes/dislikes. Long-term loyalties to suppliers

The advantages and disadvantages of range and quantity of stock-holding can and will be argued fiercely in all types of businesses. Some of the arguments are assembled overleaf.

THE VIRTUOUS CYCLE

There is a concept called the virtuous cycle. This holds that a closed-loop system will, if correctly set up and operated, lead to a marginally better result on every circuit of the loop. Over a period of time this will greatly improve the whole endeavour of which the system is a part. The more factors come into play in such a system, the less predictable the end result

Small sales area, limited number of lines

For	Against
Reduces customer confusion	Reduces customer choice
Reduces working capital tied up	Allows no clear marketing differentiation to bring customers back
Reduces stock losses	Prevents/hinders maximum seasonal displays/sales
Reduces staff costs	Prevents/hinders creation of large displays/temporary gardens
Enables clear distinction between seasons (complete stock changeover)	Reduces risk of stock-outs Protects against supplier shortages Allows substitution sales if some shortages occur

Large sales area, wide range of lines

The reverse of many of the above, also:

For	Against
Encourages trade and large private purchases, especially on an impulse basis	Requires high staff input for large stock and display areas
High value growing stock may increase in value over time	Difficulties in keeping control of stock due to sheer volume (includes security risks)
Allows high range of linked sales possibilities	

is going to be. This can be seen particularly when politicians try to justify and predict the outcomes of their favourite policies. The reality is nearly always much messier and less effective. Sometimes the end result is the exact opposite of that intended.

In garden centre terms, the virtuous spirals many businesses aspire to in terms of stock control are analysed below. However, as with politics, there may be slip-ups between planning and execution. This does not mean that it is not worth doing, but it does mean that the feedback, summarised at the foot of the diagram is critical if it is actually to be of benefit.

There are two separate but closely linked virtuous cycles shown on the next page. The first one is tactical, the second is strategic. Both rely on close observation of the stock and sales area.

STOCK LOSSES

Whatever systems are in place, there will be stock losses. This section will consider how they arise and look at some possible solutions. There is also a section considering some aspects of losses in the chapter on security. Losses have to be quantified as a first requirement. At least one of the most prestigious centres in the South-east of England does not choose to calculate its stock losses, on the grounds that its customers are all such nice people that they couldn't possibly be shoplifting. Another, totally different but also very prestigious centre (this time in the North-west of England), has a policy of allowing deliveries to be made by its suppliers, out of hours, to an unsupervised delivery area. The senior

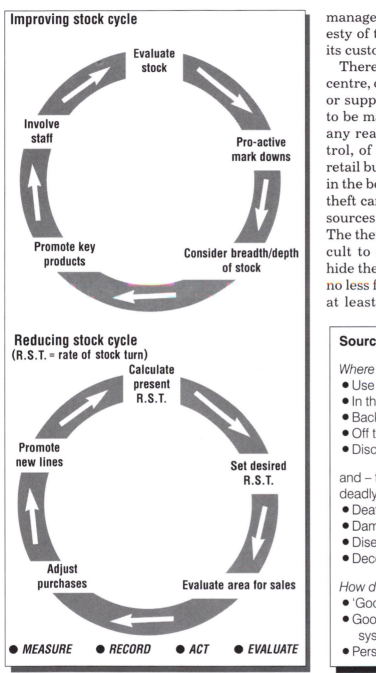

Improving stock cycle

Evaluate stock

Pro-active mark downs

Consider breadth/depth of stock

Promote key products

Involve staff

Reducing stock cycle
(R.S.T. = rate of stock turn)

Calculate present R.S.T.

Set desired R.S.T.

Evaluate area for sales

Adjust purchases

Promote new lines

● **MEASURE** ● **RECORD** ● **ACT** ● **EVALUATE**

management is as convinced of the honesty of their suppliers as the other is of its customers.

There is no intention to impugn either centre, or any particular staff, customers or suppliers in any business. The point to be made is that such policies prevent any real understanding, let alone control, of a major source of loss to every retail business in the country. Elsewhere in the book it is revealed that losses from theft can be up to 5% of turnover. Other sources of loss can total as much again. The theft problems are particularly difficult to quantify as the causes seek to hide the result. Other more innocent but no less financially devastating losses can at least be more easily measured and

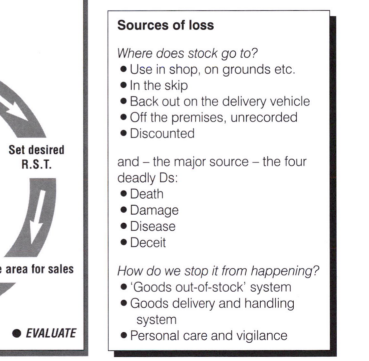

Sources of loss

Where does stock go to?
● Use in shop, on grounds etc.
● In the skip
● Back out on the delivery vehicle
● Off the premises, unrecorded
● Discounted

and – the major source – the four deadly Ds:
● Death
● Damage
● Disease
● Deceit

How do we stop it from happening?
● 'Goods out-of-stock' system
● Goods delivery and handling system
● Personal care and vigilance

these are the ones we shall start on. The diagram below can be used as a handy reference or training chart.

The first four points in the diagram are covered in some detail in the security chapter. 'Off the premises, unrecorded' can cover situations where, perhaps, a member of staff legitimately takes a selection of goods away to illustrate a talk to a local gardening group. If no record is made before the goods leave the premises, two potential problems arise. The obvious one is a loss of stock control. The less obvious one is a loss of protection for the staff member. All events and systems connected with the control of stock or other assets should consider these implications as shown below. *Mutual security is a must.*

Every time a system for the control and recording of stock is operated, it helps to:

- Protect staff and suppliers from charges of inefficiency
- Protect staff, suppliers and customers from accusations of theft
- Protect the business from financial loss.

Mutual security is a win-win situation unthreatening to, and appreciated by, all.

This concept was devised by one of the authors in a moment of inspiration (or desperation) when he was taken to task by his managing director for steeply mounting losses. All the measures considered to resolve the situation only aggravated it as they were seen to be aggressive or threatening. Once the mutual security concept was explained to staff they quickly saw the benefits. This sign was put up in the staffroom and the office, with a modified version above the tills. This had the bonus of focusing customer awareness on the benefits to them of such issues as phoning for credit card authorisation.

Event	Problem	Solution
Deliveries of goods	Death, damage, disease	Check stock carefully for condition as well as for specification. If weather is extreme, record this on delivery notes.
		Check paperwork into system, activating claims procedures immediately.
		Ensure stock is handled carefully and promptly into the right sales or storage location e.g. lift trees by pots, not stems.
Holding on sales or stock areas	Death, damage, disease	Check and action as appropriate for spacing, shelter, watering, feeding, pruning, spraying etc. Note all losses or reductions as well as the likely causes to prevent repetition.
Sales and deliveries to customers	Damage	Damage to plants can lead to longer term problems and claims as well as immediate dissatisfaction. Check suitability of transport.

Death, damage and disease, three of the four 'Deadly Ds' shown above, can also be tackled by simple but rigorously enforced systems.

It may look easy to make a set of obvious seeming statements from the security of an office but both the authors have run busy garden centres and know the practical difficulties of keeping the system going somehow during the peak season. The inevitable cry is 'lack of staff' when managers are tackled about their failure to follow systems. A few authentic examples may convince you that the price of not adhering to systems is just too high.

- A garden centre manager was contacted by the police one day and asked to inspect some stoneware found in suspicious circumstances in a nearby quarry. There were some dozens of items which had been removed from the centre over a period of time. The manager had merely thought his sales of stoneware were quite good for the time of year. The police had observed the thieves and acted on a hunch. The garden centre got lucky. After that the manager did more to reconcile his theoretical and actual stock other than at the annual stock take.

- A garden centre received 160 Danish trollies of bedding for a key weekend in April 1997. Despite frost warnings, the trollies were not wheeled inside due to the immense quantities, but were fleeced over the top. Although in an inner city site the losses the following day amounted to about 16 trollies worth! The manager has subsequently always considered his orders against protection capability as well as expected sales.

- A garden centre delivered some top-of-the-range ornamental fountain pieces to a customer. The items were very heavy but due to shortage of staff only one driver was sent. The customer was not rung as arranged prior to delivery, so the driver had to unload as best he could. The fountain was left in the wrong place, was found to be damaged from an unknown cause and the whole financial loss fell on the centre. The manager still shudders at the memory of the row between the customer and himself the following Saturday.

- A garden centre took on several teenage Saturday workers. They were given a range of mundane tasks of which one was watering the bedding. Training consisted of a few minutes with one of them being given verbal, often contradictory instructions e.g. 'make sure you water everything thoroughly but don't get in the way of the customers'. The other teenagers were then shown how by the first one. Losses soared to around 15% of bedding being unsaleable each week. The owner finally called in one of the authors to do a one day course on the care of bedding plants. The cost of the course was recouped in the first month.

Good, simple and workable systems are essential to control losses. Train staff to operate them with confidence and allow adequate time for this. Stress personal care and vigilance to your staff and listen to any suggestions they may have. It was largely as a result of staff consultation following customer complaints about speed of service some years ago that Marks & Spencer radically altered their control systems between stockroom and shopfloor. The new system gave staff more freedom to operate while still maintaining control of stock. It could actually pay many retail operations, not just garden centres, to increase staff costs by having a systems supervisor. This role is to monitor all the control systems and report on deficiencies to the manager. Such a role may be part time and should be demonstrably self-funding. The final case study gives a graphic illustration.

- A garden centre owner was worried that his gross profit in reality was almost 10% less than his predictions. He called in an outside team who observed that not only was there chronic visible overstocking of many ranges of goods, there were no stock control systems either. Worse still, there were visible tracks in the ground opposite holes in the boundary fence. Theft of stock was taking place on a wholesale basis. No-one at the centre seemed aware of the problem although it was known in the local community. The situation had existed for at least three years previously and the owners estimate of 10% losses was not far out. On turnover of around £600k p.a. that amounted to wholly avoidable losses of £60,000 (or a brand new luxury car) per year for at least three years.

In political terms it is said that the price of freedom is eternal vigilance. So it is with control of losses.

REDUCTIONS

Sometimes reductions are inevitable. They are the culmination of all the bad luck, poor weather and worse judgement we have at some time all experienced. A former boss of a famous supermarket group apparently observed that the 'first reduction is the best reduction because it is the least reduction'. This implies that reductions have to be timely; that is spotting an actual or potential problem while the stock in question still has some value in it. Even the slowest customer can usually spot the difference between a sad looking plant and a dead one.

More subtle is the flowering plant in full flower, compared with one in bud. The one in full flower may be perfectly healthy but its attraction is reduced because it will give a show of colour for a shorter time span. Regardless of the cause of the problem we have to ensure that our staff recognise and can act on it effectively.

A reduction is an acceptance of reduced profit. The dynamic tension is between trying to hang on for the full price or trying to get something for an item instead of incurring a total write off. Every centre must set its own criteria, although many have a tendency to hang on too long before reducing prices. This is particularly difficult with plants; after all, lawnmowers don't suddenly 'go over' in a hot spell! The tables below and opposite can be another good base for a system or a training session.

All the above points have universal application. Dif-

Plant reductions
• The first reduction is the best reduction because it is the least reduction
• Timeliness is the key to reducing wastage
• Reductions each side of the weekend are best
• Reduced plants must still represent good value and be of reasonable quality
• Reduced plants should have a prominent security label
• All reductions must be recorded and management notified.

ferent centres will have different views about related issues, such as the segregation of reduced plants or their retention in the main displays.

There is also a reference above to security labelling of reduced plants. The multiples and some of the other larger chains have brightly coloured plant reduction labels. The issue of these is restricted by the manager as they represent a source of loss if misused either by staff or customers. Smaller centres do not usually have such labels but may authorise only certain staff to take reduction decisions. In all cases, an accurate recording system must be operated without fail. It can be a little book at the back of the till or an account in the computerised finance system. Whatever it is, it must not only be fully and accurately used but the results must be monitored, compared with the centre's loss targets and corrective action taken.

The table suggests a range of figures for losses as used by different organisations. Losses in this sense includes total losses and markdowns on site as well as customer returns.

The data is from a range of centres, varied in type, size and location. It is not meant to be a fully representative sample. Some of the extreme figures were one-offs.

Range of losses in major plant groups		
Plant group	**Allowable losses**	**Actual range of losses**
Houseplants	3% to 10%	1.5% to 17%
Outdoor plants	2% to 6%	0.75% to 13%
Bedding plants	6% to 10%	3% to 30%

SUMMARY

One of the authors recalls the words of a former managing director, who gloomily observed that July is the month when keen managers can bankrupt their firms by continuing to purchase, while ignoring both unsold stocks and the downturn in trade. It is worth bearing in mind that all stock is perishable to some extent – plants often startlingly so. Stock losses need careful monitoring at all times, but particularly at the turn of a season or when changing established buying patterns for whatever reason.

Regardless of the mixture of space, seasonality and value that is used for determining stockholding, with whatever justification, four clear disciplines of stock control must be maintained:

- Buying – always for a purpose, not just for the sake of filling the space
- Maintenance – of quality of stock, fittings and sales area
- Security – of stock and sales area against all forms of theft
- Financial – control of the largest, most necessary and sometimes most dangerous category of working capital in your garden centre

Finally don't forget …

Plants come on to garden centres to die

Our task is to:

- control losses
- claim for everything
- identify problems
- carry out changes

and – best of all –

- sell them first!

---

8 Pricing

Applying to products. Deferred payment. Branding. Plant pricing.

Pricing is partly an art, partly a science, but it is certainly not a single formula. You may not gather this from looking at the practice within many gardening outlets where it is believed that by being able to double a cost price and add VAT you have mastered pricing! The success of a garden centre (or indeed any other type of retailer) is related to the level of innovation in the application of pricing. Experience has shown that mark-ups ranging from 10% to 1000% may all have their place, usually with some particular tactical goal in mind.

One of the first difficulties a newcomer often has when looking at this subject area is the terminology. There is no completely standard definition of certain terms such as 'margin' or 'mark-up' but below there is an attempt to give the most common understanding of many of the common terms. It is often through a misunderstanding or confusion of these terms that people have a difficulty grasping the basic concept.

The key formulae

As can been seen from above it is probably not too surprising that confusion frequently ensues for the new recruit. Indeed different sectors of the industry all seem to have their own favourite terminology. For many it is the relationship between mark-up and gross profit which is the most confusing (it may surprise many how far this confusion extends in numerous businesses).

The following example hopefully will add some clarity.

There is a table in the Appendix which lists a whole range of mark-

Simplified Definitions	
COST PRICE	What you pay for goods for resale to the public (also sometimes referred to as PURCHASE PRICE)
MARK-UP	The added value applied to those goods to give the GROSS PROFIT required; normally expressed as a percentage.
GROSS PROFIT	The amount of profit generated when a sale is made; usually expressed as a percentage (sometimes referred to as Gross Margin , Profit on Return, or Profit on Resale (POR))

The Garden Widgett

You buy a Widgett to resell...

COST PRICE	MARK-UP	SELLING PRICE
£1.00	50p	£1.50 (plus VAT)

...then you sell a Widgett...

SELLING PRICE	–	COST PRICE	=	GROSS PROFIT
£1.50 (plus VAT)	–	£1.00	=	50p

By selling the item you have made 50p **Gross Profit** on a £1.50 **Selling Price**. This is usually expressed as a percentage, so on this sale a Gross Profit of 33.3% has been achieved.

SUMMARY In the above example you achieved a **MARK-UP** of 50% and your **GROSS PROFIT** was 33.3%

FORMULAE

$$\text{MARK-UP (\%)} = \frac{(\text{Selling Price} - \text{Cost Price})}{\text{Cost Price}} \times 100$$

$$\text{GROSS PROFIT (\%)} = \frac{(\text{Selling Price} - \text{Cost Price})}{\text{Selling Price}} \times 100$$

In both these equations, it is assumed that VAT (sales tax) is removed prior to making the calculation.

Mark-up	Gross profit
33.3%	25%
50%	33.3%
66.6%	40%
100%	50%
150%	60%
200%	66.6%

NOTE: Gross profit can never reach 100% (unless you do not pay for the goods) but mark-up will frequently do so)

ups and gross profits margins side by side for ease of reference but some of the more common ones are repeated above.

APPLYING TO PRODUCTS

With the basic equations established, it is now important to look at the reasons why different mark-ups are applied to different types of goods. The precise nature of the goods themselves is the most important factor in our trade. Live goods require a higher profit margin than 'dry' goods – after all it is very difficult to kill a barbeque by underwatering it. The pricing structure for live goods needs to account for the extra losses which may be experienced due to disease, damage and death (the infamous three Ds). It is only in very specialist areas that we find dry (or dead) goods marked up to a similar extent. The precise mark-up may vary significantly in different situations so it is not a particularly useful exercise for us to attempt to produce a blueprint as it is not the intention to attempt to put a centre into a straightjacket.

There are however some main characteristics that appear to be responsible for affecting the range of mark-ups which are applied including:

- The unit value of the goods
- Vulnerability to loss
- Perceived value
- Standard practice within the trade
- Time of year
- Promotions
- Purchasing power of the retailer
- Exclusivity
- Rate of stock turn
- Competition in the area

Certain large categories are fairly well controlled as to their basic mark-ups. For example, most branded items purchased via the garden sundries wholesaler are sold at a basic price equivalent to 33.3% gross profit (50% mark-up). To confuse things yet further this is sometimes also referred to as a 'third off retail'. Clearly this is only the starting point in negotiations with such a supplier. There is quite a range of supplementary discounts which may be achieved to help increase profit margins or indeed give the flexibility to undertake selective promotional pricing to increase customer flow.

The following are just some of the areas which should be looked at carefully.

1 Shop around between suppliers – they are all keen to get your business!
2 What extra discounts are available if more business is put with one supplier?
3 Are better terms available for making a 'solus' arrangement with a supplier (i.e guarantee the business)?
4 Is your company making the best use of its buying power? (For many independent centres grouping together within an organisation such as HART may well achieve greater benefits than are possible in isolation.)
5 If discounts cannot be improved, look at areas such as 'promotional support' or delayed payment dates which may also help the profitability but have not been included in our profit calculations thus far.

It may be possible therefore to achieve a gross profit of 50% (100% mark-up) on many of these 'branded' items by the above means, bringing the profit levels in line with that of plant goods (now that's a thought!). This does assume that it is truly possible to sell an item for its recommended price because if you are able to achieve such discounts others may do too, the true market price in reality becoming far lower. (This aspect was covered more fully in Chapter 3 Advertising and promotion.)

DEFERRED PAYMENT

In addition to the straight calculation of gross profit from a particular item, there will at differing times of the year be extended credit offered by the manufacturer. But why – are they feeling charitable? As you may have guessed the real reason is far deeper. A typical 'pre-season' deal may involve the following:

'Lawnmaker' grass seed		
Orders to be placed by 1st December		
Delivery by 31st January		
10–19 packs	Trade less 27%	
20–29 packs	Trade less 32%	
Payment:	14th April	
30 packs plus	Trade less 35%	
Payment:	14th May	

Certainly on paper the above deals seem very good. There is a great opportunity to increase on the normal profit margins achieved on this line. So why does the manufacturer do it? There are some key benefits:

- With such a seasonal product range, it is useful to keep the manufacturing plant in operation throughout the year.
- Encouraging centres to take stock reduces the need for warehousing by the manufacturer.
- Delivering goods in the 'quiet season' helps to keep transport working more efficiently thereby reducing bottlenecks in the spring.
- Excessive fluctuations in demand are reduced.
- Once the product is on the retailer's shelf they are likely to keep the item in stock all season. It pays to have an early presence.

Are there benefits for the retailer?

- The discount achieved on purchasing these products in such a way can be excellent.
- With deferred payment it may be possible to sell the stock, putting profit into the till before the goods are even paid for.
- Early delivery means that the centre has longer to organise displays.
- The centre is certain of getting stocks which may be important if there is a shortage.

There are some significant downsides too:

- The retailer is carrying the cost of storage of the goods, plus the risk of stock damage and pilferage.
- If the centre does not have a sufficiently effective stock control and storage system it may even be possible to 'lose' stock in the storeroom, negating the benefits that were achieved.
- If the season does not perform as expected, the centre may be holding too much stock (most of us have seen a 'slug pellet mountain').
- Pre-season ordering still needs to be paid for – this may cause significant cash flow problems for a centre, especially in a poor season.

The benefits therefore are not so clear cut and the answer may be to almost look at the product range on a line by line basis and order accordingly. There may be little benefit in ordering large quantities of an item if its sales peak is not achieved until after the payment date. The saving will certainly be wiped out by the increase in overdraft charges and the lack of cashflow to invest in more immediate products.

Some manufacturers also privately admit that there is little benefit for them but feel that they will lose market share to rivals unless they follow suit by offering delayed payment.

So once the retailer has the product he wants to sell it. But wait, few customers would wish to buy grass seed in the middle of winter. Often the solution for the centre is to sell it at a discount. Goodbye increased profit margins!

BRANDING

Like it or not we are all brand conscious. Clearly manufacturers work hard to establish a brand image and status. The more widespread a brand, the greater the price comparison is likely to be. Many retailers have chosen to sell own-branded or unbranded goods in addition to the heavily advertised and usually dearer branded lines. Their motives may be very different but will often include:

- Offering the consumer a wider choice
- Increasing total sales within product sectors
- Reinforcement of the corporate image in-store
- Selling an item with no clear price comparison
- Advertising of your business within the home
- Increasing profit margins/offering lower prices than the brand leader

The above reasons are all very valid but anyone contemplating this route must be aware that it is not purely a 'pride' issue for the centre involved. There is clear evidence that one company pays more for its compost in its 'own brand' than if they were purchasing the brand leader, due to the short production runs involved.

Own branding does not always have to offer the cheap alternative however. Some businesses with an extremely good reputation may actually charge a premium for their own brand but such cases are a rarity.

For smaller retailers truly 'own branding' may not be an option due to the initial investment and stockholding that is required. Organisations such as Premier offer its members the option of own branded products exclusive to its membership. With a geographical restriction there will be no competition within the immediate area.

For many centres though, the brand awareness will not be sufficient to stock the own brand alone, requiring the centre to also stock the brand leading products thus opening up the retailer to all the usual price comparisons with other outlets.

The branding issue still primarily affects the dry goods area of the centre. In the UK there is still little brand awareness within the plant sector. True, certain varieties may be known well by name, often supported by point-of-sale materials, but the variation still exists in the product because that item may be grown to different specifications by a number of different growers. Even attempts by well known companies have not had the success which would have been expected. Notable examples in the 1980s saw famous name firms fail when trying to use their considerable brand awareness within the plant arena. Indeed a couple of major garden chemical and fertiliser companies failed to make inroads into the seed market either, despite heavy promotional support.

PLANT PRICING

As identified above, the main problem with plant pricing is the variable nature of the product. Two nurseries both offering the same item in the same pot size may supply items very different in terms of the actual 'volume' of the plant, plus there is no guarantee that the higher priced plant will actually be the better plant. The need to work closely with plant suppliers is of paramount importance together with the constant evaluation of the marketplace.

Plant supply – a cautionary tale

The expensive 5p bargains

A wholesaler of plants purchased a range of items from his supplier in Holland. Unfortunately, when they were delivered the consignment of clematis was not up to standard. Indeed the plants looked as if they were suffering from wilt. The plant wholesaler's initial reaction was to get these items knocked off the invoice and burn them but he was convinced by the grower that they would re-shoot again and a price of 5p each was agreed upon ...

The wholesaler then spent a whole year tending these plants, repotting, feeding and watering them at the cost of about £1.00 per plant. In the end they still did not make the grade and were thrown away!

The moral of the story is ...

The bonfire is the nurseryman's best friend!

It is now commonly expected that in addition to providing a high quality product the grower must supply a good descriptive (picture) label, pre-price and probably bar code as well. This is an invaluable service for the busy garden centre but will obviously work to a set formula. Whilst again it may be possible for the supplier to work to particular price breaks, this system still does not take into account the customer's perceived **value** of the item. Rather than blindly applying this cost-based approach to pricing there may be opportunities to increase margins by personally assessing the product lines, i.e. a more **image-based** approach.

The account below gave one of the authors his first deep insight into some of the complexities of the subject.

Plant pricing – a good mistake

A consignment of plants arrived on a busy day from a specialist nursery who do not pre-price. In the rush, a member of staff calculated the retail price by the time-honoured formula '× 100% plus VAT'. Not realising this, I took the price list lying by the batch to be the trade price, and duly carried out the standard calculation 'double plus VAT'.

I was horrified to discover that I had what looked like to be the most expensive Wisterias in the country! However, it was a very unusual variety and I promoted them hard by point-of-sale material and personal recommendation. They sold well, so I reordered. When the new batch arrived I discovered my error.

What could I do? If I halved the price overnight it would make a nonsense of all my promotional work for this unusual variety. I continued with the price for that line, earning 300% mark-up for the company plus a reputation for unusual plants too!

It may be somewhat unbelievable but it is actually possible to make an item too cheap. People start to become suspicious that there must be something wrong with the item. It is interesting to observe that in certain cases the raising of a price may actually also increase sales. The perception of 'value for money' is not purely based upon whether the item will do the job (function value) but also the look, feel or image associated with the item (esteem value).

VALUE FOR MONEY = FUNCTION VALUE + ESTEEM VALUE.

In other words, a car such as a Rolls-Royce, has a similar function value to that of a more economy model, for example a Skoda (both get you from A to B). The big difference is in the esteem value attached to them.

Is price important?

The answer is probably yes, but only up to a point. The reality probably is that many items are far less price-sensitive than the manager imagines. True there are certain items to which the consumer knows the market value quite clearly (multi-purpose compost, growing bags). As most texts on the subject will identify, the knowledge of a price and resultant price sensitivity normally relates to products which are bought frequently. In the case of gardening products this is not the case as the purchasing pattern may only be once a year. The stimulus for purchasing may well be more upon the appearance of the product rather than purely its commodity value. Perhaps this is a case to focus on products which are 'good enough to eat?'.

SUMMARY

As with stock control, there is a wide range of financial management textbooks that go into considerable detail about the various theories and techniques of pricing. This is the 'science' of pricing and should give you the bottom line figures for your decisions. The 'art' of pricing is market-led and looks to immediate tactical improvement of profit as well as long-term changes in the market. For example, by buying glut plant stocks cheaply and promoting them heavily, an immediate opportunity exists to impress and please customers and to add an unexpected bonus to the present season. This is the role of the buying department within a large organisation, something a smaller retailer may not have the time or opportunity to do in the same way. This activity is certainly one which may be covered by a 'buying group' for such organisations.

Pricing Paradox

Prices are a function of power
- When demand is strong you are free to raise prices
- If profits are good you can afford to reduce prices

Power comes from the options open to you
- If demand is weak you cannot afford to move your prices up
- If profits are poor (due to weak demand?) you are powerless!

It pays to be profitable in a strong demand market

After: Winkler, Pricing for Results

---

9 Profitability – the key to success

The Happy Book – recording and rewarding success.

In the earlier chapters we have seen various factors that help to make it possible for a business to be profitable. At the end of the day the most important reality in creating lasting, increasing profitability is to involve everyone in your business in an understanding of profit.

Profit is not about factors and percentages – you cannot pay those into the bank account. Profit is about keeping your goods in perfect condition and turning those goods into CASH as fast as possible. That cash is secured and recycled into further purchases, creating more PROFITABLE sales and so on.

Profit is lost through a number of causes. Cash itself may not be securely handled and may disappear from the system. The issues of security were addressed in Chapter 4, but suffice it to say that if cash is not secured immediately and constantly, everyone in the business suffers and profitability plummets. Equally damaging is the theft of stock or capital goods from the garden centre – this is almost as acute a problem as theft of cash and was also covered in Chapter 4.

Far more insidious, because less dramatic, are the other stock causes of profit loss. These include waste, damage and death. Together with goods taken from stock for internal use they may amount to more lost profit in a year than the problems of theft. The diagrams overleaf repeat the message from Chapter 5 about the slender net profit margin we customarily operate from.

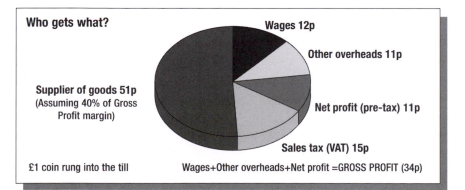

Who gets what?

Wages 12p

Other overheads 11p

Net profit (pre-tax) 11p

Supplier of goods 51p
(Assuming 40% of Gross Profit margin)

£1 coin rung into the till

Sales tax (VAT) 15p

Wages+Other overheads+Net profit =GROSS PROFIT (34p)

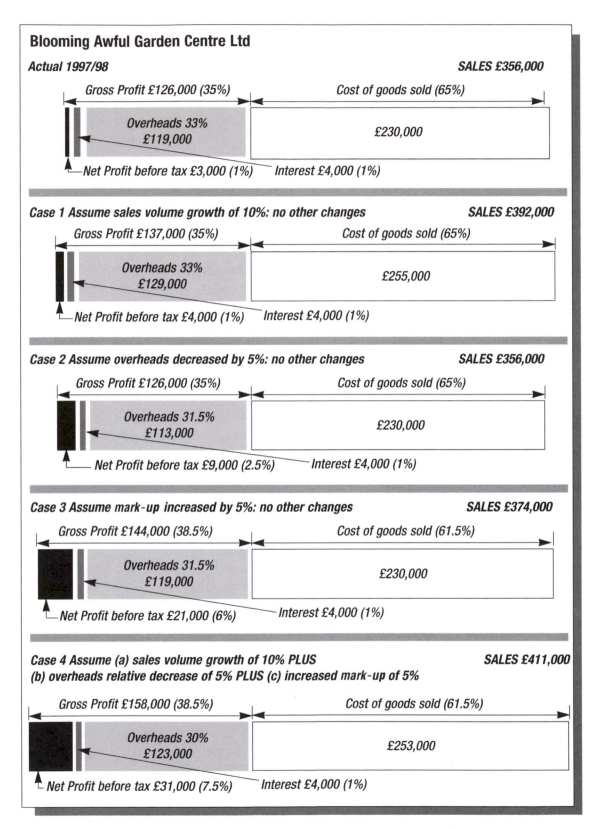

Ignoring theft of cash and stock, which will reduce takings, let us concentrate on the effects of waste, damage and death which will directly reduce gross profit and have a much worse knock-on effect on net profit. Following imaginary deliveries of products, let us see how these losses can occur.

1 Out of 40 boxes of lawn food delivered, one is broken before unloading. We mean to claim for it, but never do. **The cost of goods sold is increased by 2.5p**.

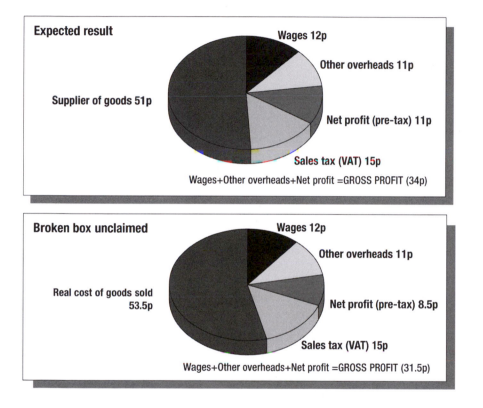

2 From a delivery of 200 boxes of bedding, 40 are not moved into a screened area and suffer wind scorch. Sell at 50% discount. **The gross profit is reduced by 15.6% and the net profit is reduced by 45%**.

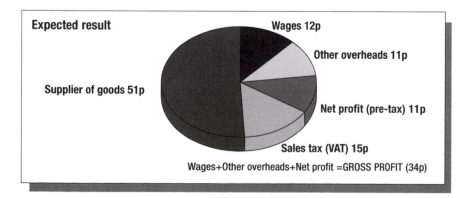

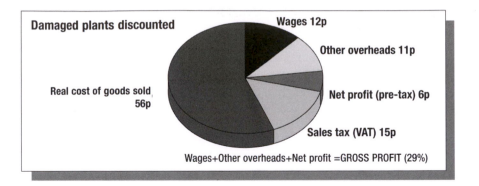

Damaged plants discounted

Wages 12p

Other overheads 11p

Real cost of goods sold 56p

Net profit (pre-tax) 6p

Sales tax (VAT) 15p

Wages+Other overheads+Net profit =GROSS PROFIT (29%)

3 Small goldfish are delivered and put in a holding tank. Unfortunately the usual sales tank has not been properly cleaned. One-quarter of the stock dies and a considerable amount of staff time, effort and embarrassment has gone into rectifying the situation. The effects on **gross profit** and on **overheads** are shown below.

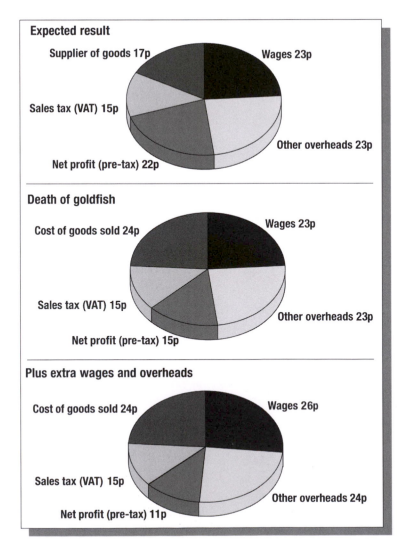

Expected result

Supplier of goods 17p

Wages 23p

Sales tax (VAT) 15p

Other overheads 23p

Net profit (pre-tax) 22p

Death of goldfish

Cost of goods sold 24p

Wages 23p

Sales tax (VAT) 15p

Other overheads 23p

Net profit (pre-tax) 15p

Plus extra wages and overheads

Cost of goods sold 24p

Wages 26p

Sales tax (VAT) 15p

Other overheads 24p

Net profit (pre-tax) 11p

By the final picture you can see what a devastating effect on profits (on real **cash**) this kind of quite ordinary occurrence can have. Net profit on this delivery of fish has been almost halved.

The final diagram in this series shows that if the damage occurs in low-profit goods (i.e. lawnmowers), **net profit** can be totally wiped out by a seemingly trivial occurrence.

4 Ten lawnmowers are delivered. There is a drought that summer and they remain in store for three months. When the drought breaks, sales start again, but so does the leak in the storeroom roof! Eventually all the lawnmowers sell, but the demo model and one which got wet in store have had to be sold at 20% off. On these mowers we are only making 20% gross profit to start with.

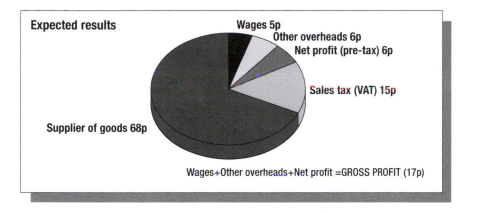

Expected results

Wages 5p
Other overheads 6p
Net profit (pre-tax) 6p

Sales tax (VAT) 15p

Supplier of goods 68p

Wages+Other overheads+Net profit =GROSS PROFIT (17p)

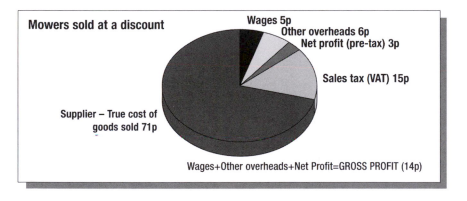

Mowers sold at a discount

Wages 5p
Other overheads 6p
Net profit (pre-tax) 3p

Sales tax (VAT) 15p

Supplier – True cost of goods sold 71p

Wages+Other overheads+Net Profit=GROSS PROFIT (14p)

Worse is to come! We bought the mowers when the business was on overdraft at the bank and during the four months between purchase and sale, the interest charges amount to 4%, increasing the **overheads**. Look at the result below.

Net profit contribution on this delivery is completely wiped out!

What can be done about it? Several important points emerge. Firstly, every delivery, from every source, carries its own risks and opportunities. Secondly, every department or section has its own pattern of profits and costs. Thirdly, *everyone* in the business needs to know the profit opportunities and pitfalls for the area they work in.

This concept often causes problems for managers and owners who fear loss of confidentiality if they disclose their trading pattern to their staff. Everyone, as defined in this exam-

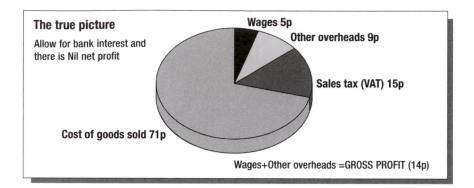

The true picture

Allow for bank interest and there is Nil net profit

Wages 5p

Other overheads 9p

Sales tax (VAT) 15p

Cost of goods sold 71p

Wages+Other overheads =GROSS PROFIT (14p)

ple, is all full-time staff and responsible, regular part-timers – these are all committed people, adult, and capable of trust (after all, you trust them with your cash and goods, don't you?). As long as you properly introduce the reasons for all your people to understand the importance of maximising profit, they will respect the confidentiality involved. Most importantly, they will feel trusted, responsible and part of the team and will react accordingly.

The examples above, particularly **4**, show how *time* is a vital hidden element in keeping profit margins up. You will see from the diagrams below that there are both obvious and subtle connections between care and control of stock and the overall profitability of the business. Improving stock quality may not at first sight seem to carry any measurable cash benefit to the company, but a little analysis proves otherwise. The act of 'roguing' or examining every stock item for poor quality starts a flow of consequences. The diagram on page 65 shows the obvious ones and the whole process generally leads to a reduction in total stock quantity simultaneously increasing stock quality. Not all stock will be equally affected. The 80/20 rule or Pareto Principle suggests that 80% of our sales comes from 20% of our stock lines. The other 80% of the stock lines therefore only generates 20% of the sales and it is in these areas that the greatest need arises for systematic and ruthless stock quality control.

Every business should have a positive policy regarding the fate of sub-standard stock. Considerations include:

(1) The nature of the goods
(2) The image of the business
(3) Extra costs involved in selling the goods

Just two examples will illustrate the point. Firstly, would you try to sell severely droughted boxes of bedding at a reduced price, or would you scrap them? If you decided to try to sell them, would you place them by your main entrance for everyone to see, or would you hide them away? If you put them by the main entrance what would this say to your customers about your plant quality and expertise? If you hide them away, how will you sell them quickly? Can you justify the security risk if reduced-price

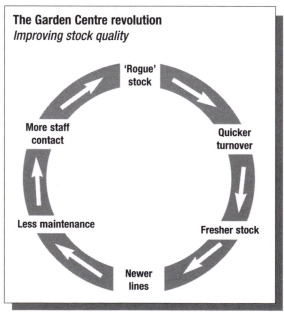

The Garden Centre revolution
Improving stock quality

'Rogue' stock

Quicker turnover

Fresher stock

Newer lines

Less maintenance

More staff contact

labels are moved to perfect quality stock? Whatever your decision, record the reason for the event and the **monetary cost**.

Secondly, how would you dispose of broken bales of peat? Would you re-bag them into smaller own-brand bags, sell them at discount as they are or use them around the garden centre for various repotting and related jobs?

Whatever you do, find out how they came to be broken and list the **costs** of disposal. Only by doing this can you avoid similar problems in the future by understanding the cost of *not* improving your goods care systems.

Simple recording system for goods out of stock

Decide on the categories to be entered, i.e.

(1) Goods dead or destroyed, not claimable from supplier
(2) Damaged goods sold at reduced price
(3) KNOWN stolen goods

Operate a parallel system for other stock losses, i.e.

(4) Goods, perfect or damaged, used by the business: for example, fencing used from stock to repair a hole in the garden centre's own fence
(5) Goods discounted in the course of sales promotions
(6) Goods discounted to special groups, e.g. staff, club members, trade discounts

According to the size of centre and the amount of people available to operate such a system, it may be made more or less complicated. To make it work keep it as simple as possible – operated by the line staff – consistently checked and queried by management.

Many companies, regardless of size, shut their collective eyes to the problems of imperfect stock. Often this is more than shortage of time: it is a positive reluctance to look at the problem for fear of what it may reveal. No-one likes to actively throw money away but you will now realise it is often the lesser evil. Remember the 5p bargains in the previous chapter? Be brave: apply the old adage that 'a bonfire can be a nurseryman's best friend' – it can be a retailer's best friend too!

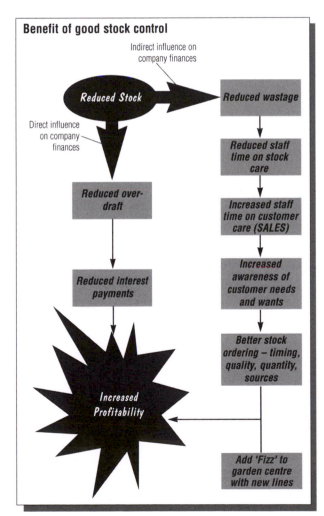

Benefit of good stock control

The outcome of good stock control policies is shown in the diagram on page 83 and is the beginning of an upward spiral of expectations that will link and reinforce improving stock to increasing customer expectations; goods to be proud of, encouraging staff to excel; increased profits being reinvested in all aspects of the business to everyone's advantage.

Once you have started on the upward trend, you will be in a position to maximise the more subtle profit earners implied in the latest diagram – the ones you have to think about. Having painted a fairly gloomy picture of the losses involved in the necessary roguing of stock we will give an example of turning potential losses into profits. A conifer nursery in the USA made a virtue and a profit out of the small percentage of trees which suffered damage or stunting while on the nursery. All the rogued stock was examined for suitability as bonsai subjects. Those with interesting shapes and damaged limbs were individually packaged as character plants for bonsai and sold at three times the price of the perfect stock! This area is one in which all staff can be involved. Try offering profit-related bonuses for successful solutions to perennial problems!

THE HAPPY BOOK – RECORDING AND REWARDING SUCCESS

This is your chance to add your ideas to ours. Below you will see some examples of potential losses turned into real profits. Check your business, with your staff, and add your even better ideas to the list.

1 Broken peat or compost re-bagged into smaller sizes and resold
2 Bonsai trees created from rogue stock
3 Surplus bulbs planted up into containers for added-value sales
4 Broken clay pots bagged and sold as drainage material (crocks)
5 Moss clumps removed from paths as a safety hazard and used in all manner of planting and floral displays as well as direct sales

Now your ideas!

For maximum long-term benefit, you will have to keep simple records of the ideas that have been tried and found effective. Often people are happy to be rewarded with recognition of their efforts by as simple a device as a Roll of Honour recording the idea and its benefit to the business, the customer, the environment, or all three.

The last area we will tackle in this chapter is the effect of overheads on profitability. You can refer back to Chapter 5 for examples of simple Trading and Profit and Loss accounts. Remembering that gross profit percentage is the best indication of the health of a business, followed by net profit percentage, we need to look closely at overheads. Broadly speaking,

$$\text{Gross profit} - \text{Overheads and Depreciation} = \text{Net Profit}$$

There is no point improving all those aspects that directly affect gross profit, only to ignore overheads and fritter all the gains away. Every overhead item demands attention, but obviously the largest ones demand the greatest attention. There are variations from business to business, but wages are invariably the largest single overhead cost, and heat/light and transport cost are also often surprisingly sizeable.

A thorough review of staff costs means an analysis of all staff grades, functions, hours and pay to determine whether this most costly resource is being used to best advantage. Typical outcomes may include the following:

- deliveries inwards should take place out of hours at least during the busier seasons using mainly non-sales part-time workers
- mechanical handling systems for heavy goods may pay back surprisingly fast in labour costs saved and added staff flexibility
- judicious use of weekend and evening student staff can release qualified full-time staff into selling and customer care at peak trading times.

The panel below shows typical wage:turnover percentages for various kinds of retailers. Service industries such as catering or repair shops are much more heavily involved in staff costs. In your coffee shop for example, wages may exceed 50% of turnover. This is one reason why such activities are best managed separately as not only are different management skills needed, but they can distort the figures of your core business.

Of the other overheads, the one with the most potential as a profit centre is transport. This wide term is usually taken to mean deliveries outwards to customers, but can include deliveries inwards and movement of people. A major London garden centre kept very

Garden Centre Customer Deliveries – Costs and Income

1995 – Basic data

Total number of deliveries by own transport	4,073
Total value of deliveries	£136,570
Delivered sales as percentage of total sales	28%
Average time taken from order to delivery	48 hours
Delivery charges levied to customers	£7,300
Total cost of own transport (vehicle & driver)	£21,850
(1 F/T + 1 P/T driver + Bedford 35 cwt pickup)	
Net cost of delivery service to company	£14,470
Equivalent to hidden discount on delivered goods of	10.6%

1997 – Basic data

Total number of deliveries by own transport	114
Total number of deliveries by contract services	3,860
Total number of deliveries by minicabs	1,053
Total value of deliveries	£187,330
Delivered sales as % of total sales	26.5%
Average time taken from order to delivery	24 hours
Delivery charges levied to customers	£10,810
Cost of hire transport	£1,680
Cost of contract services	£16,300
Cost of minicabs	£5,760
Total cost of delivery transport	£23,740
Net cost of delivery service to company	£12,930
Equivalent to hidden discount on delivered goods of	7%

accurate records in recent years of costs and receipts involved in delivering goods to its customers. The service operated six days a week, covering around 30 London postal areas. The management of the garden centre was initially shocked at their findings, but then used the information to close the gap between costs and income as well as offering their customers a better service.

How did the garden centre set about making these changes? Their first reaction on seeing the figures in 1995 was to discontinue deliveries. After careful thought they decided their reputation for service would suffer too much, but were still determined to cut the real cost to the company. The most dramatic change was to make the full-time driver redundant, sell him the Bedford truck at a notional figure and give him a cost-per-delivery contract for as much of their work as he wanted. This was supplemented by a local carrier for very heavy goods, minicabs for light and local deliveries (often combined with taking the customer home) and the occasional use of the manager's car for emergency deliveries. A perceived problem was the lack of a truck at the garden centre for occasional collections of purchased goods. After a while it was realised that most such collections had been uneconomic, and better purchase planning removed the need anyway! The figures shown above demonstrate the real benefit to both customers and garden centre from the reorganisation.

Other delivery options for retailers

The examples below are taken from current practice in DIY and garden centres in the UK.

(1) All deliveries free within a stated radius of the store.
(2) Deliveries charged for on a scale increasing with distance.
(3) The above, modified to reduce (or waive) the charge on high value purchases.
(4) Roof-racks are rented or sold to customers to fit to their own car to take the goods away.
(5) Light trucks and/or trailers are lent/hired to the customer to transport their own goods.
(6) A cab-call service is maintained for customers.
(7) In-store advertising is used to encourage customers to take goods with them, i.e. the goods you take away arrive home today.

There are so many possible areas to save costs and increase profit potential that you may feel so confused you never start on the process. Let me suggest that you write down just the first three areas that you think of, pick the simplest one and concentrate on that alone until you have achieved a better result. You will note I do not say a *perfect* result. The second reason for doing nothing is the inability to accept less than perfection. If what you have changed is measurably better, that is good enough *for now*. You will find you come back to this initial problem again sometime in the future, after you have tackled many bigger or more complex ones. You will then laugh that you ever thought it difficult and will achieve an even better result.

The more you manage to inject an element of fun and adventure into these profit-creating changes and the more you involve your staff in the whole process and the rewards, the more certain and profitable the future of your business will be.

Ten myths and old wives' tales about stock and profit

1 Double your stock to double your trade.

2 If you cannot see the hole in the fence, no-one else can.

3 Plants grow best when they are lying down.

4 Buy plenty of goods at the start of the year and profit from the inevitable price increases later on.

5 Plants increase in health and value the longer they sit at a garden centre.

6 If you have priced your goods cheaper than the place down the road you must be doing better than them.

7 Plants can always be left round the back to get better.

8 If you like it, your customers are sure to.

9 Leave the stock around for long enough and it will sell itself.

10 Dust on everything is what attracts people to garden centres.

True story: Ignore your profits and they will soon go away.

BLOOMING AWFUL GARDEN CENTRE LTD

The diagram on page 78 shows the result of applying various profit-raising ideas to the Blooming Awful Garden Centre Ltd. The top diagram is a representation of the Trading and Profit and Loss Account shown conventionally on page 46. Cases 1, 2 and 3 each show a different way of tackling the low profitability of this centre. Case 1 assumes 10% growth in sales, while achieving the *same* gross margin (i.e. real growth, not just massive discounting). Overheads are shown rising in line with sales, but do they have to?

Case 2 assumes a 5% drop in overheads. This sounds modest but it can be difficult to achieve. How would you trim £6,000 from the overheads on page 46 without compromising safety or customer service? At least all those savings go straight on to the net profit.

Case 3 assumes a 5% increase in mark-up. *Note:* this can only be done on goods without a recommended selling price (i.e. unbranded goods – usually plants, some gift lines and furniture). If plants represent half of your sales mark them up by 10% extra for an average increase of 5% on your total sales – one of the authors did this successfully at his garden centre. Note that now net profit rises from £3,000 to £21,000.

Case 4 assumes that you combine all of the above. The results are dramatic! A tenfold increase in net profit from £3,000 to £31,000. Yes it is realistic and it can be achieved.

10 Managing staff

What is a manager? Management styles. Organisational culture. The politics of the workplace. Overview of the employment process.

Human beings are the most complex organisms that we know of. They are amazingly strong, weak, resilient, fragile, innovative and resistant to change. Physical or chemical indoctrination can make them all but immune to pain and injury, while psychic or spiritual rejection can sometimes kill, without any visible harm.

In short, a person's relationship with other people and the view they have of themselves will determine their social and work effectiveness and even, in the extreme, their survival. This is not to say that a person's physical surroundings and well-being are not important. On the contrary, a poor or inappropriate environment can make a radical difference to the performance potential of most people.

There is a wide range of management textbooks on all aspects of human relationships in the workplace. A manager should be familiar with the theories despite the fact that they do not all have practical application. Indeed, many of them become, for a while, almost mystical pseudo-solutions to all business ills. They are then perceived as not being a panacea and are discarded in favour of the next magic bullet. No theory ever solved a problem on its own. However understanding a theory may provide the basis for a change in actions, or the way of looking at a particular problem. If those changes are then worked at consistently, a long-term improvement in some part of your business may result.

A summary of the major theories is shown overleaf. The authors have found elements of the work of Maslow, McGregor, Herzberg and Johnson and Blanchard useful in understanding the people they work with and in dealing with many of the difficult situations that arise in any working relationship. It will be noticed that most of these concepts have been around for quite a long time.

Apart from the theories, there are a number of 'how-to' books available for those unsure of their style with people, or who are perhaps suffering from a lack of confidence after a run of encounters with 'difficult' people. Possibly the most famous of these is *One Minute Manager* by Johnson and Blanchard. One of the authors had several of the key messages from this book Sellotaped to his office wall and referred to them regularly. The advantage of the how-to type of books is that there is little need to get involved in possibly complex

Organisational theorists, chronologically from the mid-19th century, and their dominant viewpoint*

Henri Fayol	Rational, structured approach to management of organisations
F W Taylor	Measurement and control of jobs by 'scientific management'
Frank Lilian Gilbreth	Use of method study to find the one best way of doing a job
L F Urwick	Achieving the most efficient form of organisation structure by the adoption of certain 'principles'
E F L Brech	Combination of Fayol and Urwick
Max Weber	Organisational efficiency by means of a 'rational-legal' system of authority, ie 'bureaucracy'
Elton Mayo	Social needs at work are as important as economic and physical needs
Joan Woodward	Technology and the technical demands of production make a significant impact on organisational choice
Abraham Maslow	People are primarily motivated by a range of needs arranged in an ascending hierarchy
Douglas McGregor	Underlying managerial behaviour are two basic sets of assumptions: Theory X – people need to be coerced and controlled to perform; Theory Y – people can be self-directing and self-motivating
F Herzberg	People need to find motivating factors in their jobs if they are to experience job satisfaction
Victor Vroom	People will be motivated to the extent that they can perceive links between effort, performance and rewards available
Tavistock Group	Organisations are socio-technical systems interacting with their external environment
Aston Group	Factors such as size, technology, location and type of ownership affect the structure of organisations
Lawrence & Lorsch	Different states of differentiation (specialisation and attitudes) and integration (quality of collaboration) produce different possibilities of success in achieving economic objectives

*Adapted from Cole, 1988

theories before being able to recognise and practise actual techniques of management in your everyday work.

WHAT IS A MANAGER?

A person who directs or manages an organisation, industry, shop,etc.
(Collins English Dictionary).

The dictionary definition is almost useless in throwing any light on the subject but the extracts below give a reasonable picture of the function of a manager.

The manager's job can, therefore, be broadly defined as deciding what should be done and then getting other people to do it.

(Rosemary Stewart, *The Reality of Management*)

The functions of management include:
1) Establishing overall purpose and policy
2) Forecasting and planning for the future
3) Organizing work, allocating duties and responsibilites
4) Giving instructions or orders
5) Control – checking that performance is according to plan
6) Co-ordinating the work of others

(Huczynski and Buchanan, *Organizational Behaviour*)

While this may give an outline of the technical aspects of a manager's job, it throws no light on the related but even more elusive concept of leadership. One of the accepted aspects of leadership is the sense of mission that leaders have. It is distinct from the technical skills of management but can enhance them considerably. The sense of mission can relate to the specific task the leader is engaged in, or it can be a more general view of life and purpose. Anyone who has an inward sense of purpose will usually seem to others to transmit it – which is a practical dimension of leadership. The two examples below are intended to illustrate the inner and outer aspects of leadership.

Mission or purpose

What sort of people are we?

What do we want from life?

How do we relate to others?

What do we learn from them?

What sort of people do we want to help our staff become?

What will they learn from us?

How will they answer the questions above?

Effective Expansive Personality

Bob Kaplan of the Centre for Creative Leadership identified six characteristics central to the personality of a leader. He called his model Expansive Personality. The six points are:

- A need for mastery
- An active, assertive and persistent attitude
- A belief in self
- A goal-orientated relationship
- A need for recognition
- An ability to accept the need for self-development

Hard work and dedication pays but beware becoming a workaholic.

Car parks are key elements in any garden or plant centre and their design is as important as the centre itself [courtesy Morden Hall, Haskins Garden Centre and Hadlow College Plant Centre]

Staff need to be aware of the damage pests can do, not only to the stock but to the centre's image. These Viburnum davidii are in a prominent display bed showing signs of vine weevil damage

A neat gift ideas area [courtesy Ruxley Manor Garden Centre]

A neat houseplant area [courtesy Squires Garden Centre]

And with some humour ! [Squires]

Scale of houseplants [courtesy Old Barn Nursery, Horsham]

A display of bonsai

Simple, dramatic, appropriate

A garden centre in the Netherlands

*A good display garden that could
benefit from sales impact*

*A good array
of impulse plants
which lack
point-of-sale
material*

Properly designed, a display can 'bring products to life' [courtesy Millbrook Garden Centre]

The 'nursery fresh' approach to sales [courtesy Garson Farm Garden Centre]

Colour packs
- well signposted

A well-ordered bedding area [courtesy Haskins Garden Centre]

Lewisias in the correct orientation [courtesy Millbrook Garden Centre]

Out of the many books on this subject, *Effective Teambuilding* by John Adair seems to the authors to be one of the most accessible and useful (see page 95). Whether you are a manager or a leader, you will have a certain style in the way you deal with others, which will influence how they react to you.

MANAGEMENT STYLES

A senior personnel officer from a famous retail company was asked recently by a new management recruit how it was that each store had the same logo, uniforms, and management structure and yet each store had a completely different feel to it. The answer from the personnel officer (hopefully tongue in cheek) was that they had not yet found a way of standardising people, unlike products and systems. It is certainly true that all the people who work in an organisation interact to create a unique blend or feel. It is also true that regardless of whether the business is a small independent outlet, or a branch of a multiple, the person in charge of the site (the manager) uses his or her leadership style to determine the way that outlet works.

The text on the right show various ways of understanding the different approaches managers may adopt with staff. A manager may adopt a range of different styles with different people at different times. This is not unfair or inconsistent – those words would only be appropriate if abuse of authority were present. Blanchard and Zigarmi deal with this very difficult area in another of their books *Leadership and the One Minute Manager*. When you have compared this model with the one on the next page, you will see the essential similarities.

Each person has to develop their own management style. This is an area where watching one's own bosses and taking the best of their practice, judiciously laced with a little theory and topped with your own experience is probably the best way. Whatever you do, act with integrity.

> **Leadership and the one-minute manager**
>
> The four basic leadership styles defined by Blanchard & Zigarmi (Willow Books, 1986) are:
>
> **Directing** – which involves specific instructions and close supervision
>
> **Coaching** – in which the supervision is accompanied by explanation, involvement and support
>
> **Supporting** – in which the leader gives the subordinate help and support, sharing the decision-making process
>
> **Delegating** – in which subordinates are given responsibility for decision making and problem solving

A simplified version of the model shown on the next page suitable for training junior managers is as follows:

TELL   SELL   CONSULT   JOIN   DELEGATE   <u>ABDICATE</u>

The abdicate statement (not part of the original model) is a warning that at the end of the day, managers have to manage!

Abdication is often the reaction of people who are out of their depth for whatever reason. Many inexperienced managers and most managers at the limits of their tolerance tend to fall back on the autocratic 'tell' mode of managing. While effective in getting a short-term reaction from people, it is frequently extremely counterproductive, especially with

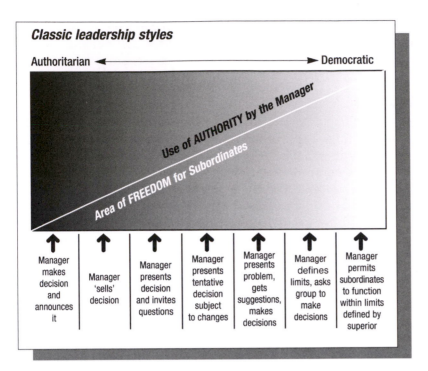

Classic leadership styles

Authoritarian ◄────────────────► Democratic

Use of AUTHORITY by the Manager

Area of FREEDOM for Subordinates

| Manager makes decision and announces it | Manager 'sells' decision | Manager presents decision and invites questions | Manager presents tentative decision subject to changes | Manager presents problem, gets suggestions, makes decisions | Manager defines limits, asks group to make decisions | Manager permits subordinates to function within limits defined by superior |

experienced or senior staff. Days, weeks or months of painstaking trust and performance building may be blighted in a single hasty or stressed moment. Almost the only circumstances when a totally authoritarian approach is necessary is at moments of physical danger or to prevent illegal acts.

ORGANISATIONAL CULTURE

Apart from the 'feel' that each manager and group of staff give to a business, there is the concept of organisational culture. This can be summarised as 'the way we do things around here'. It is most noticeable to people in an organisation when their business is taken over by another – which is happening to a growing extent in the garden centre world. This sense of change, loss and alienation often leads to resentments that cause staff in the taken over business to leave after quite a short period of time. It can also happen to people moved between teams or departments in a business, or when a new manager or supervisor is appointed to an existing small organisation. Again, of course there is a plethora of theories.

The one chosen here is from *Understanding Organisations* by Charles Handy.

Handy (1976) identified four models of organisational culture: role culture, task culture, power culture and person culture.

In *role culture* (bureaucracy) authority is drawn largely from position power and exercised through rules and procedures by top management. An example would be a government office.

Task culture puts the emphasis on getting the job done. It is characterised by teamwork and expert rather than position power is dominant. An example would be the emergency services.

In the *power culture* model, results matter most and power is in the hands of one or two people at the centre of an organisation in which the dominant influence is resource power. An example would be entrepreneurial business.

Person culture empowers the individual to do what they do best. In this model the organisation is subordinate to the individual and expert power is dominant. An example would be a barrister's chambers.

THE POLITICS OF THE WORKPLACE

Many people have come into the garden centre trade from other areas of business. Often such people quote the office 'politics' as a reason for leaving the city, the engineering works, teaching or whatever else they may have done previously. Every organisation has politics within it. It is a precondition of any group of humans that each person will see the task in hand, their role in it or the organisation itself as needing some change – often in that person's favour! When politics is blamed for dissatisfaction, falling productivity and staff leaving, it is almost always shorthand for the management not doing their job well. There is a well-known phrase in the Army that 'there are no bad soldiers, only bad officers'. While sounding rather extreme and ridiculous at first, a few moments' reflection will reveal the underlying truth in the saying. One might hazard a guess that 'there are no bad workers, only bad managers' will contain the same basic truths.

Most work in garden centres is done in small teams. With a very small business, there may effectively be only one team. As the business grows there will be a collection of teams, more or less interdependent, often with their own sub-cultures and agendas. Management will never prevent this. The trick is to recognise what is happening, how it affects the work and to harness the energy and strength of work groups to the benefit of the whole business.

The concept of power has been mentioned in the above text. This is a very specific use of the word power. Anyone with authority has some level of power and in fact, anyone in an organisation has at least the power to throw a spanner in the works and cause problems. The following text shows one of the models which seeks to explain this phenomenon.

FORMS OF MANAGERIAL POWER

According to Handy (1976) there are various forms of power available to managers: physical power, resource power, position power, expert power, personal power and negative power. Physical force is an unlikely management tool, but resource power – eg through the pay packet – can be deployed by the smaller enterprise though this is difficult in corporate concerns. Position power depends on the privileges afforded to the holder of the post, eg work allocation and access to information.

Expertise empowers the holder with expert power, but it must be recognised and valued by others. Personality (when recognised) can impart personal power while negative power arises when individuals are in a position to create dysfunctional circumstances.

Having power is one thing but using it wisely and effectively is one of the most difficult tasks any person ever faces. The corrupting nature of unchecked power is widely known. In business terms, it can cause untold damage to relationships with staff, customers and suppliers. The consequences can include legal, financial and even physical problems. Not only is it crucial to avoid the obvious problems associated with misuse of power, it is also important to avoid the unintentional difficulties caused by misunderstandings.

The teams formed in the workplace have lives of their own. This requires understanding if the best for the individual, the team and the overall business is to be achieved. People come together in all sorts of groups during their lives – family, school, church. social and sporting groups to mention just a few. Work groups or teams are not intrinsically different

Examples of how groups may exist in the workplace

Business type	Team leader	Team members	Tasks	Power types typically used	Typical cultural model adapted
Small, 6 staff	Owner/manager	All other staff	Whole range of work; little or no specialisation	Owner: most Others: expert	Often, power culture Team reaction: 'Cope or quit'
Medium, say 6 full-time and 8 part-time staff	1. Owner/manager	Part-time delivery Part-time office Full-time shop (2) Part-time shop (3)	Goods in/out Book-keeping, paperwork All dry goods, tills and general duties	Owner: most Office: expert Full-time shop: expert	Task or power: if power culture more resistance by 'experts' trying to operate a task culture in their own areas of the business.
	2. House-plant supervisor	Part-timer (1)	Houseplants and related sundries	Supervisor: expert	
	3. Outdoor	Full-timer (1) Part-timer (2)	Hardy plants, paving, pots, etc.	Supervisor and full-time plants: expert	
Large, say 20 full-time and up to 30 part-time	1. Owner/general manager	Office: Personnel Training Book-keeping Secretarial Marketing	Specialist functions as stated – full- or part-time	Owner: most Office: expert	Task or role culture – very difficult to maintain power culture without major problems
	2. Shop manager	Full-time shop (2) Part-time (up to 4)	Purchasing, display and sales of sundries	Manager: most Full-time: expert	As above
	a. Till supervisor	Full-time (up to 3) Part-time (up to 5)	Tills and other duties as needed	Supervisor: expert	As above
	b. House-plant supervisor c. Machinery supervisor d. Furniture, barbeque and Christmas supervisor	Part-time (up to 3) Part-time (up to 3) Full-time (1) Part-time (2–3)			
	3. Plant area manager (outdoor plants)	Full-time (3) Part-time (3–5)	Purchasing, display and sales of appropriate product goods	Expert	Task culture
	a. Outdoor sundries supervisor b. Buildings supervisor c. Water gardening supervisor	Full-time (1) Part-time (up to 3) Part-time (1) Part-time (1 or 2)			
	4. Teashop manager	Full-time (1) Part-time (2–6)	Purchasing, display, sales and service. Food Act 1990.		

from all the others however, there are certain characteristics of work groups worth looking at. Work groups are:

- Set up for a purpose not defined by the group members
- May be adapted or ended by others outside the group
- Must relate to the larger organisation on its terms
- Are bound by legislation as well as the internal rules of the whole organisation, along with the group's own norms and values
- May have a leader imposed from outside

From among the many books on work groups, the authors have chosen the Adair model to illustrate the way groups form and function and to show how the group leader or manager has to focus on three interrelated issues at once.

One of the key reasons for understanding and assisting the development of teams and individuals in a business is to foster a sense of professionalism. Everyone thinks they can define, or at least recognise professionalism when they meet it. The model developed and used by the authors is shown below. By focusing on specific and quantifiable issues it is felt that it may be used directly to establish and monitor norms of professional behaviour in most businesses.

Once the senior managers in a business are ready to create and act on the professional integrity of their staff, the business is poised for a radical change. Considerable additional demands will be placed on all members of the organisation. Conversely, large extra sources of energy and creativity may be tapped, with major gains in all aspects of the firm's performance. A list (by no means exhaustive) of the various areas of the business that may be improved by such a policy is shown overleaf.

The sections above show several levels of staff interacting in the workplace. There is a general view that there are three different key roles in work teams – the worker, supervisor and manager.

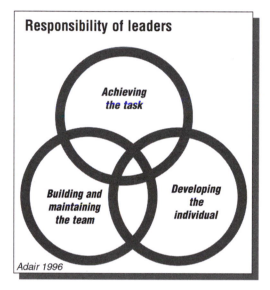

Responsibility of leaders

Achieving the task

Building and maintaining the team

Developing the individual

Adair 1996

Hallmarks of a professional

A professional is:

- self-critical
- self-motivated
- self-training

A professional supervisor/manager assists others by:

- constructive criticism
- encouraging motivation
- helping them to learn

We as professionals help others to fashion the basic tools of their professional lives. They develop the application, skills and attention to detail to become truly professional.

What we do is informed by what what we are …

Effects of widespread professionalism in a business

The effect on COMMUNICATION with ...

- ... **the Workforce**: increased willingness to communicate – questions decisions and procedures.
- ... **the Supervisory Management**: increased willingness to discuss with workforce and to question senior management.
- ... **the Line and Senior Management**: increased willingness to communicate – to review established practices and mode of operation.

The benefits for ...

- ... **the Workforce**: increased commitment to implement decisions once discussions complete.
- ... **the Supervisory Management**: increased commitment to implement decisions once discussions complete plus increased confidence in executing and enforcing decisions.
- ... **the Line and Senior Management**: chance of real improvements filtering up the organisation.

Creates atmosphere for clear enunciation, acceptance and implementation of company policy and action.

The effect on QUALITY for ...

- ... **the Workforce**: increased willingness to monitor own results and seek improvements.
- ... **the Supervisory Management**: increased willingness to monitor own results and seek improvements plus increased confidence to offer and receive help from all levels.
- ... **the Line and Senior Management**: increased willingness to accept others might be right – greater confidence in demanding the correct standards.

Creates atmosphere for quality issues to be accepted as vital and non-threatening. IIP (Investors in People) becomes a reality.

The effect of PERSONAL DEVELOPMENT on ...

- ... **the Workforce**: increased desire for training and recognition of achievements.
- ... **the Supervisory Management**: increased desire for training and recognition of achievements plus increased ability to handle counselling and appraisals.
- ... **the Line and Senior Management**: increased desire for training and recognition of achievements plus raised awareness of new issues and skills relevant to the business.

The benefits for ...

- ... **the Workforce**: increased ability to handle more complex tasks, be more flexible and able to relate to customers more effectively.
- ... **the Supervisory Management**: increased ability to handle technical and interpersonal issues with confidence, accuracy and sensitivity.
- ... **the Line and Senior Management**: increased ability to add new concepts and practices to existing fund of knowledge and experience.

Creates atmosphere for effective communications at and between all levels of the business.

The role of a supervisor is probably both the most crucial and most difficult one to undertake in any organisation. If owners can retain the support of their supervisors in any business problem, they can carry the rest of the organisation with them. Supervisors equate to sergeants in the Army. Anyone who has been in the armed forces will say without hesitation that the sergeants really run it! The same is true for virtually all businesses. The panel below shows the role and skills demanded of a supervisor, who is clearly seen as a hybrid between manager and worker.

Role of a supervisor

Worker	*Supervisor*	*Manager*
Does the job	Does the job. Is responsible for output of own team	Responsible for ensuring job is done professionally and profitably

A supervisor:

- Represents management to staff and staff management
- Must report outcomes accurately to management
- Must be clear as to responsibilities and authority
- Must be professional in outlook

Practical supervisory skills

Management expectations:

- Achieve targets
- Early notice of problems
- Best use of resources
- Good team control
- Accurate, timely reporting

Staff expectations:

- Clear targets and instructions
- Fair and consistent treatment
- Pre-work organisation
- On-site planning and leadership
- Positive reinforcement of good working practices and attitudes
- Setting a good example

All the understanding of the people processes at play in the business, and all the inspirational effort put into the people working for a business will, however, be largely wasted if the legal and organisational fundamentals are ignored. As always, there is a wide range of specialist books available. The main technical areas for all businesses to consider include those below.

OVERVIEW OF THE EMPLOYMENT PROCESS

Note: It is very important to obtain good professional advice on all relevant legal matters before employing anyone. For those who are members of the HTA or the GCA, both organisations have information and services available to their members which can greatly assist this process. The DSS and Employment Offices also have a range of leaflets which cover the basic outlines.

From the first instance where the creation of a new job or the extension of an existing one is considered, a well-organised business of any size will have a system to manage the process and any arising problems. The panels below are adapted from *Personnel Management* by G A Cole.

Recruitment planning

	Ask	*Do*
New vacancies	What extra jobs are being created?	Check demand within departments
Staff losses	Estimate of labour turnover?	Confirm monthly
Staff specification	What skills will be needed?	Match with departmental forecasts
Promotion prospects	Who is ready for an upward move?	Consult staff appraisal records
New recruits	Is the labour market bullish?	Check personnel files, local newspapers
Budgeting	How much to spend on recruiting?	Monitor the budget
Timetable	When will recruits be needed?	Confirm with departmental heads
Personnel department	Can the 'personnel' staff cope?	Check the personnel budget

---

Job descriptions

Features of the job

Job title, location, immediate superior, relationships with other tasks, overall purpose, main duties and responsibilities, level of authority, resources provided, qualifications required.

Key considerations

- Why does the post exist?
- What results are expected?
- What are the key tasks?
- How much authority goes with it in terms of spending and 'hiring and firing'?
- What budget goes with the job?
- How many staff report?
- What equipment, vehicles etc. are committed to the post?
- What qualifications/experience are required?

STAFF SELECTION

Having lined up a suitable selection of candidates, the prospective employer should remember that it is a two-way street. He/she should expect to 'sell' the organisation to the candidates during the interviews. This will be very important with any applicants who will be offered appointments.

The stages in the selection process are:

- drawing up a shortlist of candidates from the application forms and CVs
- arranging interviews
- conducting the interviews (including any tests)
- taking up references
- choosing the successful candidate(s) – if any!
- making a job offer and confirming it

Arguably, the induction process for the new staff member(s) is also part of the recruitment process. All of us remember very vividly the first day at a new school, college or job. The combination of new surroundings and being on one's best behaviour ensures that the memory and associated impressions stick. How favourable are those first

The induction experience

How do people feel when they start a new job?

What are the legal/human requirements for induction?
- Contract of employment
- Health and safety aspects
- Familiarisation: premises, staff, systems

First impressions count but:
- do not judge people on them
- integrate into work team
- explain things and support newcomer

Appraise after one month

Staff procedures

APPRAISAL

- Pro-active
- Company procedures
- Past and future work performance
  - decouple from pay
  - adequate preparation
  - mutual feedback

COUNSELLING

- Reactive
- Company procedures
- Initial assessment
  - nature of problem (masking?)
  - personal/work based?
  - reference to other agencies
  - link to disciplinary

DISCIPLINARY

- Reactive
- Statutory basis
- Breaches of law/company rules
  - escalation process
  - strict procedures
  - cost of getting it wrong

GRIEVANCE

- Reactive
- Statutory basis
- Breaches of law/company rules
  - HASAWA/COSHH
  - others involved
  - links to personal PR

Confidentiality   Preparation   Suitability of venue   Records memories? How good is your business at leaving new staff with good memories of their induction day? This and the counterpart first impressions the new staff make on you are summarised on page 99.

For all the rest of their time with you, your staff still have a call on your support, encouragement and if necessary, your disapproval. These ongoing procedures should be in line with the law and good practice. The summary on page 99 shows the relationship between the various procedures and identifies those with a statutory basis.

If you have to let a worker go, for whatever cause, do so in the most professional and generous manner possible. Your employment reputation is as valuable as any other and word travels very fast if you are perceived as better or worse than the average. Also, you may want a person to work for you again at some time; indeed you may one day have to seek work at the hands of a former employee!

SUMMARY

People are the major asset not appearing on the balance sheet. Without people to work for the business and others to patronise it, there would be no business. This chapter has looked at some of the things that must be done well in order to maximise the asset of staff. Unlike all other assets though, the human ones can assert their independence and probably more consistent care, thought and concern on the part of a manager goes into the human aspects of their business than into any other.

One final thought for those who do not think their staff deserve the best and most professional management available.

Thought for the day

We, the unwilling, led by the unknowing, have done so much with so little, for so long, that we are almost qualified to do anything, with nothing, for ever!

Anon

---

11 Training and development

The background to training. The national training picture. Training plan. Benefits from training. Investors in people.

Four words are commonly used more or less interchangeably in connection with the development of staff.

COACHING – To tutor, give hints to, prime with facts. (Collins English Dictionary)
EDUCATION – Bringing up of the young ... systematic instruction. (Concise Oxford Dictionary) – Act or process of acquiring knowledge . (Collins)
INSTRUCTION – Teaching, directions, orders. (Oxford) – Teach someone to do something, to furnish with information. (Collins)
TRAINING – Bringing a person to the desired state or standard of efficiency by instruction and practice. (Collins)

The commonly understood implication of education is that it is a general process. Basic academic skills are acquired and any facts or skills relevant to a particular trade or profession are only incidental. Most businesses seek to acquire previously educated staff but recognise the need to impart extra information relevant to the post or task in question.

Training is the word most often used to describe this task or job-specific knowledge and implies a mixture of theory and how-to instruction combined with practice of the task(s) to achieve commercial efficiency. This is the basis of NVQ qualifications.

Coaching carries the slightly different implication of being usually a one-to-one activity with the aim of improving a person's specific performance in some area of their job as well as maybe their underlying attitude and motivation.

By looking at the differences in these various terms, the range of activities and techniques for staff development should become clearer.

THE BACKGROUND TO TRAINING

College-based training and education has been the subject of means-tested grants in this country for over forty years. A division has been made between Higher and Further education which has recently acquired a real meaning. Further education (which is typically all courses below Higher National Diploma level) has been seen as predominantly vocational rather than academic. The grants are also discretionary, which means that when the money runs out; so do the grants. Higher education has mandatory grants. If you get accepted onto an approved course you will be eligible to apply for a grant, although the absolute value is declining fast.

The reason for this is that recent governments have felt it right to move the cost of full-time education and training onto the shoulders of those benefiting from it. Where courses have been run as full-time residential courses (as are the bulk of the traditional National Diploma courses in horticulture and agriculture) there has often been a marked drop off in take-up. Among other reasons this is due to the cultural expectation that the government will pick up the tab. For the same reason, most nurseries and garden centres expect to find freshly qualified staff at craft and supervisory grades emerging each year from the specialist colleges.

Methods of undertaking training

Delivery	Mode	Outcome	
College based	Full-time courses	Higher education	Degree
	Block release courses		HND
	Day release courses		HNC
	Evening classes	Further education	HNC
			ND
			NC
			1st Diploma
			1st Certificate
		NVQ	All levels
		Statutory training	
In-house training by our staff	Shop floor based informal (during working hours)	Company recognition	
	Shop floor or training centre based (outside working hours)	NVQs All levels	
	Distance learning		
Local training groups	Shop floor or training centre based – outside working hours	Statutory training	
		– forklift	
		– First Aid	
		– food hygiene	
		HTA training programme	
		Company recognition	
Personal interest	Distance learning	City & Guilds	
	Radio & TV programmes	NVQ	
	Short courses or evening classes at own cost	RHS certificate	
		College/company aware	
		Statutory training	

This is no longer true and is unlikely to be so again. The responsibility for training and developing staff is falling back on employers, individuals and their families. The advice being given by the authors and many others involved in training our industry is to 'grow your own' trained staff. The panel above shows the typical and probable future patterns of training in the industry.

The changes of funding for training will not completely change the pattern shown above. It will accelerate the tendency for full-time courses to be more localised because of the lower costs of studying from home. With subjects like English, this is not a problem, as the number of students is great enough to guarantee plenty of colleges offering the subject. Students will have a good chance of being able to study English close to home (even if not at the college of their ideal choice).

With specialist subjects like garden centre and nursery stock skills, the student pool has always been too small to support more than a few courses at any one time. This causes many students to abandon their favoured courses and so reduce the pool of students further still. This downward spiral will cause the closure of many well-known agriculture and horticulture colleges in the next few years unless they enter other areas of training and education provision. No college in the UK is currently offering a full-time garden centre course but several are including a garden centre option in their commercial horticulture courses, or are running garden centre courses as block or day release.

Hadlow College in Kent has got not one but two small garden centres as part of the training units. These trade on a fully commercial basis and act as a living laboratory for the retail and management aspects of Hadlow's courses. Several other colleges have some retail trading, but the authors believe that they operate a limited stock range and opening hours.

The national training picture

Garden centres are probably neither worse nor better than other businesses when it comes to training. As a nation, we are not good at appreciating the value of training. Recent research ranked the UK 32 out of a sample of 41 nations for in-company training and 34 out of 41 for willingness of staff to learn new skills.

The 1990s started the process of movement from maximising the physical assets of a company to maximising its people assets. This will accelerate through the next decade with the creative and learning powers of a company's people becoming the key factors for success. These creative and learning powers are not acquired by osmosis, rather they are the result of training, application and practice. With the speed of change of technology, this process will quicken and the prize will go to those businesses who have not only kept up but are near the front of the race. In this setting, training is less about cost and more about obtaining competitive advantage in the marketplace.

To give an example, it was reported in 1995 in the USA that the market for garden services (design, landscape and maintenance) had exceeded the garden products retail sale value for the first time ever and that the trend was set to continue. This is a trend which is headed the same way here in Britain. These growth areas are more service, or people-skill orientated than retail operations.

How to get benefit from training

Training is an investment of time, money, people and energy. As with any other investment, there must be a reason for the investment in the first place and it must be properly evaluated for its use to the business after it has happened.

Training: its relevance and benefit

When contemplating the provision of training, an employer needs to ask a series of questions:

- What skills does the business need or will need?
- Which aspects of the business will benefit?
- How will the business have to change to accommodate a trained workforce?
- Will training help you achieve business objectives and if so what type?
- The company will also have to decide how it is to deliver training.
- Who will be responsible?
- Departmental managers or an individual with specific, overall responsibility?
- Do those people have the necessary skills to create a training function, or will they need support, perhaps from a specialist training agency?
- How will the outcome of the training be monitored?

The latter is vital if training is to succeed and it starts with having a clear idea of what you expect training to achieve. From there you can decide how to evaluate the training provision while measuring the outcome.

Reasons for not investing in training

- In a very small business, the owner often sees training as not just irrelevant but as a triple whammy. When someone goes on a training course, the owner has to pay the wages of the trainee, the fees and expenses of the course and a second set of wages for the trainee's replacement for the duration of the course.
- Slightly larger businesses view it as a C category (nice to have) item when they are prioritising their spending plans for the next period. They do not recognise training as a key factor for business success.
- Any business insufficiently large to have a dedicated training officer is also at a disadvantage. The company may think it has a training culture but it lacks the champion in the ranks that the TO represents. Come the board meetings and training slips down the list.

Training can be initiated at various levels

- The organisation itself can undergo a quality assurance process that has the people-centred approach at the heart of business success. This is the Investors in People programme and the IIP Standard gives an excellent model for any business to follow, whether or not your particular business is going for the standard itself.
- Managers are critical to an organisation's performance. The skills of management have to be taught as much as the craft and supervisory skills. Training lower down the organisation is less efficient if managers are not themselves trained and supportive towards training. A recent survey carried out by the MCI (the management training lead body) showed a range of benefits that a range of businesses experienced as a result of management development programmes.
- **MCI survey.** MCI asked 1,000 businesses to assess the benefits of management development. It identified several measurable benefits and the top two were 'Improved efficiency/productivity' (35%) and 'Improved management ability and quality' (34%). Close behind came 'Increased competitive ability' (29%) and 'Improved quality of work' (20%). Equal fifth were 'Better staff motivation and morale' and 'Better communication skills'.

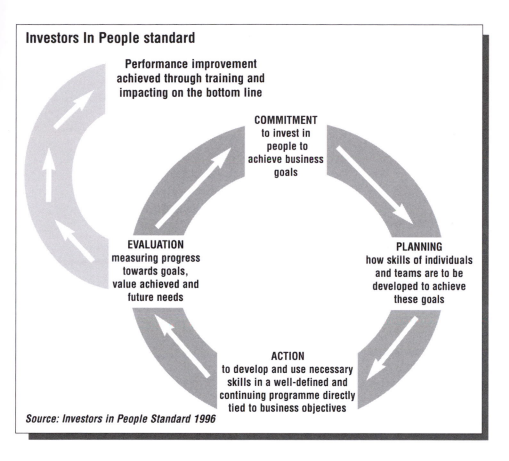

Investors In People standard

Performance improvement achieved through training and impacting on the bottom line

COMMITMENT to invest in people to achieve business goals

PLANNING how skills of individuals and teams are to be developed to achieve these goals

ACTION to develop and use necessary skills in a well-defined and continuing programme directly tied to business objectives

EVALUATION measuring progress towards goals, value achieved and future needs

Source: Investors in People Standard 1996

When should training be used?

Training is not the solution to all business problems. There are however a number of factors which point to a training solution. Where a situation has arisen which requires:

- improved confidence (with people, products, processes & place)
- specific technical skills (may or may not be statutorily required)
- increased knowledge (of 4 p's)

How to link training to business development

Objectives	How results are measured (A sample of possible measures)	Points of measurement
Mission statement	Gross profit % Net profit % Growth %	Whole organisation Departments
Long term aims (3–5 yrs)	Staff turnover rate 'absenteeism' 'development' Payback period for assets	Individuals ALSO
Seasonal aims (this year)	Average age of assets Use of new technologies	Customers Other stakeholders

- succession planning (developing people for promotion)
- motivation or re-motivation of a team or the whole workforce

then it is pretty certain that training will help the business solve the problem.

Whatever the parameters measured, consistency over time is crucial. Any failures to meet targets probably indicates a training need.

When analysing the business results consider:

(a) Were targets met?
(b) Could targets have been higher?
(c) How skilled was management in achieving the results?
(d) Are there clear skills and target links?
(e) For supervisors and workforce, ask (d) and (e)
(f) What training would help in matching or exceeding named targets?

However, isolated training is not very effective. Every business needs to make training part of its regular budgetary process. This will enable the business to plan for training in a structured and thoughtful way.

The training plan is an excellent way of getting planned, measurable benefit from the investment. Many garden centres still feel they lack the skills to organise a training plan but this can often be outlined with the help of a college or other training provider. Lantra, the management training arm of Landbase (previously the Agricultural Training Board)

Training plan

Training strategy	• Where are we now (performance measures) • What training do we need (type, cost, scope, outcomes) to reach our future goals (performance measures)
Training needs analysis	• Overall needs (as defined above) • Functional needs (e.g. checkout operations) • Personal needs (individual skills and interests) • Contingent needs (TEC requirements for modern apprentices to gain NVQ levels 2 and 3) • Business development needs (e.g. opening a teashop)
Training tactics	• Takes all the needs identified above • Cross-references to individuals and specific skills • Schedules a programme of training within an agreed budget • Identifies training providers and training types • Updates programme on a 3, 6 and 12 monthly basis • Reviews benefits/problems of training programme • Adjusts accordingly and continues

runs a widely recognised course in Training Needs Analysis. This provides a good way to get in-house expertise in this vital area. If the training planning and TNA are bought in, check that your adviser has the benefit of having been through the Lantra training in this area.

Finally, a mismatch of expectations between all the parties involved in training can cause upset and disillusionment with not only a particular programme but with training in general.

Training Provider	Trainee	Sponsor (pays for it)
Sells the training	The customer?	The customer?
Wants to deliver a standard package (ease and cost)	Often does not know what to expect; and is often not told	Wants training exactly tailored to solve present business problems
Can train in most venues unless there are technical barriers	Both on and off the work site have benefits and drawbacks	On site training causes least disruption and cost. Offsite training allows more feedback
Should have mastery of the subject	Should want to learn	Should be interested in outcomes and quality

SUMMARY

The authors have been in all three of the categories above. In their time as garden centre managers and subsequently as senior lecturers in the Hadlow College garden centre training programme they know how crucial training and development of staff is. Poaching staff from other centres is *not* a training policy despite the assertions of a senior manager in the industry quite recently. It is very difficult at the moment to offer clear advice on the best training route or package for any centre without a detailed knowledge of their plans and timescale. The HTA, GCA and NFU all have various programmes and packages available in addition to a list of college-based courses relevant to garden centres.

Training is like advertising, probably half the effort is wasted – the trick is to know which half! Training like advertising is not a luxury but a well-planned means of enhancing your business, your staff and yourself over the years.

Final thought

A garden centre owner was once approached by a trainer. In conversation the owner said, "I don't believe in spending money on training – they just go off and get jobs somewhere else after you've paid to train them!" "Ah!", replied the trainer. "But what if you don't train them and they stay?"

12 The law and the retailer

Common law and statute law. The nature of tort. Strict liability. Contract and sale of goods. FEPA and COSHH. Enforcing agencies. Sources of information.

'**A**s the creeper that girdles the tree-trunk, the Law runneth forwards and back.' So wrote Rudyard Kipling in *The Jungle Book*. It has always seemed a very apt quote when introducing legal issues to garden centre staff because the law is present in some way in every single thing that is said, done or omitted in the course of business. This chapter does not seek to replace the necessary advice all businesses need with respect to their various statutory obligations. Neither does it set out to be a legal textbook and cover all aspects of the law. Rather, it is designed to highlight those areas of the law that the trade at large seems to find onerous or difficult, or generally seems to be in ignorance of.

You will recognise the diagram below from the first chapter. In this instance it has been

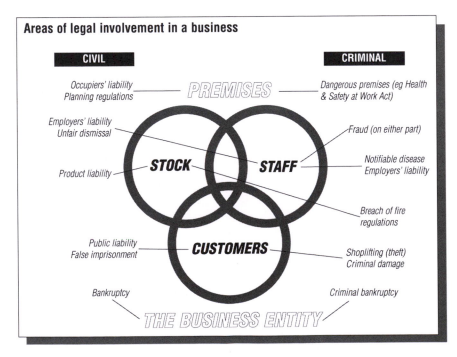

Areas of legal involvement in a business

CIVIL — CRIMINAL

Occupiers' liability
Planning regulations — PREMISES — Dangerous premises (eg Health & Safety at Work Act)

Employers' liability
Unfair dismissal — Fraud (on either part)

STOCK — STAFF

Notifiable disease
Employers' liability

Product liability

Breach of fire regulations

Public liability
False imprisonment — CUSTOMERS — Shoplifting (theft)
Criminal damage

Bankruptcy — Criminal bankruptcy

THE BUSINESS ENTITY

adapted to show all the areas of business that have some legislation concerned with them. The underlying concept is that of liability. This is a recognition of the fact that when people come onto your premises, buy your goods and services, answer your adverts or talk to your staff, they can expect a certain level of care or quality. Failure to provide such can lead to legal consequences for your business or even for you personally.

Some of the items listed above are statutory obligations, some arise from the common law. Some potential breaches will be civil, others criminal; others again may be both. A brief, non-technical summary of these concepts is given below. Like all simplifications, it is only an outline and subject to some inaccuracy.

There are many ways to classify law, the most fundamental distinction being that drawn between criminal and civil law.

Criminal law

A crime is regarded as a wrong done to the State. Prosecutions are usually commenced by the State, although they may be brought by a private citizen. If the prosecution is successful, the accused person (the defendant) is liable to punishment. Some crimes, eg rape, have specific victims while others, eg treason or speeding, can be committed without causing loss to any particular person. If there is a victim, he/she will not usually have a say in whether or not a prosecution is brought, nor will he/she benefit from a conviction since fines are payable to the State.

Criminal and civil hearings take place in different courts with different rules of procedure. There is also a different standard of proof. In a criminal trial the prosecution must prove the accused's guilt *beyond reasonable doubt*. In a civil case the plaintiff must prove his case on the *balance of probabilities*.

Civil law

Civil actions may be commenced by any person who seeks compensation for a loss which he has suffered. If the plaintiff is successful, he/she will usually be awarded damages. The damages must be paid by the defendant. Their purpose is to compensate the plaintiff for his/her loss rather than to punish the defendant. There are many categories of civil law, for example:

(a) *Contract*. This determines whether promises made by persons are enforceable.

(b) *Tort*. A tort is defined as the breach of a general duty imposed by law, for example the duty not to be negligent and the duty not to trespass on another person's property.

(c) *Property law*. This includes the law relating to freehold and leasehold land and the ownership and possession of goods.

(d) *Company law*. There is a need to regulate the relationship that a company has with its directors, shareholders, creditors and employees.

(e) *Commercial law*. This term covers contractual matters relating to business transactions, for example the law relating to sale of goods, consumer credit and cheques.

(f) *Employment law*. This also involves contractual relationships, in this case between employer and employee. The term also includes redundancy, unfair dismissal and health and safety at work.

(g) *Family law*. Marriage, divorce, nullity, guardianship and legitimacy are within the scope of family law.

Crime or civil wrong?

The distinction between a crime and a civil wrong is not found in the nature of the act itself, but in the legal consequences that follow it. Thus if a taxi driver crashes he may commit:

- A breach of contract, ie failure to deliver the passenger to his destination
- A tort, ie negligence if he causes damage to any person or property
- A crime, for example dangerous driving

In some situations the facts will therefore indicate both a criminal offence and a possible civil action. In such cases the victim will not be able to have both actions heard in the same court. He will have to start a civil action separate from any prosecution brought by the State. However the *S.11 Civil Evidence Act 1968* provides that in any civil proceedings the fact that a person has been convicted of an offence shall be admissible to prove that he committed that offence. The effect is to raise a presumption that he committed the offence unless the contrary is proved.

One of the key concepts is that the courts are at all times passive – simply waiting for problems to be brought before them. In criminal cases the State is equally passive. The most famous recent example of a criminal and civil action over the same event is that of O. J. Simpson; found innocent of murder (a criminal charge) but judged liable in the civil courts in the USA for damages arising from the victims' deaths. A shortlist of events that are covered by one or both arms of the law is shown below.

	Civil Law	*Criminal Law*
Quality of proof required for the successful prosecution of a case	The case must be shown on the balance of probabilities	The case must be proved beyond reasonable doubt
Range of penalties	Mostly financial	Financial Removal of liberty
Examples of matters under either or both arms of the law		
Murder	Damages	Prosecution
Rape	Damages	Prosecution
Theft	Damages	Prosecution
Assault and physical injury	Damages	Prosecution
Trespass	Damages	Only in case of criminal trespass
Libel, Slander	Damages	Only in case of criminal libel
Perjury		Prosecution
Contracts (general)	Damages or enforcements	Only where criminal acts (ie forgery) are present
Contracts for sale of goods	Damages or enforcements	Sale of Goods Act 1984
Names given to various parties in the cases	Aggrieved person: Plaintiff Person complained of: Defendant	Accusers: Police, Crown Prosecution Service, their lawyers – 'The Prosecution' Accused person: Defendant Their lawyer(s): 'The Defence'

COMMON LAW AND STATUTE LAW

Common law and statute law are the other main divisions within the law which it is useful to understand.

Common law is based on the largely verbal and local means of hearing complaints and obtaining justice that existed in Anglo-Saxon England. After the Norman conquest, judges travelled the country hearing cases under a variety of local laws. When they met together, they discussed and chose what seemed to them the best of these, so forming a body of Common law – the law of the people.

Statute law is that which arises from legislation in Parliament. These days it is the most important source of law in this country and in the European Union, to whose judgements the English courts are now subject. Originally, all laws came from the power of the monarch. Even today, all Acts of Parliament start with the words 'Be it enacted by the Queen's most gracious Majesty ...' although this is now a political fiction.

Statute law is now the greatest volume of law and the most important to retailers. Much of the common law has been swept up into it, although areas such as nuisance and trespass are still of importance to the garden centre trade. On the next page are some of the statutory areas of the law that a garden centre must consider.

Codes of Practice are not a full statement of the law. They are a practical means of ensuring that adequate measures have been put in place to comply with the particular legislation. They may either be published with the Act, with Regulations under the Act, or as an industry-led initiative to comply with the law. If the codes of practice are adhered to (and *documented* as necessary), a strong defence will be available if a breach of the law is alleged.

There are several important areas of common law to be considered as well. These fall under the general heading of tort – a word derived from the French 'J'ai tort' – I have been wronged.

THE NATURE OF TORT

A tort is caused by the breach of a duty owed to other people. The remedy is a civil action for damages. All of the below can affect a garden centre, although negligence is far and away the most common cause of action. To succeed in a negligence action a plaintiff must prove:

There are a variety of torts:

Type of wrong	Technical title	Practical example
Physical injury or other wrong to a person	Trespass to the person Negligence	Wrongful arrest or imprisonment Customer falls on broken paving
Interfering with the enjoyment of another's land	Nuisance Trespass to land 'Rylands and Fletcher'	Constant loud noise late at night Entering onto, or remaining on land uninvited Losing control of anything noxious held on your land
Defamation of the living	Slander Libel	Words that damage a person in a material way i.e. loss of their job Permanent form of the above i.e. in writing (can also be a crime)

Safety of:

Premises
- Health and Safety at Work Act
- Building Regulations
- Electrical Safety Act

Equipment
- Vehicle Construction and Use Regulations
- Forklift Use Regulations
- Food Act 1990 (Fridges and freezers)

Stock
- Food and Environmental Protection Act (FEPA) – Garden chemicals
- Control of Substances Hazardous to Health (COSHH)
- Phytosanitary Regulations (Imported plants)
- Sale and Storage of Fireworks Regulations
- Regulations for Sale and Storage of Liquefied Petroleum Gas (bottles & bulk)

Staff
- Health and Safety at Work Act, together with written Company Policy on safety (covers areas such as safe lifting, use of PPE ie steel toecap boots)
- Certificates of Competence and/or licences in respect of such items as:
  - Road vehicles
  - Forklift trucks
  - Chemical spraying
  - Food handling
  - Board and glass cutting equipment

Employment Law, with associated Codes of Practice for:
- Recruitment (including racial and sexual discrimination)
- Continuing employment (including unfair dismissal, Trades Union activities, racial or sexual harassment at work, TUPE – protection of workers' rights after takeovers)
- Termination of employment (including grievance and disciplinary procedures, redundancy arrangements etc.)

Finance
- Annual Returns of financial results for tax purposes
- Correct accounting and submission of VAT returns (inc. imports & exports)
- Correct and timely operation of PAYE and associated pay deductions
- Road Fund Licence for vehicles
- Rates and other local taxation

Trading
- Sale of Goods Act
- Supply of Goods and Services Act

(a) That the defendant owed him a duty of care
(b) That the defendant has been guilty of a breach of that duty
(c) That damage has been caused to the plaintiff by that breach

The burden of proof is on the plaintiff and he must prove all three points. The position is summarised on the previous page.

Trespass to land and 'Rylands and Fletcher' can be a two-way trade from a garden centre's point of view. Anything you do to your neighbours may be seen by them to be potentially actionable and vice versa. The commonsense approach is always to try to settle such disputes without recourse to the law. It may be a truism to say that only the lawyers benefit in such cases; the parties to the case very seldom do.

The duty of care owed by you to lawful visitors and trespassers is summarised here.

Occupiers' liability to lawful visitors

The duty of occupiers of premises towards lawful visitors is governed by the *Occupiers' Liability Act 1957*.

> **Significance of negligence liability for the garden centre operator**
>
> - Potential claims from most physical aspects of the operation
> - Vicarious liability for acts of employees in the course of their work (but not for independent sub-contractors)
>
> *Ways to minimise liability*
>
> - Tight business practices and systems (ie BS 5750, IIP)
> - Insurance cover
>   - employers' liability
>   - motor vehicles
>   - product liability
>   - public liability
>   - premises and stock
>   - professional indemnity
>   - legal expenses
>
> *NB: check overall costs of insurance and check policy for relevance of cover.*

(a) An 'occupier' is a person who has some degree of control over the premises. He need not necessarily be the owner. It is also possible for there to be more than one occupier.

(b) 'Premises' includes land, buildings, fixed or movable structures such as pylons and scaffoldings; and vehicles including ships and aeroplanes.

(c) 'Visitors' are persons lawfully on the premises, such as customers in shops and factory inspectors. A trespasser will be deemed to be a lawful visitor for the purposes of the Act if the occupier has granted him implied permission by habitual acquiescence in his known trespass.

The extent of the duty is laid down in S.2(2) of the Act: *A duty to take such care as in all the circumstances of the case is reasonable to see that the visitor will be reasonably safe in using the premises for the purpose for which he is permitted by the occupier to be there.*

This duty is merely an enhancement of the common law duty to act as a responsible man/woman. The Act states that all the circumstances of the case are relevant in determining the duty owed. Therefore the occupier:

(a) Must be prepared for children to be less careful than adults. In the case of very young children, the occupier is entitled to assume that they will be accompanied by an adult.

(b) May expect a person who is doing his job to guard against the ordinary risks of his job.

(c) Will not be liable if the injury results from the faulty work of an independent contractor, provided the occupier took reasonable steps to ensure that the contractor was competent and that the work was properly done.

(d) May be able to escape liability by giving an adequate warning of any danger.

However it must be remembered that under the *Unfair Contract Terms Act 1977* an occupier of business premises cannot exclude liability for causing death or personal injury through negligence and cannot exclude liability for other loss or damage unless the exclusion clause satisfies the Act's requirement of reasonableness. The Act preserves the right of the occupier to plead the defence of *volenti non fit injuria* in respect of risks 'willingly accepted' by the visitor.

Occupiers' liability to trespassers

The *Occupiers' Liability Act 1984* has replaced the common law rules governing the duty of occupiers of premises to persons other than visitors. The Act covers not only trespassers but also persons using rights of way who fall outside the meaning of 'visitor' under the *Occupiers' Liability Act 1957*.

For several years prior to 1984 the occupiers' duty to trespassers was to act with common sense and humanity. This required all the surrounding circumstances to be considered, for example the seriousness of the danger, the type of trespasser likely to enter and, in some cases, the resources of the occupier.

The main provisions of the 1984 Act are:

- *Duty owed.* The occupier owes a duty if:
  - He is aware of the danger or has reasonable grounds to believe that it exists
  - He knows, or has reasonable grounds to believe, that someone is in (or may come into) the vicinity of danger
  - The risk is one against which in all the circumstances of the case he may reasonably be expected to offer that person some protection
- *Duty broken.* The duty is to take such care as is reasonable in all the circumstances to see that the person to whom the duty is owed does not suffer injury on the premises by reason of the danger concerned.
- *Damage.* The occupier can only be liable for injury to the person. The Act expressly provides that the occupier incurs no liability in respect of loss or damage to the property.
- *Warnings.* The duty may be discharged (in appropriate cases) by taking reasonable steps to give warning of the danger. The Act also preserves the right of the occupier to plead the defence of *volenti*.

Some examples

An example of the problems associated with the duty of care to trespassers occurred in a North London garden centre. The garden centre had installed a new water meter pit near its boundary fence. The correct manhole covers were not immediately available, so three 2-foot square paving slabs were used as temporary covers. The management considered this reasonable as no vehicles would cross that area and the slabs could be walked on.

A few nights later, a potential burglar climbed the fence and jumped down onto the slabs over the pit. These broke under his weight and he was quite badly cut and bruised on his ankles and legs. He attempted to sue the garden centre for his injuries although he subsequently dropped the case! This is by no means an isolated example and it shows the lengths that managements have to go to in order to show that they have done everything reasonably possible to safeguard all potential danger areas.

The law expects a higher duty of care towards children than towards adults. This is behind the safety notices and instructions in many outlets on the safe use of trolleys;

particularly in respect of children riding in them. At least one of the multiples has a very firm policy on this. All the trolleys are clearly labelled as to their suitability for children's use. All staff are also trained in how to approach customers whose children are not in the right kind of trolley, or who are not seated safely.

Among other responses from parents asked to seat their children properly have been; verbal and physical threats, totally ignoring the staff member and walking out of the store abandoning their selected goods. One manager recalls seeing a child lying on the bottom shelf of a two-tier trolley with its head over the front end a few inches above the ground. As she watched and before she could act, another trolley came round the next corner. A potentially fatal accident was avoided by the other trolley pusher seeing the hazard and taking avoiding action. The parent was abusive when challenged and finally was asked to leave the store. If you (hopefully rarely) have to take such action, ensure that another staff member is present to act as a witness if needed later.

One of the authors had to use bottled gas cabinet heaters to supplement the houseplant heating one very cold January. Recognising the potential hazards of radiant heaters on the shop floor, instructions were given for the heaters to be turned off prior to opening time. One Sunday morning this did not happen and within ten minutes of opening a lady claimed to have burnt her full-length fur coat on one of the fires. The bill presented to the centre's insurance company was for over £4,000. Stories of claims for personal or clothing damage on shopfittings are legion. The insurance companies recognise that some people almost make a living out of such events, but cannot often do anything about it.

STRICT LIABILITY

This is liability which arises without fault on the part of the defendant. The first example is from the common law; the others from statute law.

Rylands and Fletcher

The basic rule is: 'The person who for his own purposes brings on his lands and collects and keeps there anything likely to do mischief if it escapes must keep it at his peril, and if he does not do so is *prima facie* answerable for all damage which is the natural consequence of its escape' (Lord Blackburn, Judge). The rule applies to water, animals, chemical filth and industrial use of gas and electricity. For example: vandals damage your fuel tank and a quantity of fuel oil damages your neighbour's house and land. You are liable.

Breach of statutory duty

If a person is injured as a result of a breach of statutory duty they may be able to bring a court action if:

- The Act does not prohibit it
- but not if the Act was passed for the benefit of the general public (eg *Trades Description Act 1968*)
- or if the plaintiff suffers economic loss caused by a highway authority in breach of its statutory duty to repair a highway (ie if your garden centre loses money due to the disrepair of the road you cannot sue!)

PRODUCT LIABILITY: THE *CONSUMER PROTECTION ACT 1987*

Consumer groups have argued for some time that the law governing civil liability for damage due to defective goods is unfair. For a consumer to sue a manufacturer he must either proceed via a chain of contractual actions (possibly being defeated by an exemption clause) or he must sue for negligence and prove fault. This means that the law often fails to regulate the conduct of those responsible for the damage.

Industrial groups have opposed strict product liability on the grounds that insurance would be prohibitively expensive and some smaller businesses could be forced to close. After many years of deliberation the EC issued a directive on product liability in July 1985. This has been implemented in the *Consumer Protection Act 1987*. The Act has three main parts dealing with product liability, consumer safety and misleading price indications:

Part I Product liability. Basic Rule (S.2)

To succeed in a product liability claim against a manufacturer the plaintiff must show four things:

- That the product contained a defect
- That the plaintiff suffered damage
- That the damage was caused by the product
- That the defendant was a producer, 'own brander' or importer of the product

A supplier will also be liable if he fails to identify the producer or importer when requested to do so. The effect of this section is that in future liability will no longer be decided by reference to the fault of the manufacturer or some other person, but by reference to the state of the product in question, ie strict liability is introduced. Even so the plaintiff may experience some difficulty proving that the defect in the product caused the injury.

A 'product' must be movable and industrially produced, eg cars are products, buildings are not. Products of the soil, stock farming and fishing are not products unless subjected to an industrial process eg potatoes are not products but potato crisps are.

The meaning of a 'defect'

There are three types of product defect:

(1) A manufacturing defect occurs when a product fails to comply with the manufacturer's product specifications and consequently deviates from the norm. The frequency of such defects can be calculated fairly accurately and the producer will be able to spread the risk via insurance and pricing.

(2) A design defect occurs when the product specifications are themselves at fault and present a hazard. This type of defect is far more serious and has led to major claims for compensation, particularly in defective drug cases, for example the thalidomide cases.

Part II Consumer safety

Part II is intended to provide the public with better protection from unsafe consumer goods. It primarily imposes criminal sanctions, but will also assist the plaintiff in a civil action for negligence since, if a manufacturer has been found guilty under the Act, the plaintiff will be able to rely on the breach of statutory duty rather than have to prove a breach of the duty of care. The main provisions are:

(a) A person is guilty of an offence if he supplied consumer goods which are not reasonably safe (S.10).

(b) The Secretary of State may make safety regulations (for example with regard to flammability or toxicity) governing the make and supplying of goods. Such regulations cover for example, children's nightdresses and electric blankets.

(c) The Secretary of State may serve a 'prohibition notice' upon a supplier, prohibiting him from supplying goods which are unsafe. A 'notice to warn' may also be served requiring the supplier to publish, at his own expense, a warning to customers about unsafe goods.

Part III Misleading price indications

S.20 provides that a person commits an offence if, in the course of a business, he gives consumers an indication which is misleading as to the price at which any goods, services, accommodation or facilities are available. Examples of misleading price indications include:

- An understatement of the price
- Failing to make it clear that some other additional charge will be made
- Falsely indicating that the price is expected to be increased, reduced or maintained
- Making a false price comparison, for example by falsely stating that the price has been reduced

The Office of Fair Trading has issued a code of practice on misleading price indications. Compliance or non compliance with the code may be taken into account by the court when determining whether or not an offence has been committed (S. 25).

The Act provides various defences. For example:

- That the defendant took all reasonable precautions and exercised all due diligence to avoid the commission of an offence (S. 39)
- That the defendant was an innocent publisher or advertising agency who was unaware, and who had no ground for suspecting, that the advertisement contained a misleading price indication (S. 24)

The courts have tended to interpret the 'due diligence' defence fairly strictly, although less rigorous precautions are expected of small firms.

The Rylands and Fletcher principle relates to a non-natural use of land. Damage due to things naturally on the land may cause a tort of nuisance. Interestingly, plants, as 'products of the soil', are not subject to the Consumer Protection Act. However harm caused by plants will no doubt be pursued under either negligence or the Sale of Goods Act. Garden centres are aware of the harmful properties of some of the plants they sell. The magazine *Gardening from Which?* publishes a list of such plants from time to time but a list of 'potentially lethal plants' published by *American Nurseryman* in 1996, is quite an eye-opener!

The magazine listed 66 species from *Aconitum napellus* to *Veratrum spp* together with symptoms which could result from their consumption, symptoms that ranged from visual blurring, vomiting and drowsiness to prickling of skin, convulsions and paralysis!

Two years earlier the HTA published its own *Code of Recommended Retail Practice* relating to the labelling of potentially harmful plants. This followed a study carried out by the RHS, Key and the National Poisons Unit at Guy's Hospital and listed 65 genera under three categories.

Category A plants included just three species of *Rhus* (*R, radicans, succedanea* and *verniciflua*) which were to be labelled 'Poisonous if eaten' and a warning of severe blistering on contact. **Category B** plants were generally to be labelled 'Toxic if eaten' although warnings of skin and eye irritant/allergy applied to some. The list of 26 genera ranged from *Aconitum* to *Veratrum*. **Category C** listed 37 genera from *Aesculus* to *Wisteria* which are 'Harmful if eaten', or irritant or liable to be allergenic.

CONTRACT AND SALE OF GOODS

A contract is an agreement which legally binds the parties. The essential elements of a contract are:

(a) That an agreement is made as a result of an offer and acceptance.
(b) The agreement is for value. A gratuitous promise is only binding if made by a Deed.
(c) The parties intend to create legal relations.

Common law is the basis of contract, however contracts for the sale of goods are bound by their own statute, the *Sale of Goods Act*. This has had a mass of supporting legislation spring up around it in recent years. It is still the basis for the way we contract with our customers and the outline is shown below.

Sale of Goods Act

Key points of this Act include:

- **Sale by description** Where goods are sold by description (eg '5ft bamboo canes') the goods must correspond with the description.
- **Merchantable quality** Where goods are sold *in the course of business* they must be of merchantable quality unless (a) the defects are brought to the buyer's attention or (b) the buyer examines the goods, as regards defects which the examination ought to reveal.
- **Fitness for purpose** Where goods are sold *in the course of business* and the buyer makes known to the seller the purpose for which the goods are being bought, the buyer can rely on the seller's skill and judgement.

One of the authors fell foul of the *Sale of Goods Act* in the following way. One very hot summer there was a national shortage of barbeques. He decided to make up his own kits, selling a quantity of bricks and two galvanised boot scrapers as a DIY barbeque. The boot scrapers were of merchantable quality i.e. they were a good quality metal, properly made, but were not 'fit for the purpose for which they were sold' as was evidenced by the customer who brought in silver-sparkled sausages where the heat of the fire had detached flakes of galvanising. Fortunately no-one was injured but the author rapidly withdrew the offending kits!

FEPA AND COSHH

These two Acts are part of an ongoing process (much driven by the EU) to increase safety and reduce waste and environmental damage. FEPA is concerned with the correct use of pesticides in both amateur and professional settings. It is illegal for businesses to sell to the general public anything that is not registered as suitable for amateur use in the home and garden. It also governs who may apply pesticides on a professional basis and what qualifications they must have.

COSHH governs the way that risks are assessed and acted on in terms of all substances in a business which people can be exposed to. Every business must assess the hazards and risks that its workers and customers are exposed to. All chemical products will have a hazard data sheet to aid this process. An example is shown below and all garden centres must have a full file of them for all products sold. Staff also have to know where to find them in case of an incident. The authors are frequently dismayed at the lack of awareness at all levels, in all sizes of business about this vital legal area.

ENFORCING AGENCIES

There is a range of central and local government bodies whose job is to monitor and enforce the law in all areas of business life. Additionally there are voluntary organisations who monitor consumer concerns. All of these people can report problems; in the case of the official ones they can prosecute, enforce changes and make recommendations.

It is useful to know the bodies and their officials who will visit you. Asking advice may head off a problem and if there are difficulties, a calm statement of your point of view and a willingness to listen to them is always better than creating a row.

SOURCES OF INFORMATION

The enforcement agencies themselves are a ready source of information in their own area of competence. The Stationery Office (formerly HMSO) publishes guides to clarify all the key legislation and the HTA has a range of Briefing Papers which are very good guides to many areas of retail law.

There is no substitute for *training* all staff in areas of the law relevant to their work, monitoring and insisting on compliance with all legislation, recording actions and keeping systems up to date. Personal knowledge and vigilance by all staff at all times is the best way to prevent incidents in the first place!

SUMMARY

'Ignorance of the law is no defence' sounds harsh but has an undeniable logic. Some civil law risks can be covered by insurance (e.g. public liability) but criminal law risks cannot. In extreme cases, for example death caused by dangerous vehicles, the legal penalties may include a prison sentence. This might extend to the driver of the vehicle and also the owner or other person in the organisation with overall responsibility for Health and Safety.

One way of achieving compliance in some of the more commonplace but complex areas of law (such as employment law) is to join a trade-backed scheme. The HTA, GCA, and NFU all have arrangements with specialist companies who will, for a fee, assess your business needs and provide a ready-made package. This includes procedures manuals, telephone back-up and updates to accommodate changes in the law. Such systems are built into the Store Operations manuals of multiple companies but can be beyond the scope of small firms to create for themselves.

Just having such a system is only the start. If you do not fully implement, monitor and document your actions in all areas requiring compliance, you may have little grounds for defence where an alleged breach of the law has occurred.

13 Customer care

Service: a treat or a right? What customers hate. The key roles of staff. The wise consultant. Complaints. The super seller? Developing a customer care strategy. Loyalty cards.

Ask any group of garden centre managers the reason why customers return to their stores and the most likely response will be ' ... because of the service we give'. Everybody likes to feel that they give good service, indeed textbooks and industry speakers are constantly going on about it. The question remains however, are managers really kidding themselves? No matter what attention is currently being given to this factor there is still plenty of room for improvement.

SERVICE: A TREAT OR A RIGHT?

It should be remembered that visiting a garden centre or nursery should be a pleasant experience. It is not a visit that has to be made out of necessity – people must want to pay a visit. Our whole industry is linked to the quality of life and life would continue without us!

Many retailers glibly recite that the customer is the most important person in their business (and have posters on the office wall to reinforce it) but do they really treat them in the style they deserve? If customers are truly our guests we should be treating them in a polite relaxed manner with no hassle. Often they are in no particular hurry (even if we are). Conversely there should be no excuse for slow service either.

Pressure selling is out, but customers do like contact and recognition, whether it be detailed advice, a friendly greeting or even just a smile or eye contact. The truth is that customers think that they are the most important people in your business too! Staff are doing them a service by having some sort of dialogue with them (it may even be argued that it is their right). If a customer buys the wrong item and it does not meet their requirements then they will lay the blame squarely on the supplier and they are unlikely to be a repeat customer. It is the centre's duty to give good, correct advice, either in person or by the signage they provide. Most garden centres rely heavily on the loyal support of their regular customers, so clearly management must concentrate on those factors that keep the regular visitors happy.

WHAT CUSTOMERS HATE

We all have certain shops that we would rather not visit again for variable reasons. On first reaction as a retailer, if asked which was the most common criticism by customers, our response would likely be 'rude staff'. In reality however retailing is becoming far more sophisticated and most staff understand the need for courtesy.

Results from a number of surveys seem to indicate that the most likely responses are:

- Queuing
- Lack of tills
- Staff who know nothing about the goods
- Staff who hover and pester you
- Paying for carrier bags/hidden extras/delivery service

The garden centre is judged by the high standards that the consumer experiences at the supermarket. Certainly the level of service and consumer choice have changed out of all recognition in the last ten years. Supermarket customers often experience 30+ operating checkouts and schemes to keep queues down (more than two people in a queue and another checkout is opened). It comes as quite a shock to find that when purchasing plants the queues are significantly longer (be honest, do you like queuing?).

The supermarket environment is not one that is associated with much staff/customer contact. The garden centre is different however; the product may need a lot more technical input. The resultant increased staffing costs are really only a benefit if the skills are in place to meet the customers' needs. Clearly from the comments above this is not always the case.

Features that add to the enjoyment of shopping in garden centres	
	% of all adults
Knowledgeable staff	49
Cheaper plants than elsewhere	39
Café or restaurant	36
Plants grown on site for sale	35
Free home delivery	34
Beautiful displays of flowers, shrubs	34
Help to load the car	26
Fresh fruit & veg grown on site for sale	23
Demonstration of gardening techniques	23
Unusual or exotic plants	22
Permanent displays of ponds, bedding etc	22
Decorative ideas (e.g. lighting, summerhouse)	22
Gift ideas (e.g. books, videos)	21
Homemade goods/crafts (e.g. cakes, pottery)	21
Pets & petcare	20
Children's play area	20
Wide choice of hardware	18
Discount for bulk buying	16
Better layout & signposting	13
More seating	10
Recommended service contractors	6

Source: Mintel Retail Intelligence 1997

THE KEY ROLES OF STAFF

Ask any untrained member of staff on the shop floor as to the nature of their job and they are likely to reply 'selling'. In fact this is only part of the story, as they need to master a number of different roles in their dealings with customers. Often experts divide these into three main areas, host skills, consultant skills and selling skills.

THE HAPPY HOST

Certain customers know exactly what they require when they come into the store hence will need less assistance. Nevertheless these people still like to be recognised. Signs welcoming the public are a poor substitute for human contact. A few pleasant words seem a good trade-off for the amount of money they may spend. Managers need to constantly remind staff that customers are a number one priority (who is paying the wages?).

The pricing and putting out of stock at the weekends should be kept to an absolute minimum. Staff are just too valuable in creating sales at such times. Obviously at peak times it is not possible to have detailed conversations with each customer, but eye contact and a friendly nod at least breaks the ice so that the customer knows they may approach you with any questions they may have.

What are the first perceptions of your centre upon entering?

FORGET REALITY, IT'S HOW YOU ARE PERCEIVED THAT COUNTS!

Sense	Good environmental factors	Bad environmental factors
Smell	Fragrant houseplants, pot pourri, freshly brewed coffee	The pet area, stale cooking fat
Sight	Attractive colours, smart staff, clean uncluttered layout	Dim lighting, weedy or rubbish filled pathways
Sound	Relaxing music, water features	Vacuum cleaners, heavy machinery, raucous staff
Touch	Comfortable temperature, pleasant humidity	Extremes of temperature, leaking roof, uneven floors

The uniform factor

People judge by first impressions. A customer's perception will be affected by many factors including the way the staff are dressed. A good staff uniform will help convey the knowledgeable, professional service that is being offered. It also helps to give credibility to younger members of staff (few of us meet the public's caricature of the knowledgeable gardener: old, white-haired and male). Uniforms are costly items but a necessity. Choosing a good one is difficult and the factors above will need to be evaluated.

Issues to consider when choosing a uniform:

- Easily identifiable
- Suitable for all ages
- Easy to clean
- Indoor/outdoor use?
- Colour
- Cost!
- Does not show dirt
- Suitable for both sexes
- Availability of extra items
- Comfortable
- Image of centre

Other issues which need to be addressed include the expected dress of managers. Is there a separate dress code?

Whilst certain centres have given this little attention in the past there is indeed a legal requirement to provide protective clothing for people working in harsh conditions. One also needs to budget for enough changes of clothes for a full-time worker to look presentable *every* day.

THE WISE CONSULTANT

The biggest advantage a specialist garden centre or nursery has over other retailers selling similar merchandise is that of advice. It is not possible to compete with many mass market retailers on price and in many ways it is foolish to do so, as it is not a garden centre's real strength. Good staff training is important to ensure that correct information is given from both a moral and legal standpoint. Honest advice pays off – customers will see through staff who are making up an answer. If an answer is not known, the best approach is to admit it and suggest that a more authoritative source be consulted (be it either a book or another member of staff).

Staff must be able to answer problems but will 'turn off' the public if they try to do this from a position of superiority. People dislike being talked down to. (Remember the last time it happened to you?)

When giving advice it is important not to jump to conclusions but to listen to what the customer says and use this as the basis for future questions. Analyse the way a doctor does this the next time you go to the surgery. This is the model we should follow too.

> **The Golden Rule:**
>
> "You have two ears but only one mouth . . .
>
> Listen twice as much as you speak!"

Sometimes a customer's explanation of a problem may not be that clear. It is the consultant's job to find out the real need by summarising the situation. This process can be likened to passing water through a funnel.

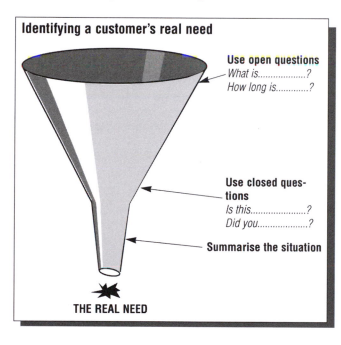

Identifying a customer's real need

Use open questions
What is.....................?
How long is.............?

Use closed questions
Is this......................?
Did you....................?

Summarise the situation

THE REAL NEED

It is far too easy to jump to conclusions. For example a customer wishing to prevent ants running up and down a tree does not need an ant killer! They need something to control the aphids or other sap-sucking insects in the tree's canopy from which the ants are collecting the sweet honeydew. It is only by the skilled use of probing questions that the real problem is discovered, a process that, admittedly, takes time. On the other hand just think of the consequences of providing the incorrect advice!

Jargon should be kept to a minimum since many people do not understand its meaning and feel too stupid to ask. (Remember when you have been on the receiving end of jargon, buying a computer perhaps?) Words like deciduous, dioecious, and ericaceous may be botanically correct but are not necessarily understood by all our visitors. A skilled, attentive employee will be able to supply information at the correct level for the recipient without talking at too high a level or conversely treating him like a half-wit.

Some garden centres go as far as issuing all their staff with business cards so that customers will have a point of contact on a return visit to the garden centre. This is a relatively inexpensive initiative but can help greatly in building loyalty to the centre and its staff. It also has the beneficial side effect that staff have even more incentive to ensure advice is accurate if they are giving out their name too.

COMPLAINTS

Despite even the greatest of care, there will always be dissatisfied customers. This is a crucial area for a garden centre to handle correctly as surveys show that this is a major reason for failure to achieve repeat business (too high prices comes further down the list).

Staff need to be trained to deal with problems quickly and efficiently. The quicker a problem can be resolved, the greater the likelihood the complainant will go away happy. Being completely honest however, most managers can recall times when they have played 'hide and seek' behind the displays rather than face such an issue head on. The truth is it won't go away!

So what advice can be given? Firstly, do not take it personally. It is very easy to take the issue to heart (the victim mentality). Focus on the problem in hand rather than the personalities involved, otherwise decisions may not be made rationally. In order to solve the problem it is vital to build a rapport with the customer. If this is not happening it is the responsibility of the staff member to change their approach rather than the customer.

People with a complaint wish to let you know all about it, and to this end, let them vent their anger (however unpleasant this may seem). If you don't, and interrupt, the result is typically a more irate customer as they feel they have not got their point across. It is reassuring to know however that even the most irate people need to breathe (they are still human after all!). When they pause for breath there is a window of opportunity to take control and start to show some sympathy for their perceived problem. It is also worth at this stage to move them to a less conspicuous position (the worst place to deal with a complaint is at the till). Often complaints become less vocal if there is no 'audience' to play to.

Questioning is vital but must be carried out with tact, avoiding antagonistic phrases such as 'You claim' or 'You didn't do that did you?'. Skilful use of open and closed questions should gain the correct information.

The customer perceives their problem as very important (that is why they are complaining), and consequently they are not interested in you or your company's problems. Trying to justify the situation does not help. Do you really imagine the customer is remotely interested in the fact that there is a greenfly problem on your supplier's nursery? Of course not – they are only concerned with your treatment of their problem!

Many garden centres offer a 'no quibble' guarantee on hardy plants but this should not be used as an excuse for not asking questions. After all what is to prevent the same problem occurring again?

> **Dealing with complaints: the seven-point plan**
>
> 1) Remain calm yourself (count to ten beforehand if necessary)
> 2) Let them vent their anger (listen!)
> 3) Empathise with the customer ('I understand how you must feel')
> 4) Ask questions
> 5) Restate content or feelings (avoid antagonism)
> 6) Find agreement (or accept their point of view)
> 7) Let others know the agreed course of action
>
> IT TAKES APPROXIMATELY 5 TIMES MORE RESOURCES TO GET A NEW CUSTOMER RATHER THAN KEEP AN OLD ONE

Despite the feeling that customers seem to complain about the slightest little thing, the opposite is actually true. It is only a small minority who will take the time to come to complain – the others try to fix the problem themselves or vote with their feet and go somewhere else next time.

THE SUPER SELLER?

Clearly the potential customer seems to be influenced by the environment within the centre prior to the actual selling process occurring. Despite the way in which many people in the garden centres feel that their industry is unique, the skills required to sell are fundamentally the same as those in other retail industries. It could easily be argued that garden centre staff are not as skilled compared to many of their counterparts. Many articles in the trade and consumer magazines highlight the lack of product knowledge that exists for example.

It is not sufficient to let the customers fend for themselves. If a garden centre is to give good service, skilled knowledgeable staff must be on hand. It's what makes a particular retailer stand out from the crowd.

Nobody can truly learn how to sell from a book although there are many basic ingredients that can be followed. These skills must be refined by dealing with 'live customers'. It is important to kill the myth that 'salesmen are born and not made'.

Approaching the customer

Customers need to feel welcome before they will enter into any sort of meaningful dialogue with a salesperson. The typical visitor to the garden centre may wish to browse awhile before seeking help. The experienced salesperson is able to spot the time is right (almost as if 'help' is tattooed on the customer's forehead).

For the uninitiated, here are a few signs:

- hovering over a product
- looking around to catch a member of staff's eye
- picking up and reading the label and putting down a product repeatedly.

Many people are too intimidated to simply come up and ask for fear of looking small. If an approach is to be made it is important not to startle the customer otherwise their automatic response is 'I'm just looking'.

Three ways to approach a customer	
The crab	A sideways scuttle, gradually edging up to the customer. Likely to put the potential customer off as the member of staff is only half in view.
The big surprise	The customer has no chance of seeing the staff member as they creep up behind them. Most likely to make the customer jump!
The full frontal	The most preferable route. A customer sees the member of staff approaching so will be well prepared. A friendly smile eases the path too.

Product knowledge

Salespeople who claim to be able to sell anything without knowledge of the product are naïve. A level of knowledge is necessary to gain the customer's confidence. People can differentiate between a salesperson who is bluffing and one who is talking from a position of knowledge.

Whilst the ideal would be to have an intimate knowledge of the thousands of product lines a centre stocks it is not normally possible. Regular staff training sessions in-store are important to ensure that all staff have the fundamentals. Even though it is difficult to quantify the results, good training is the lifeblood of good customer service. More detailed training will probably be appropriate for key staff members.

Often what is gleaned about a product is technical data i.e. mode of action, servicing etc. Customers can often be confused by this. The skill is to convert this information into benefits for the customer. In other words, what it will do for them. A person purchasing an insecticide containing pirimicarb is not concerned about the intricacies of its formulation but the fact that it will kill greenfly and blackfly (aphids) without harming beneficial insects. This is the angle that should be used to help sell the product.

Closing a sale

Once again the salesperson needs to look for signals. Over-enthusiastic staff may actually put off a potential purchaser by talking too much (it is not a contest to demonstrate to someone how much you know). It is not feasible to ask someone 'Are you ready to buy?', but actions such as helping a customer put an item into their trolley or starting to walk towards the checkout may help remind the customer in a subtle way that it is time to close. It goes without saying that the conversation should end with a 'thank you' – last impressions are indeed very important.

DEVELOPING A CUSTOMER CARE STRATEGY

The services you offer says something about your business. Ideally you should want to supply everything a customer needs to make their visit enjoyable. Whilst this humanistic approach is very commendable it has to be backed by some form of commercial strategy i.e. **to increase the store's profitability**.

The need for some cost-benefit analysis is clear but in reality may be difficult to achieve as data on a before and after basis are difficult to define accurately. For example two similar sized, similar ranged centres, situated two miles apart have considerably different turnover figures. Is this due to the fact that one has an attractive coffee shop as opposed to the other's vending machine or some other factor?

Perhaps the crucial question is 'Will I lose out on trade by not offering this item?' The value of a service to the consumer is in no way related to the cost to the operator in offering it.

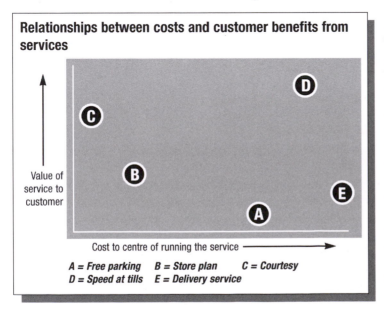

Relationships between costs and customer benefits from services

Value of service to customer

Cost to centre of running the service →

A = Free parking   B = Store plan   C = Courtesy
D = Speed at tills   E = Delivery service

Certain services and facilities are expected by the customer. These are the minimum *basic* services that don't necessarily build loyalty by their presence. On the other hand, customer loyalty will be seriously affected if they are not provided. These are sometimes affectionately known as *disappointers*. An excellent example of this is a delivery service. Customers assume that it will work efficiently and only notice when it is less than this (or when it is not offered at all). In either case it is a cause for dissatisfaction and may prevent repeat business.

On a much brighter note there are some extremely cost-effective services making a significant impression on customer loyalty (good old-fashioned courtesy fits here as does well-trained staff). These are often referred to as *loyalty retainers*.

Items that have a greater cost implication for the company but are also seen as being a real asset to the customer are classed as *loyalty builders*. These items are the 'extra' service and facilities that result in word-of-mouth recommendations to others in the neighbourhood. In this category may fall efficient checkout systems and personal notification of special offers and events by direct mail.

LOYALTY CARDS

The late 1980s saw the proliferation of gardening clubs within independent garden centres. By offering special events and discounts the aim was to encourage the customer to use the centre more frequently and in many cases to encourage the 'social' side to the visits. Whilst this is a wonderful concept the reality has been that the resources needed to run the

---

Primary Services

(Those which need to be run efficiently to prevent loss of custom)

Free car parking
Map of site
Ample trolleys
A delivery service
Good labelling
Clean toilets

Ancillary Services

(Those items which may create customer loyalty)

Trained courteous staff
Efficient tills
Garden design
Gift wrapping service
Plant finding service
Supervised crèche
Gardening clubs/special mailings

---

scheme effectively are large and it takes discipline to keep the scheme fresh after the initial burst of enthusiasm within the organisation has gone. Of those going down this route probably one of the most successful schemes has been run by Hillier Garden Centres who indeed have a specialist co-ordinator to run the scheme on behalf of its centres. In many smaller outlets this task has fallen onto the manager who in many cases has not been in a position to give it the time it requires. The difficulty is that once a scheme is underway it is difficult to withdraw it as this will have a negative effect on loyalty. Discount on purchases has also been associated with many of these early schemes and in hindsight the discount levels were often too high.

More recently there has been a great development in plastic loyalty cards throughout the whole retail industry. Indeed in the supermarket sector one major operator who publicly stated that in their opinion customers were not interested in collecting points has been forced to eat their words and follow suit due to the effect it was having on their market share.

Loyalty cards have the advantage of allowing cardholders to accumulate points on their purchases, which leads to some form of bonus or voucher at a later point (this is preferable to giving purely discount on the day as they need to return to redeem their voucher). From the retailer's point of view the level of discount may be more hidden from the customer so may be more cost effective too. The database on purchasing habits developed through such a scheme also helps the centre to target their marketing more precisely.

Within the garden centre industry Homebase has been a pioneer in this area and has a scheme that has proved to be a very effective marketing tool to target its customers at certain key times of the year. Within the independent sector, HART the marketing and buying group has developed a scheme called Garden Card which allows its members to become involved in a centrally administered scheme taking away the resource implication of a centre running a similar scheme of garden club themselves.

It is difficult to predict precisely the future development within this area. Already the prices of 'smart' cards containing a computer chip are falling in price to the point where it may be economic for the average retailer to become involved. The storage of larger quantities of data on the card will no doubt allow the development of far more sophisticated schemes together with the promise of personalised promotional offers for the consumer based upon previous purchasing patterns. The limit may truly be your imagination ...

A customer is the most important person ever in this office, in person or by post

A customer is not dependent on us, we are dependent on them

A customer is not an interruption to our work, they are the purpose of it – we are not doing them a favour by serving them, they are doing us a favour by giving us the opportunity to do so

A customer is not an outsider to our business, they are part of it

A customer is not a cold statistic, they are a flesh and blood human being with feelings and emotions like our own, and with biases and prejudices

A customer is not someone to argue or match wits with – nobody ever wins an argument with a customer

A customer is a person who brings us their wants – it is our job to handle them in a manner profitable to them and to ourselves

The moral of the story ... THE CUSTOMER PAYS OUR WAGES!

(Author unknown)

---

14 Future trends

The shape of the domestic market. UK dominant issues. Strategic business view. Present technologies, future applications.

Since John Stanley and Ian Baldwin published their *Garden Centre Manual* in 1981 there have been profound changes in the world at large as well as the garden centre trade. The breakthrough in personal computers had just begun. Clive Sinclair had launched his ZX81, which, for £49.95 gave the user (wait for it!) 1k RAM; or with a £24.90 update you could have 4k RAM. You also had to provide your own TV and tape recorder so that you could, if you were lucky, load one of the six provided programmes. A glance at any paper will show you the changes. For about five times the money (after allowing for inflation) you now get over 16,000 times as much memory – and they throw in the TV, printer, modem and dozens of programmes free!

In 1981, the recession had been underway for two years, but garden centres, at least in the south of England, were booming. Since then we have had the Lawson boom, the Clark bust, the Blair steady progress and now the Asian meltdown. How much really changes? As for garden centres, Hilliers had four, Notcutts had six, Cramphorns had over thirty retail outlets of various kinds and Mr Sainsbury had just invited a Belgian company to go into partnership with him and opened the first Homebase store at Purley Way, Croydon. Wyevale was a well-respected nursery group with seven garden centres and the Beacon Group had six centres (and were subsequently taken over by Country Gardens, who did not come into being until 1985).

In training terms, it was the third season of garden centre training at Hadlow College who were wondering how much retail knowledge was wanted by the trade. As far as we know, that was almost it in college terms, although the ATB and the HTA were running short courses and the RHS exams were, as now, the pinnacle of horticultural achievement.

What this chapter will seek to do is examine what is likely to change over the medium and long term (and the next five to twenty or thirty years) and what is likely to remain the same. Please look back at this in the year 2020 – applaud some of the lucky guesses and laugh at some of the howlers, we most certainly hope to!

THE MEDIUM TERM

Predictions for the medium term are certainly on safer ground than speculating the situation 25 years hence, but even so we are likely to see some distinct changes within the shape of the industry.

Already the industry is seeing a polarisation occurring with smaller centres relying on the higher margin, but more weather-dependent, plant specialism route while the largest centres offer a far broader experience and are more able to compensate for the vagaries of a wet spring. It is those centres that do not easily fall into either category that are under the most pressure. It is very probable that the latter will be the most vulnerable to takeover by the multiple garden centre operators. Additionally, these organisations are quite vulnerable to takeover by retail organisations (outside of our own industry) that are attracted by the relatively high margins that are still being achieved.

The speed of takeovers may also be fuelled by the fact that many of the 'first generation' garden centre owners are coming up for retirement and may wish to liquidate their assets, particularly in the absence of a member of the family ready to take over control. Lack of new green-field development sites will also increase the demand for existing operations.

The maturation of the garden centre sector will undoubtedly lead to a saturation of the market which will, in time, lead to increasing pressure on the margins achieved and inevitable erosion. However, in the meantime DIY stores are very likely to develop stand-alone garden centres – sites without the core DIY activity – as the development of large 'full-blown' outlets become increasingly difficult.

With the erosion of profit margins, the need for independent operators to work together to improve not only their buying terms but also marketing strategy will become even more important. Organisations such as the Tillington Group and HART will allow their members to compete more equally with the developing multiples. This will become doubly important as we are likely to see further amalgamation and consolidation among suppliers too. The costs of developing a new pesticide is now so great that the sums of money required are only available to a few large multinational organisations and even then is only cost effective if the application of the product is very wide.

Plant suppliers too may face increasing pressures. Barcoding and pre-pricing is already very much the norm and we are also seeing the alpine and herb sector offering a full merchandising service. The garden centre is thus ridding itself of any risk of surplus stock. Perhaps a similar move in the shrub sector is not far away – maybe the use of benches being 'leased' by the plant supplier for the season guaranteeing representation of their product.

The customer base will continue to change too as now it will continue to age. Garden centres are likely to see an increase in the expectation of the level of service required by the consumer (accompanied by an increasing willingness to resort to litigation if they are dissatisfied!). Coupled with the need for increased service, the difficulty in recruiting qualified staff is still as likely to be a key point of discussion when managers meet as it is now. The onus will clearly be on the organisation to develop their own – those employees with the right skills can certainly look forward to rapid career progression.

The demand will continue to grow for the centre to be open at times when shoppers need it. It is now possible to visit major supermarkets 24 hours a day – some are even open on Christmas day – so how long will it be before garden centres follow suit?

While those people involved in the garden centre industry feel that it is a special case (and most people do care passionately) the same case could have been argued for the specialist toy or shoe shop which used to be familiar sights in the High Street – when you last purchased a pair of shoes where did you buy them? Now justify why the specialist knowledge dealing with plants is vastly different from that of the toy industry or of fitting a pair of shoes.

The independent specialist will survive but not in the numbers we see now. Their survival will be closely linked to their management's ability to adapt to changing trends and to market themselves effectively.

After all the doom and gloom let's have a little more fun by looking further into the future towards 2026 ...

THE SHAPE OF THE DOMESTIC MARKET

One of the ways of trying to foresee the future is to look at the past. Below is a series of comparisons of overall interest in gardening and specific gardening purchases. The data for 1970 is adapted from *The pbi Garden Book of Europe* by Dr Hessayon, famous for his expert series of gardening books. The 1998 figures are from a range of sources and the 2026 figures are a simple extrapolation from the others. What is clear is that some figures simply cannot grow beyond a certain point. Wisley with three times its present visitor load? When the answer is not that simple the fun is trying to predict what new approach might be adopted.

In the case of Wisley gardens it might include:

- Timed entrance
- Limited numbers of visits per year for each member
- Floodlit visiting
- Replication of the whole garden elsewhere
- Virtual reality experience of key parts of the garden.

Statistical comparisons

	1970	1998*	2026*
Retail sales of garden products (inflation adjusted)	£1bn	£3bn	£9bn
Number of visitors to Wisley Gardens	220,000	660,000	2,000,000
National Trust members	350,000	1,400,000	5,600,000
HTA membership	1,500	1,800	2,100
Average garden size	2,000sq ft	1,200sq ft	800sq ft
Gardens with a:			
patio	10%	35%	60%
decorative walling	5%	8%	10%
garden table	7%	50%	93%
barbecue	1%	30%	60%
greenhouse	16%	25%	33%
conservatory	1%	10%	20%

projected

Using a similar technique we might predict the garden scene of 2026 to look something like this:

- An increase in the total number of gardens as more single occupancy dwellings arise.
- An increase in the amount of paid gardening undertaken for the working sector of the single occupancy dwellings.
- An increase in communal gardens for multiple dwelling unit buildings (flats and converted houses) and for the greatly increased number of old peoples homes.
- An increase in garden skills training for all age groups, delivered by garden centre gardening clubs, colleges and schools. Family learning will be the catch-phrase.
- An increase in all home-based activities and a reduction in foreign holidays. This will be caused by rising awareness of pollution and far more critically, the inevitable real rise in fuel prices over the next twenty-eight years.
- A noticeable change, not just in the climate of the UK, but in the variances between regions. Not only plant types but pests and diseases may become more diverse.
- A return to longer-lasting capital goods, such as furniture, barbeques and green-houses, particularly if of timber or oil-based materials.
- An increase in the total proportion of disposable income spent on gardening products.
- A sharper contrast between the permanent workforce (lower numbers, greater relative wealth) who will continue the trend for instant results and the ever-larger number of non-permanent workers who will be prepared to carry out the procedures for themselves and wait for the outcome. Back to the future!

UK DOMINANT ISSUES

The above predictions are the result of reflecting on the larger scale issues in the country and the world over this period. The main features to be considered are shown below.

Demographics

The balance between the age groups continues to shift. The baby boomer generation are now in the 45 to 54 age group, at the height of their spending powers in garden product terms. In ten years' time, the next cohort in this age range will be smaller. Woo them now – they will be a rarer beast! Those entering work will be a smaller yet proportion of the population and the demand for services of all kinds from the growing ranks of the elderly will mean fierce competition from other employers.

One benefit may include the reversal of the ageism that has made people over fifty almost unemployable in many sectors in recent years, regardless of their skills. One of the DIY multiples has already experimented with a store in the North of England that is predominantly manned by the over-fifties. Results include: more customer care, more product knowledge, less shoplifting (granny has sharp eyes!) and more reliance on help of various kinds for moving heavy products.

Following on from that, it may be counted as a mixed blessing that people consider it normal to continue working on into and through their seventies, as long as their health allows and need or enthusiasm demands.

Economics

One economic trend has been shown just above. As people live longer they require more resources to support them, just at the time when it is increasingly difficult to earn them. Apart from the impossible task of guessing the global economic picture in 2026, it is difficult enough to imagine whether Europe at that time will be dominated by a radical and entrepreneurial spirit as EU leaders demand; or be a stagnant economic system ruled by a Brussels bureaucracy and possibly even resembling the old Comecon bloc.

It seems reasonably likely that the EU will survive and flourish, with Britain inside it if not totally of it. Cultural and language barriers may still limit the free cross continent working that is hoped for. What will happen is an exchange of ideas and products that may extend the cachet already given to the English garden and create large-scale upmarket opportunities for UK firms in garden services and products in the European market. The EU may well be the largest and most powerful economic bloc in the world in 2026. Whether GATT will manage to increase the freedom to trade across bloc as well as national borders remains in doubt. Failure to do so, it is generally agreed, would blight economic growth for the whole of the period in question and even beyond.

In the UK one of the most disturbing predictions for the future is the creation of a large permanent underclass. As you can see, the trebling of those who feel marginalised could have powerful consequences.

In Britain as in Europe, the political cost of immigration is high and directly related to the degree of perceived difference between the immigrants and the existing population. Given the demographic trends, it is hard to see how immigration can be avoided. Garden centres may find that they give work, language and technical training to immigrant workers and get their insights into plants, retailing and customer care as well as their hours on the shop floor.

Work and asset trends in the UK		
	1995	*2020*
High assets, Secure work	10%	15%
Moderate/low assets, Secure work	50%	15%
Moderate/low assets, Part time/short contract work	30%	40%
Low assets, Spasmodic work	10%	30%

Skills

As discussed elsewhere in the book, businesses are changing their focus from the performance and development of physical assets to those of people assets. The concept of life-long training will be accepted practice by 2026. Some of those skills will still be physical (e.g. grafting, propagating etc.) but the greatest development will be in interpersonal and information skills. One rare but valuable skill may be how to set up good manual systems for running a business when the automated system crashes, as it still will!

Ecological factors

Apart from climate change and the increasing cost and rarity of raw materials, there may be a hidden benefit in the recycling culture that must prevail. Many of the sustainable technologies use plants in surprising variety and contexts. Reed beds for sewage treatment, iris beds for extraction of heavy metal pollution from water and willow meadows for biomass power stations are just three examples. The Centre for Alternative Technology would repay a visit from any garden centre owner planning for the long-term future. Those in the first wave, as with computers, may incur costs and make mistakes but they will have the right skills and attitudes ready when the need arises.

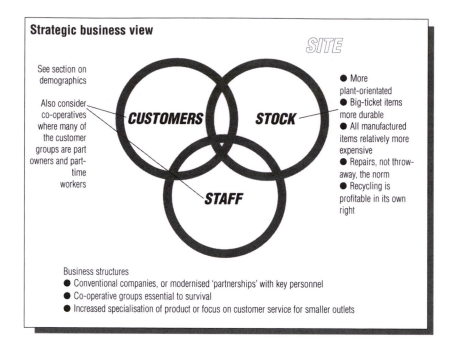

Strategic business view

SITE

See section on demographics

Also consider co-operatives where many of the customer groups are part owners and part-time workers

CUSTOMERS **STOCK**

STAFF

● More plant-orientated
● Big-ticket items more durable
● All manufactured items relatively more expensive
● Repairs, not throw-away, the norm
● Recycling is profitable in its own right

Business structures
● Conventional companies, or modernised 'partnerships' with key personnel
● Co-operative groups essential to survival
● Increased specialisation of product or focus on customer service for smaller outlets

STRATEGIC BUSINESS VIEW

Strategy means 'winning the war'. You can lose any number of individual battles as long as you achieve the fundamental goal. Insights into the future are ways of seeing how the campaign will alter shape over the coming years. Some possibilities are given below.

PRESENT TECHNOLOGIES, FUTURE APPLICATIONS

It is difficult enough to imagine what development is possible within existing technologies, let alone imagine completely new ones. The thoughts overleaf are all possibilities for the use of existing technologies in the garden centre of 2026. Our thanks must go to many of the students at Hadlow College who wittingly or otherwise have contributed to this final section.

We hope you have found this book as stimulating to read as we have in writing it. Please send us your ideas on the future of the industry, or any other topic, for further articles or the next edition.

The 'hardware'

- Speech recognition computer systems. Will allow plant searches without the need to use a keyboard.
- CD dictionaries of plant pictures. Links with the above and with CAD (computer aided design) programmes to enable a customer to research, plan, cost and contract for a single plant or a complete garden on your site or from their home. Staff intervention would be available at any stage in the process.
- Teleshopping is only a simpler version of the above idea. On-line purchase and payment can take place for trade or retail purchases or at any point in the distribution chain. Actual plants can be viewed remotely by customers at any level in the chain.
- Trolleys, buggies or goods carts can be programmed with visible route maps and product locations on the garden centre. They could also take the customer to the tills, teashop, toilet or information point if a friendly face is the preferred option.
- Self-scanning of purchases with built-in security systems.
- Multifunction smart cards with international links for banking and credit purposes and local directories for your own customer benefits (e.g. gardening club, loyalty card).
- Optical recognition systems as in-store and boundary security. 1998 has seen trials of a system where the people on the camera are recognised by the computer system and security can be alerted for example or the sales team, depending on who has been recognised!
- Multimedia in-store training centres. Practical skills can be interspersed with self-teaching technical and theory aspects. Good for customers and staff alike.
- Envirodomes where the whole centre can be under cover if desired, in as many climatic ranges as needed. Think of the Californian store with a living Santa, falling snow and nodding reindeer all 365 days of the year! (Yes, it is true. Honest!)

The 'software'

- Cloning and grafting techniques may give us plants of both a functional and curiosity value never yet dreamed of.
- The conifer that will grow to six feet in the first year, fill out in the second and then grow only marginally after that.
- The family fruit tree with a branch each of plums, cherries, peaches and apricots.
- The all-year continuously flowering shrub.
- The genetically modified ornamental plants with built-in pesticides.

Appendix

Increase in volume of business required to offset price reductions (all figures %)

Normal gross margin achieved on stock	Price reductions of 5%	10%	15%	20%	25%	30%	35%	40%	45%	50%
25%	25.0	66.7	150.0	400.0						
30%	20.0	50.0	100.0	200.0	500.0					
35%	16.6	40.0	75.0	133.0	250.0	600.0				
40%	14.3	33.3	60.0	100.0	166.6	300.0	700.0			
45%	12.5	28.6	50.0	80.0	125.0	200.0	350.0	800.0		
50%	11.1	25.0	42.8	66.6	100.0	150.0	233.0	400.0	900.0	
55%	10.0	22.2	37.5	57.1	83.3	120.0	175.0	266.6	450.0	1,000.0
60%	9.0	20.0	33.3	50.0	70.2	100.0	140.0	200.0	300.0	500.0
65%	8.3	18.2	30.0	44.4	62.5	85.7	116.7	160.0	225.0	333.3
70%	7.7	16.6	27.3	40.0	55.5	75.0	100.0	133.3	180.0	250.0
75%	7.1	15.3	25.0	36.3	50.0	66.7	87.5	114.3	150.0	200.0

Example: If an item with a usual gross margin of 50% is reduced by 20%, the retailer must sell 60.6% more to offset the reduction

Hadlow College Plant Centre, Trading year: 1 August – 31 July

Commenced trading: March 1992

Financial results (abbreviated)

Year	Turnover	Gross Profit		Net Profit	
1992–93 (17 months)	£127,000	£50,000	(39%)	Nil	
1993–94	£176,000	£72,000	(41%)	Nil	
1994–95	£220,000	£90,000	(41%)	£5,000	(2.5%)
1995–96	£245,000	£104,000	(41.6%)	£25,000	(10.2%)

Hadlow College Plant Centre, January-September 1996
Profits generated in order of importance

		£
D6	Bedding	7,700
9c	Herbaceous	3,300
9c	Bedding	1,800
7c	Bedding/Basket plants	1,800
7c	Alpines	1,600
	Garden Club members	1,100
	Lectures/demos	1,100
9c	Herbs	1,100
1L	Osteospermum	800
1L	Bedding	800
9c	Petunia trailing	550
	Apple juice	550
9c	Heathers	500
	Suttons Seedlings	400
9c	Ivy	400
1L	Geranium	400
80L	Westland Multipurpose	400
	Honey	350
9c	Tomato	350
9c	Primula	300
1L	Heathers	300
1L	Fuchsia	300
	Begonia Elatior	300
50L	Westland Tub & Basket	300
	Kompo planting compost	300
1L	Alpines	300
	Gift tokens	300
	Greeting cards	300
	Easy Grow Sack	250
23L	John Innes No. 3	200
1.5L	Hollyhocks	200
	Osmocote Plus 10 tablets	200
	Gardener's World Magazine	200

This list does not show any groups such as shrubs as they are listed individually and have not appeared on the top 30

Weekly analysis of plant centre

Day	Dates	Takings exc VAT	Number of customers	Average sale
Monday	July 11	£620.30	56	£11.08
Tuesday	July 12	£313.71	21	£14.94
Wednesday	July 13	£557.24	45	£12.38
Thursday	July 14	£430.50	35	£12.30
Friday	July 15	£245.50	34	£7.22
Saturday	July 16	£461.67	51	£9.05
	Week's Total	£2,628.92	242	£10.86

EPOS report for Week 10

Linecode	Description	Qty Sold	Value £	Cost £	Margin %
Grp 09	HERBACEOUS PERENNIALS				
4447	Herbaceous 2L Hardy A	4.0	11.16	6.12	45.2
4114	Large Herbaceous Ass 1Lt	2.0	6.04	3.00	50.3
0	1.0	0.84	0.42	50.0	
6450	Herbaceous 9cm 6 pack	32.0	184.80	111.36	39.7
2537	Small Herbaceous 9cm	139.0	152.74	80.62	47.2
288	Bergenia Bresinghm White 21	2.0	4.98	4.70	5.6
6345	Cyclamen Coum 9cm	1.0	2.00	0.90	55.0
6444	Dianthus 9cm assorted	25.0	27.98	13.75	50.9
6531	Foxglove Albino 1L	9.0	22.86	11.61	49.2
6530	Foxglove Apricot Beauty 1L	10.0	23.65	12.90	45.5
6528	Foxglove Giant Spotted 1L	9.0	21.23	11.61	45.3
6529	Foxglove X Mertonensis 1L	4,0	9.53	5.16	45.9
4473	Euphorbia Sikkimensis 10L	1.0	16.68	8.50	49.0
4726	Erysimum Ann Marie 31	1.0	3.62	1.65	54.4
4696	Hardy Fern 9cm square pot	4.0	6.64	3.20	51.5
6451	Galanthus Desdemona Clumps	2.0	8.00	4.00	50.0
6449	Helleborus Niger 9cm	3.0	5.80	2.85	50.9
6443	Helleborus Orientalis 10L Co	7.0	92.27	42.00	54.5
5647	Heuchera Palace Purple	1.0	3.02	1.70	43.7
4144	Hemerocallis L Lace 21	1.0	4.21	2.35	44.2
3896	Helleborus Orientalis 10L WH	1.0	10.17	5.00	50.8
4027	Iris Vulg Mary Bernhant 2L	1.0	3.19	1.40	56.1
1556	Pulmonaria Azurea 21	1.0	3.48	1.93	44.5
893	Gallery Lupin-Blue	15.0	37.22	19.35	48.0
894	Gallery Lupin-Pink	7.0	16.90	9.03	46.6
895	Gallery Lupin-Red	6.0	15.24	7.74	49.2
896	Gallery Lupin-White	5.0	10.94	6.45	41.0
897	Gallery Lupin-Yellow	8.00	20.07	10.32	48.6
6445	Narcissus Tete a Tete 11cm	1.0	2.26	1.50	33.6
4327	Double Primroses 1.5L	48.0	111.93	45.60	59.3
4112	Dianthus 9cm 6 pack	1.0	5.95	3.30	44.5
4134	Primula Heladoxa 21	1.0	3.53	1.75	50.4
1766	Scabious Pink Mist	2.0	6.80	3.76	44.7
	Group Totals	355.0	855.73	445.53	47.9

Simple budget and cashflow (£'000)

	MONTHS 1	2	3	4	5	6	7	8	9	10	11	12	TOTAL
BUDGET													
Sales forecast	10	20	50	90	120	80	40	30	40	50	30	40	600
Gross profit 40%	4	8	20	36	48	32	16	12	16	20	12	16	240
Expenses 30% (Wages 15%, Others 15%)	3	6	15	27	36	24	12	9	12	15	9	12	180
Net profit before interest	1	2	5	9	12	8	4	3	4	5	3	4	60
Interest on loan and overdraft (£11,200, say £12,000)	1	1	1	1	1	1	1	1	1	1	1	1	12
Net profit after	0	1	4	8	11	7	3	2	3	4	2	3	48
CASHFLOW													
Sales (from above)	10	20	50	90	120	80	40	30	40	50	30	40	600
Cost of sales 60% (Goods)	6	12	30	54	72	48	24	18	24	30	18	24	360
Expenses 30%	3	6	15	27	36	24	12	9	12	15	9	12	180
Loan repayment (£80,000 over 7 years, say £1,000 per month; interest at 10%, say £700/month)	1.7	1.7	1.7	1.7	1.7	1.7	1.7	1.7	1.7	1.7	1.7	1.7	20.4
MOVEMENTS IN OVERDRAFT													
Income	10	20	50	90	120	80	40	30	40	50	30	40	600
Expenditure	10.7	19.7	46.7	82.7	109.7	73.7	37.7	28.7	37.7	46.7	28.7	37.7	560.4
Net movement	−0.7	+0.3	+3.3	+7.3	+10.3	+6.3	+2.3	+1.3	+2.3	+3.3	+1.3	+2.3	39.6
Overdraft (before interest; starting at £50,000)	50.7	50.4	47.1	39.8	29.5	23.3	20.9	19.6	17.3	14.0	12.7	10.4	
Overdraft interest (debited quarterly at, say 10%)			1.25 cumulative			0.77			0.48			0.30	2.8
Overdraft actual (monthly balance)	50.70	50.40	48.35	41.05	30.75	25.22	22.92	21.62	19.80	16.50	14.80	13.20	

Mark-up and Margin Table (margin = gross profit)

Mark-up	Margin	Typical product groups
10%	9%	Basic foodstuffs, special lines
15%	10.3%	bought in for sales,
20%	16.67%	seasonal offers
25%	20%	Dry goods, machinery,
33.3%	25%	furniture and barbecues, promotional
50%	33.3%	plant items, cut flowers
100%	50%	The bulk of plant sales,
200%	66.6%	rare items of all kinds
300%	75%	Tropical and coldwater fish, some
400%	80%	exotic pets, some gift lines
500%	83.3%	Bankrupt or fire-sale stock – seldom regularly
1000%	90.9%	available – usually low unit value, items of great rarity value

Bibliography

Abbott, K.R. & N. Pendlebury *Business Law*, 6th edn 1996, DP Publications.

Adair, J. *Effective Teambuilding*, 1986 Gower.

Armstrong, M. *How to be an even better manager*, 1993 Kogan Page.

Blanchard, K. & S. Johnson *The One Minute Manager*, 1983 Willow Books.

Blanchard, K. & David P. Zigarmi *Leadership and the One Minute Manager*, 1986 Willow Books.

Cole, G.A. *Personnel Management*, 1988 DP Publications.

Handy, C. *Understanding Organizations*, 4th edn 1993, Penguin Books.

Huczynski, A. & D. Buchanan *Organizational Behaviour*, 2nd edn 1991, Prentice Hall.

Quinn, F. *Crowning the Customer*, 1990 O'Brien Press Ltd.

Winkler, J. *Pricing for results*, 1993 Butterworth Heinemann.

Other sources
Mintel Retail Intelligence Report 1997

Department of Transport

Royal Mail Consumer Panel

NCH Promotional Services

British Retail Consortium: *Retail Crime Survey* 1997

Index